Law in Action

Ethnomethodological and Conversation Analytic Approaches to Law

Edited by

MAX TRAVERS
Buckinghamshire College

and

JOHN F. MANZO
University of Toronto

Routledge
Taylor & Francis Group
LONDON AND NEW YORK

First published 1997 by Ashgate Publishing

Published 2016 by Routledge
2 Park Square, Milton Park, Abingdon, Oxfordshire OX14 4RN
711 Third Avenue, New York, NY 10017, USA

First issued in paperback 2016

Routledge is an imprint of the Taylor & Francis Group, an informa business

British Library Cataloguing in Publication Data
Law in action : ethnomethodological and conversation
analytic approaches to law. - (Socio-legal studies)
1.Sociological jurisprudence
I.Travers, Max II.Manzo, John F.
340.1'15

Library of Congress Cataloging-in-Publication Data
Law in action : ethnomethodological and conversation analytic
approaches to law / edited by Max Travers and John F. Manzo.
p. cm.
Includes index.
ISBN 1-84014-078-X (hardcover)
1. Sociological jurisprudence. 2. Law--Psychological aspects.
I. Travers, Max. II. Manzo, John F.
K380.L388 1997
340'.115--dc21 97-37214
CIP

ISBN 13: 978-1-138-25016-1 (pbk)
ISBN 13: 978-1-84014-078-1 (hbk)

Contents

PART II: CONTEMPORARY CONTRIBUTIONS

List of Contributors

Stacy Burns, Department of Sociology, University of California at Los Angeles
Paul Drew, Department of Sociology, University of York
Harold Garfinkel, Department of Sociology, University of California at Los Angeles
Martha Komter, Bonger Institute for Criminology, Department of Law, University of Amsterdam
Michael Lynch, Department of Human Sciences, Brunel University
John F.Manzo, Department of Sociology, University of Toronto
Gregory Matoesian, Department of Criminal Justice, University of Illinois
Douglas W. Maynard, Department of Sociology, University of Indiana
Albert J. Meehan, Department of Sociology and Anthropology, Oakland University, Rochester
Harvey Sacks (deceased), Department of Sociology, University of California at Los Angeles
Max Travers, Faculty of Applied Social Sciences and Humanities, Buckinghamshire College
Rod Watson, Department of Sociology, University of Manchester

Preface

Ethnomethodologists and conversation analysts have always been interested in the study of law and legal institutions, and there is now a large body of empirical studies, produced during the last thirty years in a number of different countries, representing a range of analytic traditions in each field. Our aim in this collection is to introduce this literature, and the research questions pursued by ethnomethodologists and conversation analysts, in an accessible form to a general audience in the inter-disciplinary field of law and society studies (see also Atkinson, 1981; Hester and Eglin, 1992). We also hope that the collection will interest students and researchers in the fields of communication studies, discourse analysis and mainstream sociology.

Ethnomethodology and conversation analysis offer a distinctive approach towards the study of law and legal institutions, through their focus on everyday talk and action, and the detailed content of occupational activities. Ethnomethodological ethnographers, in what has become known as the studies-of-work tradition, have studied the situated "practical reasoning" constituting different varieties of legal work. Conversation analysts, employing a research methodology which is based upon the analysis of audio-recordings of naturally-occurring interaction, have examined how the day-to-day business of legal settings is conducted through everyday talk. Both approaches are distinctive, both theoretically and methodologically, in that they offer a re-specification of political and philosophical debates about law, through examining the practical actions which accomplish law as a social phenomenon.

While there are many in the law and society movement who have a great interest in sociological theory, we have often found in attending conferences, and reading the law and society journals, that there is little appreciation of the fact that different sociological traditions have distinctive, and often irreconcilable epistemological and methodological assumptions which inform the way they collect research data, and produce empirical findings. Unfortunately, this has meant that, while many ethnomethodological and conversation analytic studies are well-known, and regularly cited by law and society researchers, the radical character of their assumptions are not widely appreciated by most researchers in this field, who continue to view law primarily as a macro-institution, and to keep their distance from theoretical and methodological debates in mainstream sociology. We hope that this collection will make it possible to appreciate the methodological basis of ethnomethodological and conversation analytic studies, and the wider implications for sociology of law.

We would especially like to thank Doug Maynard, Rod Watson and Deirdre Boden for encouraging us to pursue this project, and are especially grateful to Rod Watson for suggesting the title. We would also like to thank Philip Thomas, and John Irwin of Dartmouth, for their advice and support. We would also like to thank The Literary Estate of Harvey Sacks, Cambridge University Press, *Victimology*, *The Journal of Contemporary Ethnography* and *Sociological Theory* for giving us permission to publish, respectively, chapters 2, 3, 4, 7 and 8.

Finally, those with an interest in globalization (or at least in the fact that the world is becoming a smaller place) might be interested in the role of the internet in making this book possible. We have never met in the flesh, but have shared ideas, and worked through problems, via an electronic link between terminals in High Wycombe, England and Mobile, Alabama.

Max Travers and John F.Manzo, April 1997.

References

Atkinson,J.M. (1981), 'Ethnomethodological Approaches to Socio-Legal Studies', in A.Podgorecki and C.J.Whelan (eds), *Sociological Approaches to Law*, Croom Helm, London, pp.201-223.

Hester,S. and Eglin,P. (1992), *A Sociology of Crime*, Routledge, London.

1 Ethnomethodology, Conversation Analysis, and the Sociology of Law

JOHN F. MANZO

Our goal in this collection is to represent the enormous range of ethnomethodological investigations of legal phenomena. We have, to this end, organized this book into two parts. The first comprises works that we consider paradigmatic of the perspectives of ethnomethodology and the closely-related field of conversation analysis as they apply to law, concentrating on works that have heretofore been unavailable or little-known outside of specialist circles. The second part includes papers that are more recent, which are informed, to varying degrees, by the exemplary works presented in the first section. The range of topics addressed in these pieces is large, employing different approaches to data collection and analysis and with different conceptions of how best to enact the perspective of ethnomethodology and conversation analysis. Despite this variety, there are a number of themes common to all studies, inside and outside of topics related to law, in the perspective. My strategy in this chapter is to provide a somewhat cursory overview of what kind of legal sociology ethnomethodology prescribes, to address how such an approach differs from those of orthodox legal sociologies, to review some classic works not included in this collection in order to map out the history of ethnomethodology and law, and to introduce and specify the common themes of the works in this book.

Conventional Legal Sociologies: A Brief Overview

"The law" has been a theoretical and empirical focus in sociology since before sociology was recognized as a unique discipline. Each of sociology's founding practitioners addressed the law, or law-related issues, as illustrations or tests of their core concerns. For example, Weber's famous exposition of legal modernization and the attainment of formal rationality in law reflected, and indeed may represent the clearest exemplification of, his substantive historical sociology. Durkheim saw the predominance of differing types of law—repressive and restitutive—as a kind of social barometer indicating the level of organic (or mechanical) solidarity in society, and thus perceived an intimate relationship between law and other social forms. Marx, while not directly addressing law directly to the same extent as did Weber or Durkheim, saw laws as aspects of the institutional superstructure that helped to protect ruling class interests (as in his criticism of the Black Act), and Marx's intellectual heirs have helped expand this view. In each of these authors' works, we see law as a resource employed in the service of larger theoretical themes. This observation helps denote an important difference between the perspective of ethnomethodology and those of more orthodox sociological perspectives, in the sociology of law and elsewhere. We see law, and the practical activities inhering in and constituting legal settings especially, as *topics* for analysis, and not as *resources* in the service of "larger" theoretical issues. As a study policy, this distinction is vital in ethnomethodology and conversation analysis (Zimmerman and Pollner, 1971). I will address this recommendation more fully after a brief discussion of more contemporary works in the sociology of law and the differences that obtain between them and ethnomethodology.

Much of the contemporary sociology of law adheres to the perspectives of sociology's founders, at least, in theoretical and conceptual emphases. The approach of Weber has spawned studies that encompass interests in the classical Weberian topics of bureaucracy, rationality, and legitimation, as well as works that address his more micro-level interests in subjective understanding and interpretation. Durkheim's legacy is that of functionalism and its variants, such as studies that address the relationship between social forms, political structures, and reactions to crime, and any approaches (including those in social anthropology) that employ the notion of "consensus" as a basis for law. The most productive strains in legal sociology today—the approaches of conflict theory, critical jurisprudence, feminism, globalization theory, and poststructuralism— are based (or in critical reaction against) assumptions and issues derived from Marx. On balance, the contemporary sociology of law is, like sociology in general, informed by the classics.

Despite the extent of traditional themes in contemporary legal sociology, however, one notable difference between the founding fathers and their heirs is the much greater current emphasis on empirical research. In addition to, and sometimes in place of, grand theorizing are more delimited studies that attend law at a more minute level. Lawyers' work and the organization and stratification of the legal profession, courts and dispute processing, policing, penology, and governmental regulation have all been addressed, by contemporary sociologists, empirically (cf. Cotterrell, 1992). These investigations do sometimes clearly reflect theoretical orientations, but many are hardly informed by "theory" at all, as traditionally conceived. The most salient trend in the history of the sociology of law is not, in my view, the growth, demise, or resurgence of any particular theoretical perspective, but rather its transformation from a subfield concerned with evincing larger sociological theories and other more foundational issues to one that has become so (hyper-)empirically oriented that its basic theoretical motivations have, in many cases, been lost.

One way to account for this empirical turn in current legal sociology is to note that the priorities in the area are not so much those that satisfy any sociological theory, but those of law, legal practitioners, and the ideology of jurisprudence (cf. Grace and Wilkinson 1978; Berends, 1992; Travers 1993). In other words, the sociology of law has become an arena for the test of whether law, legal institutions, and legal actors are accomplishing mandates that are contained within the law itself. Sociolologists ask whether affirmative action legislation "works", whether mandatory arrest for perpetrators of domestic violence "works", whether judicial sentencing reform "works", and so on. The concerns of legal practitioners—lawyers, judges, police officers, and so forth—have become the concerns of legal sociologists. This argument militates against the view of Cotterrell (1986:20), in writing on the connections between law and sociology, who says, "the appeal made by legal scholars who seriously seek to escape the disciplinary constraints of legal science is almost always ultimately an appeal to sociology in some form". I would suggest to the contrary that sociologists "appeal" to legal science and jurisprudential priorities far more often than do legal scholars turn to sociology, whatever that might mean. Thus, whether we speak of positivist, realist, critical, feminist, or other perspectives, current sociolegal research is consistently defined by principles that are contained in the law, and the ideology surrounding legal practice.

A good example of this relationship is in research on juries, which has been the focus of much of my own work. Most conventional jury research assesses jurors and their decisions on the basis of criteria for "correct" decision-making that the law and their legal decision rules stipulate. Researchers ask whether a jury acquitted or convicted a defendant as a legally responsible act or as a "runaway" jury that has flouted its legal requirements. Although most sociologists who conduct jury research appear to be concerned with pro forma sociological questions, especially as they relate to the role of social-structural variables—race, class, and gender most especially—and their influence on the jury's decision, such concerns are not, in the main, with reference to general "sociological" questions of the influence of demographic characteristics on human behavior. Instead, the emphasis is on the *legal* stipulation that juries make decisions according to legal considerations and juries' official instructions, and without regard to the demographic or otherwise (legally) irrelevant characteristics of defendants, witnesses, or the jurors themselves (cf. Reskin and Visher, 1986). Thus, much of sociological research into jury deliberations evaluates jurors to ascertain how well, or how poorly, they meet behavioral standards that the law specifies.

The same conclusion can be drawn about much of the work in the sociology of law. The motivating question has become, "Are actors in legal settings accomplishing what the law prescribes?" and not, "What are actors in legal settings *doing* in the first place?". It is this latter question, as I will presently illustrate, that concerns practitioners in ethnomethodology and conversation analysis.

We can thus summarize much of the sociology of law, whether we speak of classical or contemporary versions, as exhibiting two often disparate concerns. In classical works, law was seen as a propitious testing ground for the theorist's larger sociological theories. Law and legal practices were not attended as topics *sui generis*, but in service to general sociological theorizing. In contemporary legal sociology, despite the longevity of classical theoretical strains, we see an emphasis on empirical studies that seem to obscure, and even obviate, bases in theory in favor of evaluative studies that address actors' adherence to, or flouting of, standards of correct procedure that legal institutions themselves prescribe. In either variety, the sociology of law is informed by priorities that exclude and preclude the study of legal actors' activities in their own terms, without deference to larger sociological questions and without prioritizing legal standards of conduct. The work in this volume is different: It scrutinizes the organization of activities that make law recognizable as a distinct form of social life. The analytic perspective here contends that the study of "law" requires this sort of attention. I will now address how this perspective has informed the sociology of law.

The Ethnomethodological Alternative

The approach of the authors in this volume is ethnomethodological. Ethnomethodology (Garfinkel, 1967; Heritage, 1984) is an area of sociology that concerns the practices of ordinary persons in daily life, in concert with other social actors, that create the appearance of enduring, stable, and predictable social order. Ethnomethodology is the study of the organization of everyday activities, the "how" of social organization. Ethnomethodological studies, based on ethnographic research, have examined the nature of practical reasoning in different casual and occupational settings (cf. Garfinkel, 1967; Turner, 1974 for exemplary collections). An area of social inquiry closely related to ethnomethodology, but with rather distinct data sources, presentation, and analysis, is conversation analysis (CA), which studies the interactional organization of *talk* and related activities in settings ranging from the everyday (for a collection see Atkinson and Hertitage, 1984) to the institutional (Boden, 1994; Drew and Heritage, 1992). Ethnomethodology and CA are, for all their difference in appearance and vocabularies, unquestionably part of the same enterprise. Both study the minutiae of social life in order to discover and explicate real actors' practical reasoning and practical activities; both address, from the standpoint of the actors themselves, how social organization is done. Thus, where I use the term "ethnomethodology" and its variants here, it should be understood that I include CA in those illustrations.

Although its title may seem to suggest otherwise, ethnomethodology is not a "method" but an independent area of inquiry that constitutes a substantive subfield of sociology. Ethnomethodology is etymologically the "study of members' methods", where "member" is an ordinary person, a participant in mundane social life; and his or her "methods" are the ordering, or sense-making, practices that persons in interaction recurrently produce and reenact (Garfinkel, 1974). Ethnomethodology is unique among areas of sociology and social science as a whole, including so-called "creative" sociologies, because it does not pursue the development of typologies or other analytic constructs (such as ethnographic models, statistical relationships, or ideal types), but attempts to specify how actual persons accomplish perceivedly stable social order as a day-to-day, moment-by-moment achievement. For ethnomethodology, actual practices need not be modified or respecified as idealized constructs, because actual practices are already endogenously organized:

> From an ethnomethodological standpoint, "raw" experience is anything but chaotic, for the concrete activities of which it is composed are coeval with an intelligible organization that actors "already" provide and that is therefore available for scientific analysis. Central to the achievement of this organization are practical activities through which actors produce and recognize the circumstances in which they are embedded. The principle aim of ethnomethodology is to investigate the procedural accomplishment of these activities as actual, concerted behaviors (Maynard and Clayman, 1991:387).

Ethnomethodological studies have concerned a variety of topics, and have been conducted in a variety of settings, as Maynard and Clayman (1991) address in discussing "the diversity of ethnomethodology". Ethnomethodology is therefore not a monolithic enterprise. It is multi-faceted. The settings in which analysts have conducted studies have varied, from the analysis of the social organization of "casual" telephone calls to a myriad of studies conducted in institutional settings, including encounters between doctors and patients, among scientists in an astronomy laboratory, in business meetings, and in many other sites of social interaction. One particularly propitious arena for ethnomethodological analysis has been the legal arena.

The history of the relationship between ethnomethodology and legal topics resonates with that between law and sociology as a whole. Some of the earliest ethnomethodological studies were of legal topics, many of which were conducted before the word "ethnomethodology" existed (Atkinson,

1981). Among these venerable studies are four that stand out, because they have so thoroughly been assimilated into "mainstream" legal sociology and criminology that non-ethnomethodologists often fail to recognize them as ethnomethodological classics. The studies are those of Sudnow (1965) on "normal crimes", Bittner (1967) on peacekeeping practices among police on "skid row", Garfinkel (1967) on jurors' reasoning practices, and Wieder (1974) on the "convict code" as reported by prison inmates. Each of these pieces treated as its central topic the methods used by "members" (attorneys, the police, prison inmates, and jurors themselves) without regard to their adequacy or appropriateness from the standpoint of legal professionals. These investigations all sought after how participants themselves described and conducted their activities, and all found that members' own descriptions were different from those of official sources, and furthermore that these members' descriptions merited study as topics in their own right.

Thus, Sudnow examined reasoning practices of a group of lawyers attempting to determine equivalent treatment in plea bargaining to illustrate how legal codes do not necessarily govern legal practice, even among "professionals". Bittner interviewed and observed police officers and discovered that police do not regard their work as either "law enforcement" or "order maintenance" (to cite terms familiar to any student of police science or criminal justice), but as "peacekeeping". This term has now become so pervasive in accounts of police work that police officers are sometimes referred to, officially and unofficially, as "peace officers". This label, in a manner that is at variance with the history of most complex organizations, was created to accommodate the officers' own view of their work, instead of having been imposed "from the top". And that view was provided in Bittner's groundbreaking research.

Garfinkel, in a piece drawn from the famed and infamous Chicago Jury Project of the 1950s, was the first (and, until my own work several decades later, the only) researcher to examine the behavior of actual jurors in deliberation. He discovered that jurors produce a set of rules that define standards of "correct" procedure that are different from, if not inconsistent with, the rules prescribed them by the judge and the rules that researchers traditionally have used as yardsticks for the veracity of their decisions. This investigation was important not only for understanding juries' interactional dynamics "from the inside" for the first time, but also in developing the entire area of inquiry that Garfinkel would call "ethnomethodology", since it was during this project that Garfinkel first came upon the expression.

Wieder found that prison inmates adhere to, and reference in their discourse, rules of conduct that separate (dishonorable) "inmates" from (honorable) "convicts" and distinguish the honorable from the dishonorable using criteria that are, at times, shockingly at odds with prison administrators' standards of conduct and notions of the "model inmate". Wieder's study has influenced theory and practice in penology ever since, because he specified part of the content of the prisoners' subculture, a subculture that encompasses discursive rules that are often at odds with the rules of the institution as conceived by prison administrators. Prison guards who bemoan the fact that "the inmates are running the prison" reference Wieder's findings and, in attempting to understand, remove, or accommodate to that control, indicate just how practical ethnomethodology can be.

Each of these classics shares at least three features, features that taken together constitute directives for conducting ethnomethodological research. First, the studies are of *members'* practices. Garfinkel's study of jurors was not an investigation into judicial directives, the court system as a whole, or any other institutional issues, but rather a study of jurors' lived activities. Second, the descriptions and other data provided by the subjects and interviewees in these works constitute the *topics* of analysis, and not *resources* for evaluative purposes or for evincing what analysts presume are the larger sociological phenomena. Third, issues of traditional concern to sociologists are set aside, or "bracketed", in favor of inspecting activities directly. For example, most sociologists would analyze prison inmates' subculture with reference to variables, such as the race, class, and age as well as penology-related issues such as criminal offense and sentence, that are assumed or predicted to affect features of that subculture. Ethnomethodologists are not concerned with variable analysis (except where "variables" are of explicit interest to *actors*, as when they themselves engage in talk on racial issues) or causal modelling. Ethnomethodologists adhere to a strict criterion of evidence for the "influence" of social-structural or otherwise external factors on participants' actions, and that criterion requires speakers to articulate that influence as features of their talk and related social activities. Even in such cases as where speakers explicitly note the salience of social-structural issues, however, ethnomethodology prescribes that such accounts not be taken as evidence for the analyst's hypotheses, but as features of the *speaker's* discourse and displayed reasoning procedures. An ethnomethodologist would not take a recorded statement such as, "The problem here is minorities", as straightforward "evidence" of the speaker's racial or ethnic biases. Instead, an ethnomethodologist would consider how such statements are organized and attended in social interaction to uncover the interactants' uses of such terminologies. Such an analytic policy calls upon the researcher to set aside issues of traditional sociological concern—race, gender, "false consciousness", group cohesiveness, and so on—and to observe activities as objectively as possible.

All three of these foregoing research policies inform all ethnomethodological studies. Ethnomethodology concerns practical activities in their details, and it treats as topical and notable what other avenues of social research either ignore or obscure by transforming those activities into resources that stand as evidence for interpretive or hypothetico-deductive claims. Ethnomethodology lets actors speak for themselves, and treats that "speaking"—which comprises all practical social activities— as the central topic of study.

Ethnomethodology has encompassed a large and growing number of law-related works in addition to those just reviewed. Among these, the most popular empirical setting, as determined by the number of studies conducted there, has been in the courts. Influential among these are several monographs: Atkinson and Drew (1979), on the organization of trial talk and related behaviors, Cicourel (1968) on practices in the administration of juvenile justice, Matoesian (1994) on rape trials, and Maynard (1984), on criminal plea-bargaining. The focus of each of these studies has been the organization of discourse in these settings, and so these works are estimable examples of studies in conversation analysis as well as in the sociology of law. In addition to these monographs, shorter pieces that address trial and trial-related processes include works by Garfinkel (1956, 1967a), Garcia (1991), Komter (1994), Pollner (1979), Pomerantz (1987), Pomerantz and Atkinson (1984), Travers (1992), and Watson (1990).

With regard to police work, Cicourel's (1968) work on juvenile justice stands as a seminal monograph on this topic as well as with respect to practices in juvenile courts. Sacks' (1972) piece on the ways in which police evaluate arrestees' character, and, more recently, Meehan's (1986, 1989) research on police and their practices of record-keeping have continued and expanded Bittner's interest. Studies of juries have also constituted an important vein in legal ethnomethodological scholarship. Studies on juries have been conducted by Holstein (1983) Manzo (1993, 1995, 1996) and Manzo and Maynard (1993). Each of these studies relies and expands upon Garfinkel's (1967a) earlier work by emphasizing what jurors do, in real time and in their own terms.

Ethnomethodology, conversation analysis, and studies of law-in-action share a long history, and this history warrants our collection here. But the amount of law-related work begs the question concerning why ethnomethodologists have addressed law for so long and with such thoroughness. One reason, as addressed by Atkinson (1981), is the straightforward fact that research relating to law and criminology is more readily fundable than much of the rest of sociology. Any perusal of advertisements for academic positions in sociology can verify that law and its cognate areas, such as deviance, criminology, criminal justice and juvenile delinquency, are clearly the "growth areas" of the discipline, and researchers and teachers must go where the money is. But, although this reason should not be de-emphasized, the answer is more complex than economics alone. I believe that ethnomethodology is well-equipped, and in fact best-equipped among approaches to such study, to address how legal work is *done*. This is because "law" consists, in the first place, of concerted work by real persons in real time. Ethnomethodological law-related research reflects an assumption that legal decision-making (among other phenomena constituting law in action) can be best explicated by inspecting closely the activities that constitute it. As Pomerantz and Atkinson (1984:286) note,

> Persons involved in legal work, then, cannot enjoy the luxury of speculating about how truth claims can be validated, or whether it would even be possible to specify independent and decontextualized procedures for so doing. The local interactional business at hand is such that, somehow or other, participants have to make decisions about matters of fact and responsibility that are treated as definite "for all practical purposes". For the ethnomethodologist, that somehow or other provides the main focus for analytic attention.

For most conventional legal sociologists, the activities that constitute work in legal settings - the talk that makes up plea bargaining, that makes up jury deliberation, that makes up conversations between lawyers and clients - is an annoyance, a stumbling block that exposes the gap that exists between idealized theoretical or philosophical constructs surrounding "law" and the work of legal actors. This gap between what might be labelled "theory" and "practice", often referred to as "*The* Gap" (which mirrors perfectly the distinction between idealized social forms and the "disorganization" in concrete social activities that animated Parsons and has informed formal analytic sociology ever since), has always been a central concern in jurisprudence and the sociology of law. The Gap helps explain the curious disjunction between classical theoretical works and the empirical studies of contemporary analysts discussed earlier in this chapter. The activities that obtain in legal settings do not fit the idealizations developed in theory (either sociological or jurisprudential), and so in lieu of attempts to bridge "theory" and "practice", many researchers have chosen to abandon such attempts altogether.

Ethnomethodology offers a unique solution to the problem of The Gap, and I believe that this signals ethnomethodology's unique contribution to the sociology of law. Whereas other sociological orientations, such as symbolic interactionism and interaction process analysis, propose studying micro-interactional phenomena as ethnomethodologists usually do, such approaches are still limited by hypothetico-deductive presumptions (as with IPA, which imposes pre-existing codes on observed actions) or conceptual foundations that delimit analytic interpretation to make observations "fit" such foundations (as with SI and its imposition of notions of symbolic communication). Ethnomethodology and conversation analysis employ designs of research that are grounded in the truest sense. Neither approach imposes hypothetical constructs on the activities under scrutiny. Findings are informed by *members*' interpretations and not the interpretations of the analyst. Ethnomethodology is about the social organization of lived activities. It is about the real work of real persons, a phenomenon that constitutes, in other approaches to law, a distraction that must be ignored or explained away as error on the part of the persons under study. The Gap is a problem only if analysts disallow actors from speaking for themselves. This speaking is, again, the empirical and theoretical focus of ethnomethodology and conversation analysis. As such, our perspective bridges The Gap.

The topics of ethnomethodology are what Garfinkel has called the "seen but unnoticed" features of social life, features whose presence is so taken for granted that they are only "noticed" when they are missing (as when somebody ignores certain tacit interactional rules, such as those governing interpersonal distance, the volume of conversational speech, how to comport one's self in an elevator, and so on) or topicalized by ethnomethodologists. Ethnomethodological studies present social life in fine-grained detail, they allow one to see "the trees for the forest", by uncovering phenomena that participants are at once completely dependent upon and usually completely unaware of. Findings in ethnomethodological studies often militate against the views as prescribed in organizational maps, in law, in rules of procedure, and in other institutionally-imposed environments, not because these "rules" are wrong or wanting, but because they blind us to the exquisite accomplishment of practical social organization. This accomplishment in the legal area is the topic of each of the pieces in this book.

References

Atkinson, J.M. (1981), 'Ethnomethodological Approaches to Sociolegal Studies', in A. Podgorecki and C.J. Whelan (eds), *Sociological Approaches to Law*, Croom Helm, London, pp.201-223.

Atkinson, J.M. and Drew,P. (1979), *Order in Court: The Organisation of Verbal Interaction in Judicial Settings*, Macmillan, London.

Atkinson, J.M. and Heritage, J. (1984), *Structures of Social Action: Studies in Conversation Analysis*, Cambridge University Press, Cambridge.

Berends, M. (1992), 'Review Essay: An Elusive Profession? Lawyers in Society', *Law and Society Review*, vol.20, pp.161-188.

Bittner, E. (1967), 'The Police on Skid Row: A Study of Peace Keeping', *American Sociological Review*, vol.32, pp.699-715.

Boden, D. (1994), *The Business of Talk: Organizations in Action*, Polity, Cambridge.

Cicourel, A.V. (1968), *The Social Organisation of Juvenile Justice*, Wiley, New York.

Cotterrell, R. (1986), 'Law and Sociology: Notes on the Constitution and Confrontation of Disciplines', *Journal of Law and Society*, vol.13, pp.9-34.

Cotterrell, R. (1992), *The Sociology of Law: An Introduction*, Butterworths, London.

Drew, P. and Heritage,J. (1992), *Talk at Work: Interaction in Institutional Settings*, Cambridge University Press, Cambridge.

Garcia, A. (1991), 'Dispute Resolution without Disputing: How the Interactional Organization of Mediation Hearings Minimizes Argument', *American Sociological Review*, vol. 56, pp.818-835.

Garfinkel, H. (1956), 'Conditions of Successful Degradation Ceremonies', *American Journal of Sociology*, vol. 61, pp.241-244.

Garfinkel, H. (1967), *Studies in Ethnomethodology*, Prentice Hall, Englewood Cliffs, N.J.

Garfinkel, H. (1967), 'Some Rules of Correct Decision-Making that Jurors Respect', in H.Garfinkel, *Studies in Ethnomethodology*, Prentice Hall, Englewood Cliffs, N.J.

Garfinkel, H. (1974), 'On the Origins of the Term "Ethnomethodology"', in R.Turner (ed.), *Ethnomethodology*, Penguin, Harmondsworth, pp.15-18.

Grace,C. and Wilkinson,P. (1978), *Sociological Inquiry and Legal Phenomena*, Collier Macmillan, Middlesex.

Heritage, J. (1984), *Garfinkel and Ethnomethodology*, Polity, Cambridge.

Holstein, J. (1983), 'Jurors' Uses of Judges' Instructions', *Sociological Methods and Research*, vol.11, pp.501-518.

Komter, M. (1994), 'Accusations and Defences in Courtroom Interaction', *Discourse and Society*, vol.5, pp. 165-187.

Manzo, J. (1993), 'Jurors' Narratives of Personal Experience in Deliberation Talk', *Text*, vol.13, pp.267-290.

Manzo, J. (1994), '"You Wouldn't Take a Seven-Year-Old and Ask Him All These Questions": Jurors' Use of Practical Reasoning in Supporting their Arguments', *Law and Social Inquiry*, vol. 19, pp.601-626.

Manzo, J. (1996), 'Taking Turns and Taking Sides: Opening Scenes from Two Jury Deliberations', *Social Psychology Quarterly*, vol. 59, pp.107-125.

Matoesian, G. (1994), *Reproducing Rape: Domination Through Talk in the Courtroom*, University of Chicago Press, Chicago.

Maynard, D.W. (1984), *Inside Plea Bargaining: The Language of Negotiation*, Plenum, New York.

Maynard, D.W. and Clayman,S. (1991), 'The Diversity of Ethnomethodology', *Annual Review of Sociology*, vol. 71, pp.385-418.

Maynard, D.W. and Manzo,J. (1993), 'On the Sociology of Justice: Theoretical Notes from an Actual Jury Deliberation', *Sociological Theory*, vol.11, pp.171-193 (reprinted in this volume).

Meehan, A.J. (1986), 'Record-Keeping Practices in the Policing of Juveniles', *Urban Life*, vol.15, pp.70-102 (reprinted in this volume).

Meehan, A.J. (1989), 'Assessing the "Police-Worthiness" of Citizens' Complaints to the Police: Accountability and the Negotiation of "Facts"', in D. Helm (ed.), *The Interactional Order: New Directions in the Study of Social Order*, Irvington, New York, pp.116-140.

Pollner, M. (1979), 'Explicative Transactions: Making and Managing Meaning in Traffic Court', in G. Psathas (ed.), *Everyday Language: Studies in Ethnomethodology*, Irvington, New York, pp.227-253.

Pomerantz, A. (1987), 'Descriptions in Legal Settings', in G. Button and J. Lee (eds), *Talk and Social Organisation*, Multilingual Matters, Clevedon, UK, pp.226-243.

Pomerantz, A. and Atkinson, J.M. (1984), 'Ethnomethodology, Conversation Analysis, and the Study of Courtroom Interaction', in D.J. Mueller, D.E. Blackman, and A.J. Chapman (eds), *Psychology and Law*, Wiley, New York, pp.283-297.

Reskin, B. and Visher, C. (1986), 'The Impacts of Evidence and Extralegal Factors in Jurors' Decisions', *Law and Society Review*, vol. 20, pp.424-434.

Sacks, H. (1972), 'Notes on Police Assessment of Moral Character', in D. Sudnow (ed.), *Studies in Social Interaction*, The Free Press, Glencoe, pp.31-75.

Sudnow, D. (1965), 'Normal Crimes', *Social Problems*, vol. 12, pp.255-276.

Travers, M. (1992), 'Persuading the Client to Plead Guilty: An Ethnographic Examination of a Routine Morning's Work in the Magistrates' Court', Manchester Sociology Occasional Papers, No.33, University of Manchester.

Travers, M. (1993), 'Putting Sociology Back into the Sociology of Law', *Journal of Law and Society*, vol. 20, pp.438-451.

Turner, R. (1974), *Ethnomethodology*, Penguin, Harmondsworth.

Watson, D.R. (1983), 'The Presentation of Victim and Offender in Discourse: The Case of Police Interrogations and Interviews', *Victimology*, vol.8, pp.31-52 (reprinted in this volume).
Wieder, D. L. (1974), *Language and Social Reality*, Mouton, The Hague.
Zimmerman, D. and Pollner, M. (1971), 'The Everyday World as a Phenomenon' in J. Douglas (ed.), *Understanding Everyday Life*, London, Routledge and Kegan Paul, pp.80-103.

PART I
EXEMPLARY STUDIES

Introduction to Part I

MAX TRAVERS

The exemplary or paradigmatic studies we have selected for this part of the collection are intended to illustrate some of the key research questions pursued by ethnomethodologists and conversation analysts in studying law. Inevitably, some important and well-known studies are missing, for example, the work of Sudnow, Bittner, Garfinkel and Wieder, summarized by John Manzo in the previous chapter, as well as pieces of research which will be unfamiliar to academics working in the fields of sociology of law and criminology, but are highly regarded within ethnomethodology (for example, Pollner's 1974 analysis of "explicative transactions" in a traffic court). In this introduction, I will refer to some of this wider literature, but my main concern will be to explain what is ethnomethodological about these studies, and how they provide a distinctive contribution to the study of law.

To begin the collection, we have reprinted Garfinkel's (1967) paper on "Practical Sociological Reasoning" which is a clearer and more developed version of the section in the first chapter of *Studies in Ethnomethodology* about the work of the Los Angeles Suicide Prevention Center. Garfinkel has always had a great interest in legal settings, and his study of how jurors make decisions, and (1956) analysis of the courtroom as a "degradation ceremony" will already be familiar to law and society scholars. He also wrote an article in the 1940s which is concerned with the phenomenological significance of inter- and intra-racial homicides for lawyers in a court-room in the southern United States (Garfinkel, 1948), and has used legal work as one of his main examples in promoting what became the studies-of-work program in the late 1970s.

Like many of Garfinkel's early empirical studies, this is a powerful and theoretically complete statement of how ethnomethodology can contribute to the study of human group life, but it also has particular implications for understanding legal settings. The occupational task of investigators in this office was to produce the official, legal record of how people in Los Angeles had died. Garfinkel shows how this was, through and through, a practical task, so that what investigators found depended, amongst other things, on the time and resources they had available, and other organizational contingencies. Most decisions were recognized by practitioners as imperfect, and potentially revisable, but adequate "for all practical purposes".

Garfinkel uses the work of suicide investigators as a case-study to explicate the key ethnomethodological concepts of reflexivity, accountability and indexicality, and to recommend a policy for studying any social institution in terms of the methods used by members to demonstrate the adequacy and rationality of their actions. The study has tremendous implications for those sociologists and criminologists who continue to use official statistics, as if these represented, at least in principle, an accurate measure of phenomena one can objectively measure in society (see also Atkinson, 1978; Eglin, 1987). For me, however, the piece is most valuable as an illustration of how everyday practical action, in settings like police stations, or law courts, can be investigated as a sociological topic, in a way that preserves the understandings and methods of reasoning used by people doing day-to-day legal work. Anyone wishing to study institutional processes (for example, how the police, social workers or the courts reach, and account for, decisions) should be able to find inspiration, and analytic resources, from this exemplary ethnographic study.

The second piece in this section is a previously unpublished paper by Harvey Sacks that, according to his literary executor Emanuel Schegloff, was probably written in 1962. Sacks is best known as the founder of conversation analysis, but this paper is ethnomethodological in character, and illustrates the influence of Garfinkel's ideas at this early stage of his work, as well as his interest in law as a sociological topic.

Sacks structures the paper around two observations about the role of lawyers in society. He suggests that, in their daily work, they are involved in "the management of routine" (in maintaining the "massive stability" of social life); while in their court work, they are involved in "the management of continuity" (in treating each new case as an instance of a category or principle of existing law).

In the course of the paper, Sacks also addresses a central jurisprudential question, the relationship between law and society. Ehrlich argued that social life was governed by what he termed the "living law" - customary practices governing commerce and the family -which existed outside legal regulation by the state. One theme in Sacks' paper is that everyday social life is normally pursued successfully without following legal rules: for the lawyer, emphasis upon "written matter, on coherence, clarity, completeness, impersonality [and] predictability...provide solutions to matters not treated as problems in the everyday world of others". Sacks also suggests that the operation of the legal system depends upon non-legal practices (such as unspoken agreements between opposing attorneys not to argue every point); that lawyers orient to non-legal relevances in day-to-day practice; and that the legal system colludes with jurors reaching decisions using community, rather than legal values. Garfinkel's study of jurors is presented as being significant for jurisprudence, and perhaps the whole ethnomethodological and conversation analytic enterprise (in showing how common-sense skills and knowledge underpin legal practices) can be viewed in this light.

The next two papers, by Paul Drew and Rod Watson, form part of a program of research informed by Sacks' later writings, which has become known as conversation analysis. Although conversation analytic studies of law, such as Atkinson and Drew (1979), or Maynard (1984) are regularly cited in the field of language and law (see, for example, Levi and Walker, 1990; and Mertz, 1992), it is worth noting that there has, so far, been little appreciation or engagement with methodological issues, as these are understood by researchers working in this tradition.

Most readers will be familiar with the basic method used by conversation analysts: the audio-recording, and transcription of naturally-occurring conversation. The questions they seek to address through this method are, however, less widely appreciated. Why, for example, do they view obvious features of courtrooms - such as the fact that barristers ask the questions, or that everyone stands when the judge enters the room - as posing difficult sociological problems? The reason is that the main object of conversation analysis, like ethnomethodology, is to analyze the taken-for-granted methods which we are using to produce the orderly character of the everyday world. The most obvious feature of conversation identified by Sacks was the fact conversationalists take turns at talk. Since then conversation analysts have studied how turn-taking works in everyday and institutional settings, including the court-room (Atkinson and Drew 1979). However, understanding how turn-taking works as a basic mechanism of conversation is only one part of a wider program that examines the taken-for-granted communicative and interpretive methods used in conversation.

The paper we have published by Paul Drew - which is an abridged version from an influential (1992) collection edited by Drew and Heritage called *Talk at Work* - is concerned with some of the methods used by witnesses and attorneys in the course of cross-examination during rape trials. It is mostly concerned with a short exchange that took place during a particular cross-examination (sixteen lines of transcript) in which a lawyer is trying to discredit the evidence of the alleged victim of a rape. This exchange is then analyzed, in considerable detail, to explicate the methods or "devices" used by the witness and attorney in presenting "contrasting versions" of the event. Drew shows how both attorney and witness are engaged in a struggle to influence the jury, but that this is often conducted obliquely, rather than by direct rebuttal or challenge. This offers a far more subtle and grounded appreciation of "power relations" than one finds in most conventional treatments of this topic, as well as again illustrating how everyday skills and resources (such as the ability to construct alternative descriptions) are used in courts of law.

Watson's paper, which was first published by *Victimology* in 1983, is also about the use of common-sense knowledge and reasoning in the criminal justice process, specifically the methods which offenders use to describe their victims in murder interrogations, in a way which makes available their motives, and, in some cases, attempts to make the victim responsible, wholly or partly, for the offence. In another (1990) paper, Watson has also analyzed the cultural and communicative resources used by police in persuading suspects to confess.

The best way to approach this paper is to begin with a careful reading of the data: in each interview the suspect, to some degree or other, uses the identity or actions of the victim (as a "negro", or a "faggot" or a woman who behaves in a "pricky" way, or as one of the suspect's "black sisters who sleeps with white men") to excuse the crime. Watson shows that, in order to read these interviews in this way, we are using a highly-organized body of common-sense knowledge, which can be analyzed using Sacks' ideas about "membership categories": the everyday terms we use in describing members of society. Categories are understood conventionally in relational pairs (so that we understand the term "negro" as part of the pair "black-white" in the first data extract); as belonging to "Membership Categorization Devices" (so that we make sense of references to a person as being a "negro" or a "faggot" in terms of their membership of collections of categories, such as "racial groups", or "modes of sexual orientation"); and as having category-bound attributes (for example, conventional expectations on how women should behave). These methods are not simply of academic interest: they are used by the police, defendants, criminal lawyers and jurors to recognize "victims" and "offenders" in particular circumstances. In this sense, membership categorization analysis allows us to understand the moral basis of society.

The final piece in this part of the collection is a previously unpublished paper by Michael Lynch, which is based on observing hearings in a criminal court in Canada in the mid-1970s. Lynch has recently co-written a book which adopts an ethnomethodological approach to the Iran-Contra hearings in America (Lynch and Bogen, 1996). This early paper is also about the courtroom, and focuses on the publicly visible work of the judge in the course of criminal proceedings. This includes the management of procedural contingencies, as well as the delivery of moral lectures when sentencing defendants. The actual or projected presence of the judge is also a hearable feature of the work of prosecution and defence lawyers.

Lynch notes that this approach to studying the courtroom cannot give access to the technical skills and knowledge used in legal practice, but "it points to a rich topic of inquiry: the public accountability of judicial actions and reasons as constituents of courtroom hearings". It is instructive to note how much he is able to demonstrate about the interactional work involved in accomplishing a legal hearing from the careful description and analysis of courtroom events. Like the other papers in this collection, it illustrates how ethnomethodology offers a distinctive approach to understanding legal institutions, through examining mundane interactional phenomena which are ignored or idealized by conventional approaches.

References

Atkinson, J.M. (1978), *Discovering Suicide: Studies in the Organization of Sudden Death*, Macmillan, London.

Atkinson, J.M. and Drew, P. (1979), *Order in Court: The Organisation of Verbal Interaction in Court Setting*, Macmillan, London.

Drew, P. and Heritage, J.(1992), *Talk at Work: Interaction in Institutional Settings*, Cambridge University Press, Cambridge.

Eglin, P. (1987), 'The Meaning and Use of Official Statistics in the Explanation of Deviance', in R.J.Anderson, J.A.Hughes and W.W.Sharrock (eds), *Classic Disputes in Sociology*, Unwin Hyman, London, pp.184-212.

Garfinkel, H. (1948),'A Research Note on Inter- and Intra-Racial Homicides', *Journal of Social Forces*, vol.4, pp.369-381.

Garfinkel, H. (1956), 'Conditions of Successful Degradation Ceremonies', *American Journal of Sociology*, vol.61, pp.241-244.

Garfinkel, H. (1967), 'Practical Sociological Reasoning: Some Features in the Work of the Los Angeles Suicide Prevention Center', in E.S.Schneidman (ed.), *Essays in Self-Destruction*, International Science Press, New York, pp.171-187.

Levi, J.N. and Walker, A.G.(eds) (1990), *Language in the Judicial Process*, Plenum Press, New York.

Lynch, M. and Bogen, D. (1996), *The Spectacle of History: Speech, Text and Memory at the Iran-Contra Hearings*, Duke University Press, Durham.

Maynard, D. W. (1984), *Inside Plea-Bargaining: The Language of Negotiation*, Plenum, New York.

Mertz, E. (1992), 'Language, Law and Social Meanings: Linguistic/Anthropological Approaches to the Study of Law', *Law and Society Review*, vol.26, pp.1215-1230.

Pollner,M. (1974), 'Explicative Transactions: Making and Managing Meaning in Traffic Court', G.Psathas (ed.), *Everyday Language: Studies in Ethnomethodology*, Irvington, New York, pp.227-256.

Watson, D.R. (1990), 'Some Features of the Elicitation of Confessions in Murder Interrogations', in G.Psathas(ed.), *Interaction Competence*, University Press of America, Lanham, Maryland and London, pp.263-295.

2 Practical Sociological Reasoning: Some Features in the Work of the Los Angeles Suicide Prevention Center

HAROLD GARFINKEL

The purpose of this chapter is to treat "certification practices" of the Los Angeles Suicide Prevention Center (SPC) as an occasion for reflections about practical actions and practical sociological reasoning in order to formulate several of their features as problematic sociological phenomena. Insofar as these phenomena exhibit characteristic properties of their own, they constitute a legitimate area of inquiry in themselves. The certification practices of the Suicide Prevention Center provide an experience with which these phenomena may be examined.

The plan of the chapter is as follows: Practical action and sociological reasoning are characterized in the first part in sections devoted to features of "common-sense situations of choice" learned about elsewhere but which are repeated in the circumstances and practices of the SPC; to singular features of SPC accounting practices; and to some structural equivocalities in SPC accounts. These remarks are then used as a context for the second part in which three problematic features of practical sociological reasoning are formulated.

Practical Sociological Reasoning

Doing Accounts in "Common-Sense Situations of Choice"

The SPC and the Los Angeles Medical Examiner-Coroner's office joined forces in 1957 to furnish coroner's death certificates the warrant of scientific authority "within the limits of practical certainties imposed by the state of the art". Selected cases of "sudden, unnatural death" that were equivocal between suicide and other modes of death were referred by the Medical Examiner-Coroner to the SPC with the request that an inquiry, called a "psychological autopsy", be made.[1] Subsequently, in joint consultation, the mode of death is decided and a proper title for the death is entered on the death certificate.

The practices and concerns of SPC staff to accomplish their inquiries in common-sense situations of choice repeated the features of practical inquiries that were encountered in other situations: studies of jury deliberations in negligence cases; clinic staff selections of patients for out-patient psychiatric treatment; graduate sociology students' coding of the contents of clinic folders into a coding sheet by following detailed coding instructions; and countless professional procedures in anthropological, linguistic, social psychiatric, and sociological inquiry.[2] The following features in the work at SPC were recognized by staff with frank acknowledgment as prevailing conditions of their work and as matters to consider when assessing the efficacy, efficiency, or intelligibility of their work and SPC testimony added to that of jurors, survey researchers, and the rest: (1) there was an abiding concern on the part of all parties for the temporal concerting of activities; (2) there was a concern for the practical question *par excellence*: "What to do next"; (3) there was a concern on the inquirer's part to give evidence of his grasp of "what anyone knows" about how the settings in which he had to accomplish his inquiries work and a concern to do so for actual occasions when decisions were to be made by his exhibitable conduct in choosing; (4) matters that at the level of talk might be spoken of as "production programs", "laws of conduct", "rules of rational decision-making", "causes", "conditions", "hypothesis testing", "models", and "rules of inductive and deductive inference" in the actual situation were taken for granted to consist of recipes, proverbs, slogans, and partially formulated plans of action; (5) inquirers were required to know and be skilled in dealing with situations "of the sort" for which "rules of rational decision-making" and the rest were intended so that they would "see" or, by what they did, insure the objective, effective, consistent, complete, and empirically adequate; i.e., the rational character of recipes, prophecies, proverbs, and partial descriptions in actual use of the rules; (6) for the practical decider, the actual occasion as a phenomenon in its own right exercised overwhelming priority and decision rules or theories of decision-making were without exception subordinated in order to assess the rational features of the occasion rather than those of the rules; and finally, and perhaps most characteristically, (7) all of the foregoing features, together with the inquirer's system of alternatives, his decision methods, his information, his choices, and the rationality of his accounts and actions were constituent parts of the same practical circumstances in which inquirers did the work of inquiry - a feature that inquirers, if they are to claim and recognize the practicality of their efforts, know of, require, count on, take for granted, use, and gloss.

SPC Accounting Practices

The work by SPC members of conducting their inquiries was part and parcel of the day's work. Recognized by staff members as constituent features of the day's work, their inquiries were thereby intimately connected with the terms of their employment, various internal and external chains of reportage, supervision, and review, and similar organizationally supplied "priorities of relevances" for assessments of what "realistically", "practically", or "reasonably" needed to be done and could be done, and how quickly, with what resources, seeing whom, talking about what, for how long, and so on. Such considerations furnished the "we did what we did what we could, and for all reasonable interests here is what we came out with" its features of organizationally appropriate sense, fact, impersonality, anonymity of authorship, purpose, reproductibility - i.e., of a *properly* rational account of the inquiry.

Members were required in their occupational capacities to formulate accounts of how a death for all practical purposes *really* happened. "Really" made unavoidable reference to daily, ordinary, occupational workings.

Members alone were allowed to invoke such workings as appropriate grounds for recommending the reasonable character of the result *without necessity of furnishing specifics*. On occasions of challenge, ordinary occupational workings would be cited explicitly, in "relevant part". Otherwise such features were disengaged from the product. In their place an account of how the inquiry was done made the how-it-was-actually-done out as appropriate to usual demands, usual attainments, usual practices, *and* to usual talk by SPC personnel in speaking as *bona fide* professional practitioners about usual demands, usual attainments, and usual practices.

One of several titles (relating to *mode* of death) had to be assigned to each case, being legally possible combinations of four elementary possibilities - natural death, accident, suicide, and homicide.[3] *All* titles are so administered in order to withstand the varieties of equivocation, ambiguity, and improvisation that arise in every actual occasion of their use; but these titles are so administered that they *invite* that ambiguity, equivocality, and improvisation. It is part of the work not only that equivocality is a problem - is *perhaps* a problem - but also that practitioners are directed to those circumstances in order to *invite* ambiguity, equivocality, improvisation, temporizing, and the rest. It is not that the investigator, having a list of titles, performs an inquiry that proceeds stepwise to establish grounds for electing among them. The formula is not "here is what we did and among the titles as goals of our research *this* title finally interprets in the best fashion what we found out". Instead titles are continually postdicted and foretold. An inquiry is apt to be guided heavily by the inquirer's imagined settings in which the title will have been "used" by one or another interested party, including the deceased; the inquiries do this in order to decide from whatever "datum" might have been searched out that which can be used to mask the situation if that needs to be done - or they equivocate, gloss, lead, or exemplify, and so on. The prevailing feature of the inquiry is that nothing about it remains assured except the organized occasions of its uses. Thus a routine inquiry is one that the investigator uses particular goblins to accomplish, and he depends upon particular goblins to recognize and to recommend the practical adequacy of his work. Viewed with respect to practices for making it happen, a routine inquiry is not one that is accomplished by rules. It seems much more to consist of an inquiry which is openly recognized to have fallen short; but its adequacy is acknowledged in the ways it falls short, and no one offers or calls particularly for explanations of its shortcomings.

What members are *doing* in their inquiries is always somebody else's business, in the sense that particular, organizationally located and locatable persons acquire an interest as a result of an SPC member's account of whatever it is that might have been reported to have "really happened". Such considerations contribute heavily to the perceived feature of investigations, namely, that they are directed in their course by an account for which the claim will have been advanced that it is correct for all practical purposes. Thus one of the investigator's tasks is to render an account of how a particular person died in society that is a reasonable one for all practical purposes.

"What really happened", over the course of arriving at it as well as after the "what really happened" has been inserted into the file and the title has been decided, may be chronically reviewed as well as chronically foretold in light of what might have been done or what will have been done with the decisions. On the way to making a decision, what might come from it is reviewed and foretold in light of its anticipated consequences. *After* a recommendation has been made and the coroner has signed the death certificate the result can still be "revised", as they say. It can thus become a decision that needs to be reviewed "once more".

Inquirers wanted very much to be able to give the assurance that they could arrive at the end with an account of how the person died that would permit the coroner and his staff to withstand claims by arguing that the account was incomplete or that the death happened differently from - or in contrast to or in contradiction of - what members to the arrangement "claimed". Reference here is neither only nor entirely to complaints of the survivors. Such issues are dealt with as a succession of episodes, most of which are settled fairly quickly. Greater contingencies consist of enduring processes that result from the fact that the coroner's office is a political office. Its activities produce continuing records of its activities; and records are subject to review as products of the scientific work of the coroner, his staff, and his consultants. Office activities are techniques for accomplishing reports that are scientific for all practical purposes, and they involve "writing" as a warranting procedure, for the report by reason of being written proceeds into a file. That the investigator "does" a report is thereby made a matter for public record, for the use of some other only partially identifiable persons. Their interest in why or how or what the inquirer did would have in some relevant part to do with his skill and entitlement as a professional. But investigators also know that other interests will inform the "review", for the inquirer's work will be inspected to see its scientific-adequacy-for-all-practical-purposes as professionals' socially managed claims. Not only for investigators but for all sides there is the relevance of "what was really found out for all practical purposes", which consists unavoidably of how can one find out, how much can one reveal, how much can one mask, how much can one conceal, and how much can one hold as none of the business of some important persons, *investigators* included. All investigators acquire an interest by reason of the fact that as a matter of occupational duty they are making written reports of how for all practical purposes a person really died and really died *in* the society.

Decisions have an unavoidable consequentiality. By this is meant that investigators need to say *in so many words* what really happened. The important words are the titles that are assigned to a text to recover that text as the title's "explication". But what an assigned title consists of as an explicated title is at any particular time for no one to say with any finality, even when it is proposed "in so many words". In fact, *that* it is proposed in so many words, *that*, for example, a written text was inserted into the file of the case, furnishes grounds that one can invoke in order to make something of the "so many words" that will have been used as an account of the death. Viewed with respect to patterns of use, titles and their accompanying texts have an open set of consequences. Upon any use of texts it remains to be seen what can be done with them, what they will come to, what remains to be done "for the time being" pending the ways in which the environment of that decision may organize itself to "reopen the case", "issue a complaint" or "find an issue", and so on. Such ways for SPC'ers are, as patterns, certain; but as particular processes for making them happen, they are in every actual occasion indefinite.

SPC inquiries begin with a death that the coroner finds equivocal as to *mode* of death. They use the death as a precedent by means of which various ways of living in society that could have terminated with the death are searched for and read "in the remains" - in the scraps of this and that, such as the body and its trappings, medicine bottles, notes, bits and pieces of clothing, memorabilia: anything that can be photographed, collected, and packaged. Other "remains" are collected too: rumors, passing remarks, and stories - material in the "repertoire" of whomever might be consulted through the common work of conversations. These "whatsoever" bits and pieces that a story or a rule or a proverb might make intelligible are used to formulate a recognizably coherent, standard, typical, cogent, uniform, planful, i.e., a professionally defensible, and thereby for members, *recognizably* rational account of how the society worked to produce these remains. This point will be clearer if the reader consults a standard text-book in forensic pathology. In it he will find the inevitable photograph of the victim with a slashed throat. Were the coroner to use that "sight" to suggest the equivocality of the mode of death he might say something such as this: "In the case where a body looks like the one in that picture, you are looking at a suicidal death because the wound shows the 'hesitation cuts' that accompany the great wound. One can imagine these cuts are the remains of a procedure whereby the victims first made several preliminary trials of a hesitating sort and then performed the lethal slash. Other courses of action are imaginable, too, and so cuts that look like hesitation cuts can be produced by other mechanisms. One needs to start with the actual display and imagine how different courses of action could have been organized such that *that* picture would be compatible with it. One might think of the photographed display as a phase-of-the-action. In any actual display is there a course of action with which that phase is uniquely compatible? That is the coroner's question".

The coroner (and SPC'ers) ask this with respect to each *particular* case, and thereby the work of achieving practical decidability seems almost unavoidably to assume a prevailing and important characteristic. SPC'ers must accomplish that decidability by considering the "this's": they have to start with *this* much; *this* sight; *this* note; *this* collection of whatever is at hand. And *whatever* is there is good enough in the sense that whatever is there not only *will* do but *does*. One makes whatever is there do. By this is not meant that an SPC investigator is too easily content or that he does not look for more when he should. What is meant rather is that the "whatever" it is that he has to deal with is what will be used to find out, to make decidable the way that society operated to produce *that* picture, to have come to *that* scene as its end result. In this way the remains on the slab serve not only as a precedent but as a goal of SPC inquiries. Whatsoever SPC members are faced with must serve as the precedent by means of which they read the remains in order to see how the society could have operated to have produced what it is that they have "in the end", "in the final analysis", and "in *any* case". What the inquiry can come to is what the death came to.

Structural Equivocalities of Practical Accounts

The structurally equivocal features of the methods and results of both lay and professional sociologists of making practical activities observable were epitomized by Helmer and Rescher,[4] who point out that when members' accounts of everyday activities are used as prescriptions for locating, identifying, analyzing, classifying, making recognizable, finding one's way around in comparable occasions, the prescriptions are lawlike, spatiotemporally restricted, and "loose". By loose is meant that though they are intended as conditional in their logical form, "the nature of the conditions is such that they can often not be spelled out completely or fully". The authors cite as an example a statement about sailing-fleet tactics in the eighteenth century. They point out that the statement carries reference to the state of naval ordinance as a test condition.

> In elaborating conditions (under which such a statement would hold) the historian delineates what is typical of the place and period. The full implications of such reference may be vast and inexhaustible; for instance . . . ordnance soon ramifies *via* metal working technology into metallurgy, mining, etc. Thus, the conditions which are operative in the formulation of an historical law may only be indicated in a general way and are not necessarily, indeed, in most cases cannot be expected

> to be exhaustively articulated. This characteristic of such laws is here designated as looseness...
>
> A consequence of the looseness of the historical laws is that they are not universal, but merely quasi-general in that they admit of exceptions. Since the conditions delimiting the area of application of the law are often not exhaustively articulated, a supposed violation of the law may be explicable by showing that a legitimate, but as yet unformulated, precondition of the law's applicability is not fulfilled in the case under consideration.

Consider that this holds in every particular case and not from logical necessity, i.e., not by reason of the meaning of "quasi-law" but because of the investigators' actual, particular practices. According to these practices one uses such a formulation and counts it a correct formulation despite the fact that the conditions under which one might specify its appropriate or proper or correct use on *that* particular occasion would have been relaxed, yet the result and the usage considered adequate. Accordingly, Helmer and Rescher point out:

> The laws may be taken to contain a tacit caveat of the "usually" or "other things being equal" type. An historical law is thus not strictly universal in that it must be taken as applicable to all cases falling within the scope of its explicitly formulated or formulable conditions; rather, it may be thought to formulate relationships which obtain generally, or better, which obtain "as a rule".
>
> Such a "law" we will term quasi-law. In order for the law to be valid it is not necessary that no apparent exceptions occur, it is only necessary that, if an apparent exception should occur, an adequate explanation be forthcoming, an explanation demonstrating the exceptional characteristic of the case in hand by establishing the violation of an appropriate, if hitherto unformulated, condition of the law's applicability.

These and other features can be cited for the cogency with which they describe SPC members' certification practices. Thus: (1) Whenever a member is required to demonstrate that an account analyzes an actual situation he invariably makes use of the practices of "et cetera", "unless", and "let it pass" to demonstrate the rationality of his achievement. (2) The definite and sensible character of the matter that is being reported is settled by an agreement that reporter and auditor make with each other to furnish one another with whatever unstated understandings are required. Much of what is actually reported is therefore not mentioned. (3) During the time required for their delivery, accounts are apt to require that auditors be willing to wait for what will be said in order that the present significance of what has been said will have become clear. (4) Like conversations, reputations, and careers, the particulars of accounts are built up step-by-step over the actual uses of and references to them. (5) An account's materials are apt to depend heavily for sense upon their serial placement, upon their relevance to the auditor's projects, or upon the developing course of the organizational occasions of their use.

In short, the recognizable sense, fear, methodic character, and impersonality of SPC accounts are not independent of the socially organized occasions of their use. Their rational features *consist* of what members do with and what they "make of" the accounts in the socially organized actual occasions of their use. SPC accounts are reflexively and essentially tied for their sense to the socially organized occasions of their use, for they are *features* of the socially organized occasions of their use.

Some Problems Dealing with the Practical Accomplishment of Rational Action

Objective and Indexical Expressions

Properties that are exhibited by accounts (by reason of their being features of the socially organized occasions of their use) are available from studies by logicians as the properties of indexical expressions and indexical sentences. Husserl spoke of expressions whose sense cannot be decided by an auditor without his necessarily knowing or assuming something about the biography and the purposes of the user of the expression, the circumstances of the utterance, the previous course of the conversation, or the particular relationship of actual or potential interaction that exists between the expressor and the auditor.[5] Russell observed that descriptions involving them apply on each occasion of use to only one thing, but to different things on different occasions.[6] Such expressions, wrote Goodman, are used to make unequivocal statements that nevertheless seem to change in truth value.[7] Each of their utterances, "tokens", constitutes a word and refers to a certain person, time, or place but names something not named by some replica of the word. Their denotation is relative to the speaker. Their use depends upon the relation of the user to the object with which the word is concerned. Time for a temporal indexical expression is relevant to what it names. Similarly, just what region a spatial indexical expression names depends upon the location of its utterance. Indexical expressions and statements containing them are not freely repeatable; in a given discourse, not all their replicas therein are also translations of them. The list can be extended indefinitely.

Virtually unanimous agreement exists among students of practical sociological reasoning, both laymen and professionals, about the properties of indexical expressions and indexical actions. Impressive agreement exists as well that (1) although indexical expressions "are of enormous utility" they are "awkward for formal discourse"; (2) a distinction between objective expressions and indexical expressions is not only procedurally proper but unavoidable for whosoever would do science; (3) without the distinction between objective and indexical expressions, and without the preferred use of objective expressions, the victories of generalising, rigorous, scientific inquiries - logic, mathematics, some of the physical sciences - would fail, and the inexact sciences would have to abandon their hopes; (4) terms and sentences can be distinguished as one or the other in accordance with an assessment procedure that makes decidable their character as indexical or objective expressions; and (5) in any particular case only practical difficulties prevent the substitution by an objective expression of an indexical expression.

In philosophers' studies the distinction and substitutability are motivated by a search for and a concern with theories of consistency proofs and computability of terms and sentences. Areas in the social sciences where the promised distinction and substitutability occurs are countless. These are supported by and themselves support immense resources which are directed toward developing methods for the strong analysis of practical actions Promised applications and benefits are immense.

Nevertheless, wherever studies of practical actions are involved the promised distinction and substitutability of objective expressions for indexical expressions remain programmatic in every particular case and on every actual occasion in which the distinction or substitutability must be demonstrated. In every actual case without exception conditions will be cited that a competent investigator will be required to recognize such that in *that* particular case the terms of the demonstration can be relaxed and the demonstration nevertheless be counted an adequate one.

For "long" texts, or "long" courses of action, for events where members' actions are features of the events that their actions are accomplishing, or wherever tokens are not used or are not suitable as proxies for indexical expressions, the programs' claimed demonstrations are satisfied as matters of practical social management. The distinction and substitutability are always accomplished *only* for all practical purposes, and thereby the first problematic phenomenon is recommended to consist of the reflexivity of the practices and attainments of science in and of the organized activities of everyday life, which is an essential reflexivity.

The Essential Reflexivity of Accounts

SPC members' practical theorizing is sober, serious business. Their concerns are for what is decidable "for practical purposes", "in light of this situation", "given the nature of the actual circumstances", and the like. SPC members are acutely aware that the practices that make up their work circumstances are the same measures whereby a suicide rate is produced. Further SPC practices are treated by its personnel as somewhat approximating scientifically adequate procedures. Accounts with the use of which each problematic death is made out under the auspices of "the case" are treated as being some approximation of "what really happened". Suicide rates are treated as being in some approximation to "real suicide rates".

SPC members cite the relevance of practical considerations to their work of sociological theorizing as defects of their work. Such defects are also invoked as challenges or sources of the virtues in their work. Their brag consists of reciting the frustrations that nature and man impose on the tasks of doing science while certifying cause and mode of deaths. In its terms *how* they are doing *what* they are actually doing is glossed: "We are, after all, doing the best we can, which is better than most".

It is the case for the members of the SPC just as it is for jurors and for professional sociological researchers that practical circumstances and practical actions refer to many organizationally important and serious matters: to resources, aims, excuses, opportunities, tasks, and of course, to grounds for arguing or foretelling the adequacy of procedures and the findings they yield. One matter is excluded from the SPC members' interests: practical actions and practical circumstances are not in themselves a topic, let alone a sole topic, of their inquiries; nor are their inquiries addressed to the tasks of sociological theorizing undertaken to formulate what these tasks consist of as practical actions. In no case is the investigation of practical actions undertaken in order that SPC personnel might be able to recognize and describe what they are doing in the first place. Least of all are practical actions investigated in order to explain to practitioners their own talk about what they are doing. Indeed, SPC personnel find it altogether incongruous to consider seriously that they be engaged in the work of certifying mode of death in such a way that they would concert their efforts with a person seeking to commit suicide so as to assure the unequivocal recognition of "what really happened".

To say they are "not interested" in the study of practical actions is not to complain, nor to point to an opportunity they missed, nor is it a disclosure of error, nor is it an ironic comment. Neither is it the case that because SPC members are "not interested" that they are "precluded" from sociological theorizing. Nor do their inquiries preclude the use of the rule of doubt, nor are they precluded from making the organized activities of everyday life scientifically problematical, nor does the comment bear on the difference between "basic" and "applied" interests in research and theorizing.

What does it mean then to say that they are "not interested" in studying practical actions and practical sociological reasoning? And what is the import of such a statement?

There is an aspect of accounts of singular and prevailing relevance in that it restricts the other features to their specific character as recognizable properties of practical sociological inquiries. It consists in this: with respect to the problematic character of practical actions and the practical adequacy of their inquiries members take for granted that a member must at the outset "know" the settings in which he is to operate if his practices are to serve as measures to bring particular, located features of these settings to recognizable account. They treat as the most passing matter of fact that members' accounts of every sort in all their logical modes; with all of their uses, and for every method for their assembly, are constituent features of the settings that they make observable. SPC members know, require, count on, and make use of this reflexivity to produce, accomplish, recognize, or demonstrate the scientific adequacy for all practical purposes of their procedures and findings.

Not only do SPC members, like jurors and others, take that reflexivity for granted, but they recognize, demonstrate, and make observable for each other the rational character of their actual - and this means their occasional - practices while respecting that *reflexivity* as an unalterable and unavoidable condition of their inquiries.

When I propose that SPC members have no interest in studying practical actions I do not mean that members have none, little, or a lot of it. That they are not interested has to do with reasonable practices, with plausible arguments, with reasonable findings - with "accountable for all practical purposes" as a discoverable matter, exclusively, only, and entirely. To be interested would consist of undertaking to make the reflexive character of practical activities observable - to examine the artful practices of rational inquiry as organizational phenomenon without thought for correctives or irony. SPC members and members wherever they engage in practical inquiries, though they would like to, *can* have none of it.

The Analyzability of Actions in Context as a Practical Accomplishment

In indefinitely many ways SPC inquiries are constituent features of the settings they analyze. In the same ways, their inquiries are made recognizable to members as scientifically adequate for all practical purposes. Thus, that deaths are made accountable for all practical purposes are practical organizational accomplishments. Organizationally, the SPC consists of practical procedures for accomplishing the rational accountability of suicidal deaths as recognizable features of the settings in which that accountability occurs.

In the actual occasions of interaction such an accomplishment is for members omnipresent, unproblematic, and commonplace. For members doing sociology to make this kind of accomplishment a topic of practical sociological inquiry seems unavoidably to require that they treat the rational properties of practical activities as "anthropologically strange". By this I mean to call attention to reflexive practices such as the following: when by his accounting practices the member makes familiar, commonplace activities of everyday life recognizable as familiar, commonplace activities; when on each occasion that an account of common activities is used, that they be recognized for "another first time"; when the members treat the processes and attainments of "imagination" as continuous with the *other* observable features of the settings in which they occur; and when proceeding in such a way that at the same time that the member "in the midst" of witnessed actual settings recognizes that witnessed settings have an accomplished sense, an accomplished facticity, an accomplished objectivity, an accomplished familiarity, and an accomplished accountability the organizational hows of these accomplishments are unproblematic, are known vaguely, and are known only when done skilfully, reliably, uniformly, with enormous standardization, and as an unaccountable matter.

The accomplishment consists of doing, recognizing, and using ethnographies. In unknown ways that accomplishment is a commonplace phenomenon for members. And in the unknown ways that the accomplishment is commonplace it is an awesome phenomenon, for in its unknown ways it consists of (1) members' uses of concerted everyday activities as methods with which to recognize and demonstrate the isolable, typical, uniform, potential repetition, connected appearances, consistency, equivalence, substitutability, directionality, anonymously describable, planful - in short, the rational properties of indexical expressions and indexical actions, and (2) the analyzability of actions in context, given not only that no concept of context in general exists, but that every use of "context" without exception is itself essentially indexical.

The recognizedly rational properties of their common-sense inquiries - their recognizedly consistent, methodic, uniform, or planful character - are *somehow* attainments of SPC members' concerted activities. The rational properties of their practical inquiries *somehow* consist in the concerted work of making evident from fragments, from proverbs, from passing remarks, from rumors, from partial descriptions, from "codified" but essentially vague catalogues of experience, and the like, how a person died in society, and of doing so for deaths from enormously diversified settings of everyday activities. *Somehow* is the problematic crux of the matter.

Programmatic Considerations

The earmark of practical sociological reasoning wherever it occurs is that it seeks to remedy the indexical properties of members' talk and conduct in order to demonstrate the observability of organized actions. Endless methodological studies are directed to the tasks of providing a remedy for indexical expressions, for their properties are pervasive and obstinate nuisances to members in their abiding attempts, with rigorous use of ideals, to recover common conduct and common talk with full structural particulars.

The properties of indexical expressions and indexical actions are ordered properties. These consist of organizationally demonstrable sense, facticity, methodic use, and agreement among "cultural colleagues". Their ordered properties consist of organizationally demonstrable rational properties of indexical expressions and indexical actions. Those ordered properties are ongoing achievements of the concerted commonplace activities of investigators. The demonstrable rationality of indexical expressions and indexical actions retains over the course of its managed production by members the character of ordinary, familiar, routinized, practical circumstances. As process and attainment, the produced rationality of indexical expressions consists of practical tasks subject to every exigency of organizationally situated conduct.

For the study of the forgoing problem, the following interpretive policies are recommended:

1. Let the SPC, like any setting, be viewed as self-organizing with respect to the intelligible character of its own particular, actual, perspectively located appearances as appearances of a social order. Like any setting, the SPC organizes its activities to make its properties as an organized environment of practical activities detectable, countable, recordable, reportable, analyzable - in short, accountable. Its organized arrangements consist of various methods for accomplishing the accountability of its organizational ways as a concerted undertaking. Every claim by SPC practitioners of effectiveness, clarity, consistency, planfulness, or efficiency, and every consideration for adequate evidence, demonstration, description, or relevance obtains its character as a phenomenon from the corporate pursuit of this undertaking and from the ways in which its various organizational environments by reason of their characteristics as organizations of activities "sustain", "facilitate", "resist", etc., these methods for making their affairs accountable matters for all practical purposes.

In exactly and only the ways that SPC is said by its members to be organized it consists of members' methods for making evident to each other their settings' ways as clear, coherent, planful, consistent, chosen, knowable, uniform, reproducible, connections i.e., as rational connections. In exactly the way that SPC personnel are members to organized affairs, they are engaged in serious and practical work of detecting, demonstrating, and persuading through displays on the ordinary, actual occasions of their interactions the appearances of consistent, coherent, clear, chosen, planful arrangements. In exactly and only the ways in which the SPC is said by its members to be organized its activities consist of methods whereby its members are provided with accounts of the setting as countable, storyable, proverbial, comparable, picturable, representable - i.e., accountable events.

2. Of course, not only the SPC but any actual occasion of activity whatsoever can be examined for the feature that "choice" among alternatives of sense, of facticity, of methodic practice, of cause, of communal agreement among "cultural colleagues", and of practical actions is a project of members' actions. When such a possibility is used as a prescription for search and interpretation it turns up inquiries of every imaginable kind, from coroner's inquests to experimental astrophysics, all of them alike in claiming our interest in them as socially organized, artful practices. Every way of doing

inquiry without exception acquires its eligibility for our interest from the various ways that the social structures of everyday activities furnish contexts, objects, resources, justifications, and topics. The work of doing water witching, mathematics, chemistry, and sociology, as well as the psychological autopsy, whether done by lay persons or professionals, would be addressed according to the policy that every feature of sense, of fact, and of method for every particular case of inquiry is the managed accomplishment of organized settings of practical actions; further, that particular determinations in members' practices of consistency, planfulness, relevance, or reproducibility of their practices and results are acquired and assured only through particular, located organizations of artful practices. Every kind of inquiry without exception would consist of organized artful practices whereby the rational properties of indexical expressions - of proverbs, advice, partial description, elliptical expressions, passing remarks, fables, tales, and the rest are demonstrated. The demonstrable rationality of indexical expressions and indexical actions is an ongoing achievement of the organized activities of everyday life. And here is the heart of the conjectural matter. The managed production of this phenomenon in every aspect, from every perspective, and in every stage must retain the character for members of serious, practical tasks, subject to every exigency of organizationally situated conduct.

Notes

1. The following references contain reports on the psychological autopsy procedure developed at the Los Angeles Suicide Prevention Center: (1) Theodore J. Curphey, "The Forensic Pathologist and the Multidisciplinary Approach to Death", a chapter in this volume; (2) Theodore J. Curphey, "The Role of the Social Scientist in the Medicolegal Certification of Death from Suicide", in Norman L. Farberow and Edwin S. Schneidman (eds), *The Cry for Help* (New York, McCraw-Hill Book Company, 1961); (3) Edwin S. Schneidman and Norman L. Farberow, "Sample Investigations of Equivocal Suicidal Deaths", in *The Cry for Help*; (4) Robert E. Litman, Theodore J. Curphey, Edwin S. Schneidman, Norman L. Farberow, and Norman D. Tabachnik, "Investigations of Equivocal Suicides", *Journal of the American Medical Association*, 184: 924-929, 1963; and (5) Edwin S. Schneidman, "Orientations Toward Death: A Vital Aspect of the Study of Lives", in Robert W. White (ed.), *The Study of Lives* (New York, Atherton Press, 1963), reprinted in the *International Journal of Psychiatry*, 2:167-200, 1966.
2. Reported in the author's *Studies in Ethnomethodology* (Englewood Cliffs,N. J.,

Prentice-Hall, Inc., 1967).

3. The possible combinations include the following: natural, accident, suicide, homicide, possible accident, possible suicide, possible natural, accident-suicide undetermined, natural-suicide undetermined, natural-accident undetermined, and natural-accident-suicide undetermined.
4. Olaf Helmer and Nicholas Rescher, *On the Epistemology of the Inexact Sciences*, P-1513 (Santa Monica, California, RAND Corporation, October13, 1958), pp.8-14.
5. Marvin Farber, *The Foundation of Phenomenology* (Cambridge, Mass., Harvard University Press, 1943), pp. 237-238.
6. Bertrand Russell, *Inquiry into Meaning and Truth* (New York, W. W. Norton & Company, Inc., 1940), pp. 134-143.
7. Nelson Goodman, *The Structure of Appearance* (Cambridge, Mass., Harvard University Press, 1951), pp. 287-298.

3 The Lawyer's Work[1,2]

HARVEY SACKS

1. The lawyer is involved in his daily work in the management of routinization, and in his court-oriented work in the management of continuity. In neither of these is he 'the special' operative; in both, however, his contributions have special features. It will be noted that legitimation, authority-orientation, and the like, those widely conceived specialities of the lawyer, are not so treated in this formulation. The reasons for this should shortly become clear.

2. In the first sphere of his activity he faces the fact that the massive stability, ordering of affairs involving interaction takes place in a world where persons take it all for granted, i.e., where action is not oriented to the production of the product. Indeed, nonchalance with respect to the product may be seen to be the condition for its maintenance.

2.1 The lawyer, whether it be due to his failure to grasp how this can go on (this massive ordering) given the known failings of men, i.e., their poor senses, minds, intentions, or whether it be his feeling that *when he* is called in, the matters taken for granted cannot be or are not working, doesn't so rely. The sources of routine are treated by him as problematic. He has got to solve the problem of keeping things going without relying on the attitude of daily life. So he (a) adopts a suspension of knowledge about how things ordinarily go on, and (b) then attempts to provide forms for interaction which have as their goal the complete specification of the necessary components of routine interaction; thus the emphasis on written matter, on coherence, clarity, completeness, impersonality, predictability; for the lawyer these provide solutions to matters not treated as problems in the everyday world of others.

2.2 It is commonly said that where that lawyer participates in organizations that have on-going purposes he is constantly engaged in the use of legalisms that interfere with the prosecuting of those purposes. From his perspective, however, it is taken to be the case that the organizations cannot hold together and perform their jobs 'on trust'. He fears that at each point where there might be a departure from that which is a public guide to where we are and how we are to move anywhere else which all can see and locate us and they by, then there is danger that the routineness by which goals may be accomplished and responsibilities assessed will break down. This requisite, that anyone on the interest of the organization be able to assess what it is doing and how, can only be satisfied, it seems to him, by virtue of the care that goes into the drafting of organizational constitutions, rules of performance, codes of duties, and the producing of the documents that attest to their being followed in every action.

In short, the lawyer feels that he must give explicit concern to the production of the features of society which seem otherwise to be produced without any attendance to their production.

2.3 One of, if not the main beauty of the legal resolution of the problem of managing routinization is that it permits dealings between those who have no respect for each other's motives, interests, statuses, etc., where if the need to be able to check out the common public world were present, things could probably not go on. Insofar as there are connections between everyday actions and the definitions of actions in the legal world (unidirectional connections; there need be no warrant that once an action is 'conceived legally' we can ever find out again 'what actually went on') then there is no need to acknowledge each others private world, or rather then there is no need as a condition of interaction that one or another's private world be acknowledged as a common public world (of statuses, motives, values, etc.). The conveyance of aims, terms, reasons, can be made with reference to a standard set of aims, terms and reasons, having standard meanings, i.e., the meanings the legal system provides. The development and wide use of such possibilities of conducting 'impersonal' transactions, transactions in which there is no call to 'involve oneself' seems to be of especially critical importance in the de-traditionalizing society. The legal system provides a complete set of features for one engaging in an interaction which are defined in terms of the particular type of interaction and not in terms of the features generally known to be possessed by persons in the generally known and valued conceptions of the social structure, and in this way avoids calling into question any of the features typically assigned to members having various locations in their valued conceptions of the social structure.

3. In the second sphere of his activity, the lawyer is engaged in the management of continuity. We have, of course, a huge 'continuity-managing'

industry and the lawyer's part, while key, is far from the whole show.

3.1 Lawyers, of course, try to win cases, but here we are interested in how they go about producing cases from the conflicts clients bring. What is key is that cases 'represent' conflicts; for the fact seems utterly clear (and has been widely noted, especially by those closest to the scene, e.g., Learned Hand) that if it is conflict-resolution one is aiming for, few more awkward devices than the judicial process are conceivable.

What seems to be involved are

(a) the fact that each case is treated as an 'instance' whose resolution has been provided for, rather than as a new development (which intrinsically seems to threaten the stable frame of reference).

(b) consequent upon the 'instance' matter is the stable frame of reference matter. What is involved is not 'ordinary' stable frames, but the frame of reference to the impersonal features of interactionists, which the law is specialized to maintain.[3] The law case is a stable way of transforming conflicts into the terms of this frame wherein issues can be resolved quite without respect to features of the known-in-everyday-terms situation. Maintenance of this frame is key not only (as we have suggested) to permitting interactions across class lines, but to permitting actions that the moral systems might now allow were it necessary that they be conceived in their terms. The law maintains this stable frame in the face of constant pressures from various other motive-and-justification producing-and-warranting systems (church, ideology, etc.) as well as (more recently) from specialist groups who claim to redefine the situations in terms of their expert understanding of what 'really is going on' (e.g., the psychiatrist). These pressures explain why the most tension fraught issues of our time in the legal system have involved the question of the possible shift from 'objective' to 'subjective' standards; for example, in the law of contracts, where *understanding* of terms is concerned, the question classically was not what *the* party understood, but what 'such a one' who wrote this contract 'would' understand, and not with respect to everyday knowledge, but with respect to 'the state of the law' on the matter. The conflict between postulated understandings and understandings in terms of naive and systematic psychology are a peculiarly subtle issue because when the psychiatrist advances his claims to define competence in terms of the problem of mental-conditions-taken-seriously he does not merely give better answers to an old problem, he causes to be faced the question whether it seriously matters what a party's mental condition actually is.

3.2 The constraints in the operation of the legal system are due to those just mentioned and to the limited commitment even those most involved in its processes have to *its way* as compared with their normal ways of proceeding, a limitation of commitment due to the fact that even in their business they function in the sphere of everyday life. The lawyer can't maintain a full commitment to his professional skills because the other institutions he feels fealty with are typically involved even in his most professional actions. Thus for example, there are few lawyers who will take any case regardless of how 'controversial' it is, i.e., how closely its 'issues' impinge on matters of great concern for other areas of normative reference; the sex deviate, the political agitator, and periodically others have difficulties in getting lawyers because in these areas the lawyer is caused to feel that he in doing his job 'associates himself with' the acts of his clients.

Then, too, no lawyer fully exploits in any particular case his full repertoire of technical skills. Thus for example while any fact each of the opponent's witnesses assert can be questioned (not only as to truth, but as to whether it can be said, whether it is relevant, etc.) the lawyer does not do so. Together the two opposing attorneys construct a 'hypothetical fact situation' which is to be taken as the base from which quite narrow, consensually arrived at, issues are framed as the subjects of the decision-to-come. No lawyer need agree to any assertion whatsoever made in court,[4] but if he doesn't the system breaks down. Indeed it has happened that those concerned to break the system down have proceeded in precisely this way. In the *Dennis* case, where the first string communist leaders were tried, their lawyers systematically questioned every point their opponents attempted to make, caused the judge to rule, then appealed each ruling so far as they could. The consistent pressure they put upon the judge, by further not granting him the deference usual given, resulted in him giving up 'the dignity of the judge' and engaging in personality attacks quite as vicious as those the lawyers used on him - to produce this response which would 'demonstrate' the corruptness of the legal system to the world.[5]

The great instructiveness of that case can be seen when we note that perhaps the greatest problems that have gotten in the way of constructing an adequate sociology of law (of the court process, that is) have been due to the failure of observers to see that

(a) there are NO rules of the legal system which cannot be questioned, made the subject of a ruling in any single case; all the rules of the system are operable contingently on their not being questioned in a particular case, and therefore, the game model that some rules (say that rules defining a valid move) are not to be questioned in the course of any game, modified by a move itself is not applicable. (This is strictly true in the absence of legislated codes; where such codes are present, the problem shifts somewhat to an issue I won't deal with here, 'interpretation'.)

(b) 'facts' cannot be taken as a given by the observer; the largely consensual construction of an hypothetical set of facts is an utterly key activity of the lawyers.

When others, witnesses, technical experts, juries, who have much more fleeting involvements with the legal system's ways get caught up in its processes, their attachments to its devices are correspondingly more tenuous than the lawyer. The jury's limited attachment is indeed often felt to be a safety valve through which community values impinge on the legal system 'despite' its attempts to keep them out.[6]

Finally, it might be suggested that that function which has been most extensively focused on, i.e., that the role of the legal system is to regulate behavior by way of a specific set of norms is perhaps secondary to a more basic function, that of socializing the members of a society to the obligation to be prepared to produce answers to 'why' questions. What is most interesting about this socialization function both in the case of religion and law is that this function seems, very early in the development of complex societies, to become a matter taken care of by a specialized skilled group who produce, maintain and indeed evaluate between themselves whether those answers which *they* offer for "lay" members of the society are adequate.

Notes

1. Editorial Note by Emanuel A. Schegloff, Literary Executor for Harvey Sacks: In a volume concerned with ethnomethodological and conversation-analytic contributions to the study of law, it may be in point to suggest that Sacks' "The Lawyer's Work" should be understood not as conversation-analytic (despite the

association of Sacks' name with that enterprise) but as ethnomethodological in inspiration. At the time of the writing of this draft, most likely during the 1961-62 academic year, no hint of "conversation-analysis", in any of its subsequent versions, had yet appeared. The draft manuscript of a paper entitled "The Lawyer's Work" which is published here carries no date. Juxtaposing it with drafts of other papers from his student years and setting them in the context of Sacks' academic itinerary in the years following his completion of Yale Law School, it seems most likely that the paper was drafted during either the 1960-61 or the 1961-62 academic year. Sacks had completed law school in the Spring of 1959, and had moved for the 1959-60 academic year to Cambridge, MA, spending time both at M.I.T. and at Harvard. It was at Harvard, in the context of an ongoing seminar run by Talcott Parsons (that year specially concerned with the law), that Sacks met Harold Garfinkel, who was spending a sabbatical year in Cambridge. Sacks was much taken with Garfinkel's work and its seriousness, and when he moved to Berkeley in the fall of 1960, he brought with him much of Garfinkel's current writing in manuscript form and his intellectual engagement with it. In Berkeley, Sacks went to work for Philip Selznick at the Institute for Industrial Relations, with a focus specially turned on collective bargaining - work in which the engagement with Garfinkel and ethnomethodology was not particularly evident. During that initial period in Berkeley, Sacks was writing other papers related to law, also not *prima facie* ethnomethodological in manner - for example, a paper on the sociological jurisprudence of Eugen Ehrlich, and another entitled "Introduction: The Problem of Viable Law". Sacks spent the summer of 1961 at UCLA, and by the year 1962-63 he had moved to the new center which Selznick had founded as a home for socio-legal studies at Berkeley, the Centre for the Study of Law and Society, by which time the paper had already been drafted. Most likely it had been written during 1961-62. Its extensive acknowledgement of indebtedness to Garfinkel marks the convergence of Sacks' engagement with Garfinkel's ideas with his own, at that time central, interests in how the law as an institution can work. The manuscript has been edited only with respect to matters of orthography, punctuation and bibliography.

2. The general orientation of this paper is due to Harold Garfinkel. This may be considered one of a number of studies which might be produced were wider attention given to his work. Anyone interested in this paper for other than its topical features ought to turn to Garfinkel's general theoretical writings, in particular to his "Common Sense Knowledge of Social Structure" [1962; reprinted in Garfinkel, 1967]. Then, perhaps, the extent of my debts to him might be appreciated.
3. While I shall not deal with those just occasionally involved in the system, it is worth mentioning a certain peculiarity. Often whether a party can be treated as a person is an issue (e.g., is he insane?). If it is decided that he can be treated as a person then the law proceeds to treat him as a case, i.e., he is treated

impersonally only if he can warrant that he is not a person, can't bear the usual imputations, the law simply won't process him, and typically he is committed to some other sphere's care.

4. I have considered this and point (a) below much more extensively in a paper concerned with assessing some alternative formal models of the legal process.
5. Verbatim samples of their interchanges are available in Frankfurter, J.'s appendix to his opinion in *Sachar v. U.S.*
6. On the jury, see the as yet unpublished paper by Garfinkel and Mendlovitz.

References

Garfinkel, H.(1962),'Commonsense knowledge of social structures: the documentary method of interpretation in lay and professional fact finding', in J.M. Scher (ed.), *Theories of the Mind*, The Macmillan Company, The Free Press of Glencoe, Inc., New York, pp.689-712.

Garfinkel, H. (1967), *Studies in Ethnomethodology*, Prentice-Hall, Englewood Cliffs, N.J.

4 Contested Evidence in Courtroom Cross-Examination: The Case of a Trial for Rape[1]

PAUL DREW

Introduction

In the adversarial Anglo-American criminal judicial system, cross-examination is essentially hostile. Attorneys test the veracity or credibility of the evidence being given by witnesses, with questions which are designed to discredit the other side's version of events, and instead to support his or her own side's case. When being cross-examined, witnesses are, of course, conscious of this purposefulness behind the questions they are asked. They are alive to the possibility that a question or series of questions may be intended to expose errors or inconsistencies in their evidence, and hence to challenge and undermine it. This awareness on the part of witnesses is manifest in the guarded and defensive ways in which they answer certain questions. For instance, in this extract from a rape trial from which the data for this paper are principally taken,[2] the alleged rape victim gives an answer which is designed to manage what she perceives to be the damaging implications - for her version of events - of the defence attorney's questions. (In all the data extracts in this chapter, the attorney is designated as A, the witness as W, and the judge as J.)

(1) [Ou:45/3A:270]

A: An during that enti:re: (0.3) eve:ning. (0.8)
Miss ((name)), (0.5) its your testimony: (2.0)
that there was: (0.9) no indication (.) as far
as you could te:ll, (0.3) that the defendant
had been drinking.
(0.2)
W: No:,

8		(2.2)
9	A:	Now: Miss: ((name)) (1.2) when you were
10		interviewed by (.) the poli:ce (.) some times
11		later (.) that evening (1.0)
12		didn't you tell the police that the
13		defendant had been drinking?
14		(0.2)
15	W:	No[::
16	A:	[Didn' you tell 'em that=
17	W:	=I told then there was a cooler in the ca:r
18		an I never opened it.
19	A:	The answer: uh: (.) may the balance be: uh
20		stricken y'r honour:, an the answer is no:?
21	J:	The answer is no:

The attorney's questions in this extract are plainly designed to imply an inconsistency in the witness's story - an inconsistency, that is, between her present testimony that the defendant had not been drinking, and what the attorney alleges she told the police shortly after the incident. The witness first denies that she told the police that the defendant had been drinking (line 15). However, she adds to that denial an explanation about what she actually told the police at the time (ie. that there was a drinks cooler in the defendant's car; lines 17-18). In providing this supplementary explanation, which the attorney asks to be stricken from the record (lines 19-20), the witness constructs her answer in such a way that her versions then and now are consistent, whilst also implying an account for the attorney's 'mistaken' interpretation of what she told the police, a matter which would not be resolved by her denial alone. Thus the defensiveness of the witness's answer orients to the potential inconsistency in her story which the questions are attempting to imply; it is designed also to rebut the damaging inferences which might otherwise be drawn about the apparent discrepancy between the attorney's version of what she told the police, and her own.

This chapter focuses on such disputes as these in cross-examination, when attorney and witness offer alternative and competing descriptions or versions of events. It will focus particularly on a device for producing inconsistency in, and damaging implications for, a witness's evidence. The device is therefore associated with an attorney's management of questioning to attempt to discredit a witness. A line of questioning[3] is designed in such a way that it ends by juxtaposing and contrasting items of discrepant information, as in extract [1], or information from which certain damaging inferences might be drawn about a witness's version of events. The systematic properties of this contrast device will be explicated.

The Data

The particular focus of the present analysis is an extract from a trial for rape, recorded in a municipal criminal court in a large city in the eastern United States. In this extract the alleged rape victim is being cross-examined by the defence attorney. Just before this the witness has agreed that she knew the defendant for "two or three years" before the alleged rape; and she has testified that he had been to her house before. The questions in this extract concern an occasion before the night of the alleged rape, when the witness met the defendant (not by arrangement) in a place which the attorney describes as a "bar" and the witness a "club".

(2) [Da:Ou:2:1]

A: An' at tha:t ti:me (0.3) he: asked ya to go
ou:t with yu (0.4) isn't that c'rect
(2.1)
W: Yea[h
A: [With him. (.) izzn'at so?
(2.6)
W: Ah don't remember
(1.4)
A: W'l didn:'e: a:sk you if uh: (.) on that night
that uh::: (.) he wanted you to be his gi:rl
(0.5)
A: Didn'e ask you that?
(2.5)
W: I don't remember what he said to me that night.
(1.2)
A: Well yuh had some uh (p) (.) uh fairly lengthy
conversations with thu defendant uh: did'n you?
(0.7)
A: On that evening uv February fourteenth?
(1.0)

W: We:ll we were all talkin.
(0.8)
A: Well you kne:w. at that ti:me. that the
defendant was. in:terested (.) in you (.)
did'n you?
(1.3)
W: He: asked me how I'(d) bin: en
(1.1)
W: J- just stuff like that
A: Just asked yuh how (0.5) yud bi:n (0.3) but
he kissed yuh goodnigh:t. (0.5) izzat righ:t.=
W: =Yeah=he asked me if he could?
(1.4)
A: He asked if he could?
(0.4)
W: Uh hmm=
A: =Kiss you goodnigh:t
(1.0)
A: An you said: (.) oh kay (0.6) izzat right?
W: Uh hmm
(2.0)
A: An is it you testimony he only kissed yuh
('t) once?
(0.4)
W: Uh hmm
(6.5)
A: Now (.) subsequent to this...

What is plainly at issue in this extract, quite explicitly so in lines 23-25, is what the witness could or should have known about the defendant's "interest" in her. What evidently is being proposed in the attorney's questions in [2], and what the witness is contesting, is the matter of what she and the defendant 'were to each other' prior to the incident in which it is alleged the witness was raped. What is therefore also being contested is whether as a result of what happened on this earlier occasion the witness had grounds for suspecting or anticipating that the defendant was (sexually) "interested" in her.[4]

In each of his questions in extract [2] the attorney attributes to the defendant behaviour which might manifest sexual interest, namely asking her to go out, asking her to be his girl, having lengthy conversations together, that the evening they met was February 14th (ie. Valentine's Day), being interested in her, and kissing her goodnight. It is also clear that in answer to these points the witness is being defensive, and is contesting whether from what happened on that occasion she would have been aware of the defendant's sexual interest in her. The analysis of these data will begin by considering the witness's defensiveness, before turning to focus on the point in lines 30-31 where the attorney employs the discrediting contrast device.

Alternative Descriptions

After the witness's claims not to remember whether the defendant asked her to go out with him, or asked her to be his girl, the attorney pursues his line of questioning with two further formulations of the defendant's 'interest' in her.

A: Well yuh had some uh (p) (.) uh fairly lengthy
conversations with thu defendant uh: did'n you?
(0.7)
A: On that evening uv February fourteenth?
(1.0)
W: We:ll we were all talkin.
(0.8)
A: Well you kne:w. at that ti:me. that the
defendant was. in:terested (.) in you (.)
did'n you?
(1.3)
W: He: asked me how I'(d) bin: en
(1.1)
W: J- just stuff like that
A: Just asked yuh how (0.5) yud bi:n (0.3) but
he kissed yuh goodnigh:t. (0.5) izzat righ:t.=

When the attorney proposes that the witness had "fairly lengthy conversations with the defendant" (lines 16-19), she counters that version with the answer that "we were all talkin" (line 21). And again, her reply that "he asked me how I'(d) bin: en j- just stuff like that" in lines 27-29 appears to deny that she "knew that the defendant was interested" in her (lines 23-25). That latter reply is used by the attorney when he constructs the contrast in lines 30-31: and that contrast will eventually be the focus of analysis in a later section.

But for now I shall focus on how the versions which the witness constructs in her replies work to dispute the versions which the attorney proposes in his prior questions. How, for instance, does her account that "He: asked me how I'(d) bin..." manage to dispute the attorney's claim that she knew that the defendant was interested in her? Since this will involve a quite extended treatment of how her alternative descriptions are designed to compete with and rebut the attorney's versions, it may help if I summarize the stages in the analytic argument.

A first observation, discussed in the following subsection, is that although it is clear that the witness's versions are designed to rebut and replace those of the attorney, her answers in lines 21 and 27 above, as elsewhere, do not contain overt markers of rejection or correction. Thus the contrastive force of her versions derives almost entirely from properties of the descriptions which she constructs. That observation leads to a consideration of how a description of something that happened, for example her account in line 27-29 of the defendant's greeting, can be taken to represent or characterize the scene-as-a-whole, or to stand as a gloss for the scene. But in order that her description/characterization be heard to differ from and rebut the attorney's versions, her description, again for example of the defendant's greeting to her, is required to be heard as representing 'the most' that happened between them. This maximal property associated with the contrastive or disputatious force of her descriptions is discussed in the third subsection: after which the more general relevance, for conversation, of this maximal property of next and contrasting descriptions is considered in the final subsection.

The Absence of Overt Correction Markers

One option which the witness has as a way to dispute a version of events proposed in the attorney's question is to explicitly reject that version, with a overt negative marker "No" followed by a correction. That option was selected in extract [1], when the witness rejected the attorney's version of what she had told the police regarding the defendant's drinking, and then gave a correct version of what she told them.

[from extract 1]

A: Now: Miss: ((name)) (1.2) when you were

10 interviewed by (.) the poli:ce (.) some times
11 later (.) some time later that evening, (1.0)
12 didn't you tell the police that the
13 defendant had been drinking?
14 (0.2)
15 W: --> No[::
16 A: [Didn' you tell 'em that=
17 W: =I told then there was a cooler in the ca:r
18 an I never opened it.

This option of overtly rejecting and correcting the attorney's version is likewise used in these fragments:

(3) [Da:Ou:6:2]

A: And it was at this point that you say that
the defendant (2.0) started to kiss you
is that right
W: --> No we started talkin'

(4) [Da:Ou:1:4]

A: He take you out to the ca:r?
(1.3)
W: --> No he walked outsi:de with us.

An alternative option for disagreeing with a version proposed by the attorney is, however, more indirect: the witness does not preface her version with a negative rejection marker, and the description she offers implies a different characterization of an event or scene than that conveyed by the attorney's description. The witness uses this option in [2], for instance when she is asked about her knowledge of the defendant's interest in her.

23 A: Well you kne:w. at that ti:me. that the
24 defendant was. in:terested (.) in you (.)
25 did'n you?
26 (1.3)
27 W: He: asked me how I'(d) bin: en

(1.1)
W: J- just stuff like that

The witness is plainly disputing the attorney's contention that she knew that the defendant was interested in her: but she does so by producing an alternative description which implies that she did not know. Her alternative description competes with or challenges the attorney's account, but it does so by reporting something which implies a rather different relationship between her and the defendant than is proposed by the attorney's use of "interest" (line 24). Here are two further instances illustrating this option of producing alternative competing descriptions without prefacing them with overt rejection markers occur elsewhere during this cross-examination.

(5) [Da:Ou:1:2]

A: Its where uh (.) uh gi:rls and fella:s
meet isn't it?
(0.9)
W: People go: there.

(6) [Da:Ou:1:3]

A: An' during that eve:ning: (0.6) uh: didn't
Mistuh ((name)) come over tuh sit with you
(0.8)
W: Sat at our table.

In each of these extracts, as in lines 23-25 of [2], the question is designed to elicit an answer which is either 'Yes' or 'No', that is which will either confirm or disconfirm the version proposed in the question. So the first thing to notice about her answers is that the witness is avoiding what the question asks, and declining either to confirm or disconfirm. Secondly, although her answers implicitly work to disconfirm the attorney's versions, her descriptions or versions are in some respects not intrinsically oppositional to his. In extracts [3] and [4], where the witness uses an overt disconfirmation marker, there was also a direct contrast between her versions and the attorney's, that is between 'sitting across from' and 'sitting next to' and between 'started talking' and 'started to kiss you'. However, in a case such as [6], not only is her version not prefaced as a disconfirmation, but the description she offers, "Sat at our table" does not intrinsically exclude the attorney's version, "sit with you". Whilst hers are qualified, guarded versions of what the attorney suggests, that they manage to be defensive as well as to rebut his versions is an almost entirely implicit property of the descriptions which she selects.

I have said 'almost entirely' because there are elements of contrasting references in some of the witness's versions. For example, in lines 16-21 of [2] there are two such contrastive elements.

A: Well yuh had some uh (p) (.) uh fairly lengthy
conversations with thu defendant uh: did'n you?
(0.7)
A: On that evening uv February fourteenth?
(1.0)
W: We:ll we were all talkin.

The first is the turn initial component "We:ll", which marks a certain disjunction between the second speaker's opinion or position, and that expressed by the first speaker. That preface therefore projects that the witness's version will differ from and disagree with the attorney's position (Sacks, 1987, p.59; Pomerantz, 1984, p.72 and fn 12). The second contrastive element is that the witness substitutes "we...all" in place of "you...with the defendant"; whilst "we" in her answer would include her and the defendant, her adding "all" specifically includes others besides the two of them (ie. the girlfriends she was with).

Despite the way in which her version of "we...all" directly contradicts his version of 'you two', such a straightforwardly exclusive contrast does not seem to capture how "all talkin" is designed to be heard as standing in place of "fairly lengthy conversations", and thereby as disputing the attorney's version. The terms 'all talking' and 'fairly lengthy conversations' are not by themselves incompatible, and might easily be applied to the same activity or scene. It is possible to imagine one person having 'lengthy conversations' with another in the course of a bunch of people 'all talking'. Clearly one respect in which the witness's version is designed to challenge his version is the sheer matter of the sequential position in which it is produced. The witness produces her versions as next or second to the attorney's, by virtue of the sequential occurrence of answers: and insofar as she has declined to confirm the version in the question, and has instead produced in next position a different version of the 'same' incident or circumstances, the descriptions which the witness reports can be heard as candidate replacements. They are not further specifications which add something to the attorney's versions, but as *alternative* versions designed to qualify and *replace* the versions initially produced by the attorney. Sequential position is, then, a primary interpretative resource in understanding that the witness's answers are designed to counter or to dispute his versions.[5]

Reporting a 'Detail' Implies a Characterization of the Scene

However, within that context of their sequential position, her answers have other interpretative properties through which they are designed to dispute his versions. We can return to the observation that the alternative consecutive descriptions of the attorney and witness might appear not to be mutually exclusive. Even though the witness's answers contain alternative references, for example "people" in place of "girls and fellas" in [5], nevertheless her alternative descriptions are not necessarily, inevitably or invariably inconsistent or contrasting ways of describing the same thing. Just as on occasions two people having "fairly lengthy conversations" can go along with "we were all talking", so too the term "people" certainly includes "girls and fellas" in [5]; and in [6] there is a mutual or necessary connection between "sitting with" someone and "sitting at" their table. In each question-answer pair, therefore, the subsequent description by the witness does not exclude, in a directly contrastive sense, the prior description which she has been asked to confirm.

The witness's answers display a marked cautiousness insofar as she takes a stand, through her re-descriptions or qualifications of the attorney's versions, on matters which might not otherwise, in other forms of discourse, seem to make much of a difference. For instance in a conversational setting it may be doubted that in describing someone joining one at one's table for a drink, there is sufficient difference between that person 'sitting with' one and 'sitting at one's table' for it to be worth troubling to insist on the latter version. The two versions are not intrinsically mutually exclusive.

These alternatives might then be used interchangeably as *equivalent*, as *partial* but equally adequate or correct descriptions of the same scene. However, in not allowing the attorney's versions to pass unamended, the witness orients to the differences between these versions for her story. Focusing on lines 16-29 of [2], her versions are designed not merely to add to or supplement those proposed by the attorney, but to replace his. In so doing she is attempting to correct some impression or implication which might be conveyed by the attorney's portrayal of the facts. When in line 21 she answers "We:ll we were all talkin" and in line 27 that "He: asked me how I'(d) bin:", she is treating his prior versions not as having been partial and needing filling out, but as having been wrong. And a first requirement for treating her descriptions as combative, as correcting his, is that they are not just detailing more which could be said about a scene, but re-characterizing the scene as a whole.

The witness does not manage this recharacterization by disputing the attorney's version head on; by which I mean that she avoids some rather direct ways of challenging his version that she knew that "the defendant was interested in you". "Interested" here can be considered a *gloss* for some details of what was said between them that night, what the defendant did, the way he looked at her, how they acted towards one another and so on - instances of which could be detailed as evidence in support of that gloss (Garfinkel and Sacks, 1970). At least a couple of direct ways in which the witness might have challenged that gloss would have been simply to dispute it, along the lines of "No he didn't seem much interested in me"; or to have substituted her own contrasting gloss, for example "Well, he was interested in everyone that night, he was having fun". Alternatively she might have challenged the gloss "interested" in a more indirect fashion. Given that a gloss might be unpackaged into its constituent or component activities (Jefferson, 1986), the witness might have focused on one of those constituent activities or details as a means of challenging the gloss, for example by answering in lines 21 or 27 that "Well he didn't talk to me any more than he talked to the others". In her answer in line 27 she does not use any of these methods of disputing the attorney's gloss "interested in you".

Instead she answers by reporting particulars of the occasion which stand as constituent or evidential details for a quite different gloss than that proposed by the attorney. In reporting "He: asked me how I'(d) bin:", the witness details a greeting which is conventionally one between people who know one another, but have not been in touch for some length of time ('How have you been?' indicates passage of time 'since we last met'). It is a greeting which indicates acquaintance and familiarity but not close intimacy. Such a greeting would not be the kind of detail to be reported as evidence of the sexual interest of the one performing the greeting: so that the witness is detailing something about the scene - finding in the scene something to report - which would *not* be used as evidence to support the attorney's gloss or characterization of the scene. This has an important corollary which underlies the manner in which her version specifically but implicitly challenges the attorney's version: that is, selecting to report a detail which does not support his version implicitly asserts (provides the grounds for recognising) that there is nothing in what happened which *could* be reported in its support.

A gloss with which a scene or someone's behaviour is characterized (eg. "interested in you") can be taken to stand for a collection of particulars of that scene/behaviour (for more on which see Jefferson, 1986; Garfinkel and Sacks, 1970), particulars which if necessary can be cited as evidence in support of that gloss. Outside of that collection are other details which may not 'fit' the proposed gloss, not in the sense that they necessarily contradict it (though they may), but just because they are conventionally unconnected or not associated with, or not constituent behaviours of, the gloss in question. For example, the fact that the birds are singing might well be reported as part of the evidence for the gloss that it is a 'beautiful day'; but if the day being described as 'beautiful' happened to be a Tuesday, that fact would not ordinarily be included in a collection of the particulars of a 'beautiful day'(for related issues, again see Sacks, 1984). Thus if one speaker were to propose that "It's a beautiful day" and the other replied "It's Tuesday", the second speaker would be heard to imply something like "What's beautiful about it, it's Tuesday": where even if the first speaker did not know what it was that the other had against Tuesdays, why for him it was a bad day, the first speaker would at least be able to discern that it *was* a bad day for the other, that the other was not assenting to it being a 'beautiful day', and might therefore perhaps ask in reply "Why, what do you have on Tuesdays?".

Thus there is a reflexive property of reporting a detail outside of the conventional collection of particulars for a proposed gloss; which is that in so reporting an 'unassociated' detail, that other (second) speaker dissents by implying that an alternative gloss is the correct version. So that the indirectness or delicacy of the witness's method of disputing the attorney's characterization of the witness as "interested" in her is that she does not dispute the characterization itself, nor even its supposed constituent particulars from the collection of details reportable as evidence for that characterization. Instead she reports a detail from *outside* that constituent collection, thereby implying but not stating that nothing occurred which could support the attorney's version. In coming to this generic formulation of the methodical procedures which underlie the manner in which the witness's answer disputes the version proposed by the attorney, the aim is to free the methodical practises of reasoning from their local environment. In this way we can begin to discern the procedures for reasoning and for interpretation through which one version might be disputed by an alternative competing version, in an implicit fashion and without using explicit markers of rejection or correction.

The 'Maximal' Property of Descriptions

This brings us closer to an analytic account of how the witness's version in lines 27-29 is designed to dispute the attorney's prior version; but the account is not yet exhausted. Her report "He: asked me how I'(d) bin: en (1.1) j- just stuff like that" has a discernible property with respect to the attorney's prior version, which can best be approached by considering the attorney's subsequent question, and the contrast on which the analysis here is coming to focus.

23 A: Well you kne:w. at that ti:me. that the
24 defendant was. in:terested (.) in you (.)
25 did'n you?
26 (1.3)
27 W: He: asked me how I'(d) bin: en
28 (1.1)
29 W: J- just stuff like that
30 A: Just asked yuh how (0.5) yud bi:n (0.3) but
31 he kissed yuh goodnigh:t. (0.5) izzat righ:t.=

The contrast in the attorney's question in lines 30-31 suggests an inconsistency between the version she offered in lines 27-29, that he just asked her how she had been, and another 'detail' of the scene/behaviour to which she has previously attested, that the defendant kissed her goodnight. This inconsistency trades off an interpretation that when she claimed that the defendant asked her how she had been, she is reporting not just a detail of what happened, his greeting, but is suggesting that nothing more happened between them as regards intimacy, 'interest' and so forth than might be depicted by that greeting. Whereas the attorney is proposing that something more intimate did occur, namely kissing. So that the contrast in the attorney's question displays his understanding that the witness is claiming that the defendant's behaviour towards her was only as friendly (ie. non-intimate) as his greeting indicates.

That is, of course, just what the witness's answer in lines 27-29 is designed to indicate. She reports this one detail, a friendly greeting, and then adds "just stuff like that". By completing her detailing with that generalized phrase, she makes explicit that whatever else occurred between them that evening was nothing more than is suggested in the lack of intimacy in the greeting.[6] The generalized completer is informative about other unspecified details of the scene, indicating that all the other reportable but unspecified details are commensurate with the nothing-more-than-friendly greeting (the "just" indicates 'no more than', and "stuff like that" refers to the greeting).

The result of this is that the witness is indicating that everything that occurred between her and the defendant that evening is part of a collection which is adequately represented by the kind of greeting she reports. But we still need to account for the implication that the form of greeting she reports is as much by way of "interest" that the defendant showed towards her. This account rests on a further interpretative or pragmatic property of her description of his greeting, through which it can convey that 'nothing more intimate happened' than that. This can be referred to as the 'maximal' property of the description - 'maximal' because the description "He: asked me how I'(d) bin:" depicts the most, in terms of intimate behaviour, that happened between them.

In sum, the witness challenges the descriptive adequacy of the attorney's characterization by selecting an alternative candidate version which is informative about the 'most that can be said' concerning some locally occasioned, contextually bound essential feature of the scene. The 'maximal' property of a sequentially next description, produced in answer to the attorney's prior version, is then the interpretative device through which the witness's answers are designed to stand in place of, and hence to rebut, the attorney's versions. This is evident in two of the witness's answers in the target data.

A: Well yuh had some uh (p) (.) uh fairly lengthy
conversations with thu defendant uh: did'n you?
(0.7)
A: On that evening uv February fourteenth?
(1.0)
W: We:ll we were all talkin.
(0.8)

A: Well you kne:w. at that ti:me. that the
defendant was. in:terested (.) in you (.)
did'n you?
(1.3)
W: He: asked me how I'(d) bin: en
(1.1)
W: J- just stuff like that

Her answers in lines 21 and 27-29 are designed to specify details which, without directly negating or contradicting the attorney's prior versions, do not support his versions. Her subsequent characterizations are formulated to represent a scene in which there was no more intimate talk between her and the defendant than that they were "all talking", and no more interest shown in her by the defendant than is indicated by his friendly but not intimate greeting. Her alternative characterizations stand on behalf of a different gloss than that conveyed in the attorney's versions. Certainly her characterizations do not assert that all that happened was that the defendant asked her how she had been, and that he did not speak to her after that greeting. Instead they imply that whatever else did happen or was said, alluded to but not detailed in "just stuff like that" in line 29, amounted to nothing more intimate than is indicated by that greeting. Just as an invitation to 'come over to watch the game' may not preclude 'munchies', and perhaps beers, sitting, talking and so on - but that nothing more in some essential respect (ie. dinner) will be provided - so too her characterizations are partial in leaving unspecified whatever else happened, but assert that in some essential respect (i.e. intimacy) nothing more than that happened.

It is precisely this maximal property of the witness's paired alternative characterizations, designed to dispute his versions, to which the attorney orients in constructing the contrast "Just asked yuh how (0.5) yud bi:n (0.3) but he kissed yuh goodnigh:t." (lines 30-31).

Contrast Structures, and the 'Power of Summary'

We can now turn to consider the attorney's question in line 30-31 of [2], in which he appears to contest the witness's version that nothing more happened between her and the defendant that evening to suggest the defendant's "interest" in her than is indicated by his greeting.

W: He: asked me how I'(d) bin: en
(1.1)
W: J- just stuff like that
A: Just asked yuh how (0.5) yud bi:n (0.3) but
he kissed yuh goodnigh:t. (0.5) izzat righ:t.=
W: =Yeah=he asked me if he could?
(1.4)
A: He asked if he could?
(0.4)
W: Uh hmm=
A: =Kiss you goodnigh:t
(1.0)
A: An you said: (.) oh kay (0.6) izzat right?
W: Uh hmm
(2.0)
A: An is it you testimony he only kissed yuh
('t) once?
(0.4)
W: Uh hmm
(6.5)
A: Now (.) subsequent to this...

The contrast which the attorney proposes between "Just asked yuh how (0.5) yud bi:n" and the defendant having subsequently "kissed yuh goodnigh:t" is plainly designed to discredit the veracity of the witness's characterization of the defendant's lack of "interest" in her that evening. The attorney manages that contrast by bringing together two things to which the witness has already attested. Twelve lines before extract [2] the witness confirmed that the defendant kissed her goodnight:[7] and she has just in her prior answer (line 27) volunteered that version of the defendant's greeting.

Now the chance to 'bring together' what has previously been said, pieces of prior evidence, and to juxtapose them to make a point, is available only to the questioner. Anyone in the position of answering is restricted to dealing with just what is asked in the prior question: though the question may be understood in the light of what has come before, and what is anticipated to be the line of questioning being developed, nevertheless it is the prior question which demands to be answered. And it will be recalled that this restriction is enforced in extract [1] when the witness, after disconfirming that she told the police that the defendant had been drinking, added to her answer an explanation of what she had told them: the attorney's request to the judge that the "balance be here stricken" being a specialized instance of the familiar admonishment to witnesses to "Just answer the question, yes or no". As Sacks observed, the opportunity to bring together pieces of information to make a point gives to a questioner some sort of control.

> "What we find...is that the person who is asking the questions seems to have first rights to perform an operation on the set of answers. You can call it "draw a conclusion". Socrates used the phrase "add them up". It was very basic to his way of doing dialectic. He would go along and then say at some point, "Well, let's see where we are. Let's add up the answers and draw some conclusions". And it's that right that provides for a lot of what look like strugglings in some conversations, where the attempt to move into the position of questioner seems to be quite a thing that persons try to do...As long as one is in the position of doing the questions, then in part one has control of the conversation." (Sacks, 1992, p.54)

Bearing in mind the pre-allocation of speaker turns in courtroom examination, the 'strugglings' to which Sacks refers for the position of 'doing the questions' in conversations do not occur. The specialized speech exchange system allocates to the attorney and witness the fixed roles of questioner and answerer respectively: so that the element of control that Sacks describes, in which the questioner has 'first rights' to pull together evidence and 'draw conclusions', lies always with the attorney. The witness is left in the position of addressing and trying to deal with the attorney's selection of which items to pull together: she has no control over the connections which are made between pieces of information or testimony, nor over the inferences which may be drawn from such juxtapositioning - although she may attempt to rebut those inferences, as she does in extract [1], and in her answer to the attorney's contrast here (line 32, "Yeah=he asked me if he could?").

So out of the prior testimony the attorney selects two items to be pulled together, the descriptions of the greeting, "Just asked yuh how (0.5) yud bi:n", and of the farewell, "but he kissed yuh goodnigh:t.". In considering them together here, the attorney manages to juxtapose the claimed non-intimacy of the greeting with the acknowledged (or apparently acknowledged) intimacy of the farewell. The contrast achieved through this juxtaposition is a special kind of object, because it does not simply propose that if one is right (e.g. if the defendant did kiss her goodnight) then the other must be wrong (ie. it must have been a warmer greeting than she is admitting). Whatever inconsistency is being implied in the contrast is not one which would be resolved by simply discounting one or other of the versions, of the greeting or farewell. Instead the difference between them in terms of intimacy/non-intimacy generates a puzzle about how it could have come about that the witness and defendant ended the evening on much warmer or closer terms than it is claimed they began it. Thus the manner of their farewell is represented in the contrast as *accountable*; not that it is being disputed, but insofar as it needs to be explained (for a more general consideration of which see Hart and Honore, 1959, chapter 2, especially p.43). The puzzle which the contrast poses implicitly is, therefore, what happened between the greeting and the farewell which could account for the intimacy of the latter, when they had apparently begun on a non-intimate footing?

Whilst in other circumstances the change in intimacy between a greeting on arrival and a farewell on departure might be construed in a happier light, here that change is damaging for her having implicitly proposed - through the maximal property attributed to her detailing that "<u>He:</u> asked me how I'(d) <u>bin</u>:" - that everything else that happened between them that evening was 'nothing more' intimate than is indicated by such a greeting. The damaging force of the puzzle which can be inferred from the contrast is that something else must have happened for them to have ended on such apparently intimate terms. The contrast works, then, to challenge not her characterization of the greeting itself, but the credibility of that as an adequate representation of everything else that happened, of all the scene's other essential particulars and how they are to be glossed.

This understanding of the implication conveyed in the contrast is displayed in the witness's reply in line 32, "Yeah=he asked me if he <u>c</u>ould?". She first confirms the descriptions out of which the contrast is built (she has, after all, already attested to these versions): but she then straightaway (note the latching of the second part of her reply to her confirmation) adds an explanation which attempts to account for the apparent and puzzling discrepancy. In that explanation she specifically details something else that happened, namely that the defendant asked to kiss her. She thereby constructs an account which attempts to 'reconcile' the farewell, the kissing, with the greeting, just as in [1] she added an explanation which attempted to account for the apparent contradiction. She simultaneously holds on to her version that the greeting represents the 'most' that happened between them; her characterization of how the defendant came to kiss her, that is after asking her permission, being rather too formal for intimacy, thus indicating that no special understanding had developed between them that evening such that he could have counted on kissing her (to ask permission for something is not to take it for granted).

So the attorney juxtaposes the witness's version of the greeting and what it 'stands for' in terms of the defendant's interest in her, with the manner of their farewell. In this we can see that participants mutually orient to the properties underlying the disputatious work which the witness's detailing of the greeting is designed to accomplish. That is, the puzzle in his contrast trades off the understanding that her description of the greeting was intended to convey 'all/the most that happened' between them. Hence the attorney's construction of the contrast builds on just those properties through which her detailing "He: asked me how I'(d) bin:" was deployed in challenging the attorney's alternative characterization. The same pragmatic resources which were available to the witness implicitly to rebut the attorney's version of the defendant's "interest" in her are equally available to the attorney in pulling together these two pieces of information and generating out of that a puzzle which is damaging to her version.

Although the attorney's construction of a contrast in lines 30-31 has been examined in some detail for this instance alone, such contrasts appear to be quite recurrent in cross-examination. The pre-allocation of speaker roles and turn types affords the attorney control over 'putting facts together' from prior testimony. This is done in hostile cross-examination (i.e. apparently not, or not in this form, in direct examination) by juxtaposing 'facts' in such a way as to achieve a contrast which has some damaging implication for the witness's testimony.[8] Such contrasts have in common a number of organizational/structural and interactional features: for this reason they may be regarded as instances of a *contrast device* recurrently used in cross-examination (for an account of contrast structures used by political speech makers as applause elicitation devices, see Atkinson, 1984; there are close parallels between the interactional properties of contrasts in political speeches and in cross-examination). The features of this device's organization are the following.

i) In consecutive questions the witness is asked to affirm or confirm a pair of 'facts' or characterizations which are recognizably not discrete: taken together through their sequentially adjacent position, they are juxtaposed in such a way as to generate a puzzle. The puzzle arises from some 'lack of fit' between one fact and the other, some discontinuity for which there should be, or needs to be, an explanation which is nevertheless not given. That is, the puzzle is created by implying that some discrepancy is accountable, without a possible account being provided.

ii) In each instance the puzzle is left unresolved. Although the contrast has generated a puzzle which needs to be explained, the attorney does not subsequently ask what the explanation might be. Thus he breaks off that line of questioning at the point where an explanation is relevant, but has not been given. By not asking the witness for her explanation, he withholds giving her the opportunity to provide an account which might satisfactorily resolve the puzzle.

iii) Whilst left unresolved at an official, explicit level, the puzzling discrepancy implies what might be termed an 'unless' clause. Here in [2], the defendant's kissing her goodnight is only puzzling unless something more happened between them in the course of the evening than the witness is admitting in her characterization of his not seeming to be particularly "interested" in her.

Nothing very technical is meant by the 'unless' clause; it serves only to draw attention to the way in which the contrasts work to favour the implication of explanations which are prejudicial to the witness's accounts, or work to discredit aspects of her testimony. It might be that there are 'innocent' explanations for what is inferable from the contrast: the contrasts, however, are designed not to imply any such innocent circumstances or account. They are designed specifically and systematically to imply an 'unless' clause which is damaging to the witness's testimony, by casting doubt upon her veracity, or upon the motives of her actions at the time.

iv) However, these damaging inferences are only implied in the contrasts. They are not stated explicitly: it is left for hearers to recognize what the damaging implications are which arise from the contrast. The jury are thereby given the opportunity to draw their own conclusions and to find 'for themselves' the discreditable implications of the contrast. By pulling together pieces of evidence in this way, the attorney manages not only to provide the jury with the materials with which to decide for themselves what conclusions to reach from the evidence in the contrast: he also avoids having to state explicitly what those conclusions (ie. damaging implications) are. If he were to state them explicitly, given the turn-taking organization for (cross)-examination, he would have to formulate such conclusions/inferences in a question; which would then give the witness the opportunity to challenge or deny them.

Recalling the point made earlier in this chapter, that the talk between attorney and witness is designed to be understood by non-speaking recipients, such contrasts are a means of conveying something to the jury over the head of the interaction with the witness. It is specifically in the contrasts where damaging conclusions from the evidence-so-far are implied: making out these implications is the work which non-speaking recipients do.

v) Associated with the way in which contrasts are designed to enable the jury to draw their own conclusions from the testimony, is that they are given time to do so. After the completion of each of a contrast, the attorney then delays asking his next question for a pause of 6.5 seconds in line 46 of [2]. This is a considerably longer pause than is to be found elsewhere in cross-examination, the next longest pauses clustering around 3-4 seconds and occurring in quite different environments. This indicates a close connection between the clustering of pause lengths and the interactional work achieved in the prior question-answer pairs: the longer pauses of 6 seconds and more which occur in the environment of the production of a contrast appear to highlight the significance of the contrast, by giving the jury time to recognize and consider the damaging implications for the witness's testimony. Given the multi-party recipiency of the questions and answers, the pauses are designed to be slots for audience appreciation[9] of what they have just heard. As recipients, the jury do not display their understanding or appreciation verbally; therefore in the absence of any means for the attorney to check the jury's comprehension, the pauses are extended to maximize the time in which they can assimilate the points implied in the contrasts.

vi) Contrasts are summaries of sorts: they pull together some selected points from the prior testimony, and complete that line of questioning. In each case, after the pause which follows the contrast the attorney moves on to question the witness about some other aspect of the case. The topic on which the attorney subsequently focuses may be related to the topic of the prior line of questioning, but it is nevertheless a distinct shift to a discernible next matter. For example, after the contrast in [2] which concludes his line of questioning about the defendant's "interest" in the witness on the evening they met in a club/bar, the attorney begins (line 47) to ask about the subsequent period between that meeting and the occasion of the alleged rape. Such shifts in the focus or topic of questioning after the contrast further deprive the witness of the opportunity to come back to the prejudicial point implied in the contrast. So to the earlier comment about the questioner exercising some control through having rights to summarize 'where we are now', we can add that in cross-examination - unlike conversation - the attorney not only has first rights to perform that operation (see the above quotation from Sacks, 1992), but also has effectively the only right to do so. This is because he also has control over changing topic or topical shifts in questioning.

It is by virtue of these organized features of the production of contrasts that they can be considered to be devices, the use of which has a special and central role in the hostile, disputatious questioning of cross-examination. They are the means by which the attorney can selectively bring together points from the witness's testimony, and juxtapose them in such a way as to generate a puzzle, the implication of which is something discrediting about the veracity of the witness's evidence. The damaging inferences which may be drawn from the contrasts are not stated but left implicit. It is left to the jury to draw the conclusions which the contrasts are designed to convey. A contrast is a summary and completion of a line of questioning: hence the attorney manages to bring a line of questioning to a conclusion on what is, for the witness, a damaging point.

Conclusion

This paper has focused on phenomena associated with 'contrasting versions' produced by participants in courtroom cross-examination. The first sense of 'contrasting versions' explored here concerns the alternative and competing versions which the attorney, and then the witness, produce to describe the 'same' action, event or scene. A version is first proposed by the attorney in a question: the witness, in her subsequent answer, produces an alternative description, through which she is heard to dispute or challenge the attorney's version. Without necessarily directly rejecting and contradicting the attorney's versions, the witness nevertheless disputes these by designing her descriptions in such a way that they stand for a quite different characterization of a scene than that proposed by the attorney. The witness's descriptions achieve their (implicitly) disputatious force, through a combination of their sequential placement, as being done as 'nexts' - and hence as alternatives to - the attorney's; of their being qualified versions, which do not endorse the attorney's prior versions; and of their 'maximal' property.

The second sense of 'contrasting versions' explored here concerns a device through which the attorney manages to convey to the jury a contrast between the witness's account of what happened, and what is likely in fact to have happened. The attorney designs a question, or a pair of adjacent questions, in such a way as to juxtapose facts, the contrast between which implies a version which is at odds with, and hence seeks to discredit, the witness's versions of events. So in response to the witness's attempts to rebut the attorney's versions, he produces contrasts which in turn are designed to damage her rebuttals.

Both these kinds of contrasts are the products of the attempts by each participant to challenge or discredit the other's version of events. Their competing versions are implicated in, and portrayed through, the descriptions of 'facts' which each produces. In this way 'facts' are left to 'speak for themselves'; or rather, their production is designed to enable the jury to make the proper inferences from them. Descriptions are designed to provide the jury with the materials from which they can discover for themselves what to make of the facts. And both contrasts are associated with a measure of control which each seeks to gain over what emerges from the cross-examination. Whilst this is perhaps more obviously the case for the contrasts which the attorney produces, as a procedure for summarizing by putting together facts in ways which are inconvenient or discrediting for the witness's position, the witness's attempts to counter the attorney's descriptive strategies, and hence herself control the information which is available to the jury, should not be overlooked. Her resistance to the attorney's versions is an attempt to deny him the materials with which he can develop a line of questioning towards some projected and, for her awkward, point: and therein lies the defensiveness of many of her answers.

Whilst the specialized speech exchange system which is characteristic of cross-examination provides the necessary structural position and resource within which the attorney and witness respectively 'fit' their turns, and hence their competing versions of events, this paper has not focused on participants' management and implementation of the organization of turn-taking for cross-examination. The focus has instead been the activities in which each is essentially engaged in cross-examination - those of substantiating and defending their respective versions of events, and disputing the other's versions. What has concerned me is not the management of turn-taking itself, but the interactional management of activities in the turns which participants take.

Notes

1. The analysis here is based in part on research I undertook whilst visiting lecturer in Language and Institutions, Tilburg University, Netherlands, in the spring of 1983. I am most grateful to Tilburg University's Department of Language and Literature, and to Professor Konrad Ehlich, for giving me the opportunity to do this research. Versions of this paper have been given at various places: I am grateful particularly to the EPOS group at UCLA for their comments and critical suggestions when I gave it there in 1987. I am grateful also to John Local and to

John Heritage for their comments on an earlier draft. This is an abridged version of a paper which was published in P.Drew and J.Heritage (eds), *Talk at Work: Interaction in Institutional Settings*, Cambridge, Cambridge University Press, 1992. The permission of the publishers to reprint this version is gratefully acknowledged.

2. I am much indebted to Brenda Danet, of the Hebrew University of Jerusalem, and to Mack O'Barr, of Duke University, North Carolina, for their generosity and colleagueship in making available to me data which they have so painstakingly collected. Most of the transcripts are my own, although in some cases they are based on those of Bob Dunstan.
3. For further discussion of how lines of questioning may be managed in cross-examination, and how witnesses attempt to counter perceived lines of questioning, see Atkinson and Drew 1979, especially pp.173-181.
4. It is clear from the defence attorney's closing speech that this is the significance which he attaches to this line of questioning, and to aspects of the evidence about the defendant's claimed "interest" in the witness/alleged victim. Referring to this part of the testimony in his closing speech, he says: "Now it seems to me (a) situation that uhr: (0.5) that uhr, (0.7) uhr::, whe:re yuh have two (0.2) young people (0.6) who (0.6) appea:r, (0.4) from their testimony to be interested in each other.... he kissed her goodnight, (0.5) an' I reckon she wannah, (0.8) no question about that (0.3) a'right? here's two people who ar:e er interested in each other...".
5. This formulation makes reference both to a speaker's *production* of a turn/description, and to a recipient's *interpretation* of that turn. There is an assumption here that there is a fundamental symmetry between production of conduct and its interpretation, because they are both "the accountable products of a common set of methods or procedures" (Heritage, 1984, p.241), these common methods and procedures underlying the shared competence of participants, and thereby underlying 'stable meanings'. And it is clear in [2], though the data for extracts [5] and [6] are too extensive to be shown, that the attorney understands her answers to be disputing his versions. This is displayed in the manner in which he pursues an issue, by rephrasing the point of a question and asking it again.
6. Jefferson's account of the work of such generalised completers in the context of three-part lists is relevant here also:

   "...the [2 item and generalised completer] lists may be 'relevantly incomplete'; ie. not only do the named items not exhaust the possible array of nameables, but a third item would not do such work; ie. there are 'many more' relevant nameables which will not, and need not, be specified" (Jefferson, 1990).
7. The attorney asked "Did'e kiss ya goodnight?", to which the witness replied "Yei:s".
8. The contrast in [2] is managed within a single speaking turn or single question: elsewhere during the same cross-examination similar contrasts are established in

consecutive question-answer pairs, as in the following example:

[Da:Ou:45/2B:1]

A: Now (.) subsequent to this: uh (0.6) uh you
say you received uh (0.8) a number of
phone ca:lls?
(0.7)
W: Yei:s
(0.4)
A: From the defendant?
(1.2)
W: Yeis
(0.8)
A: And isn't it a fa:ct (t)uh (.) Miss ((name))
that you have an unlisted telephone number?
(0.3)
W: Yeis
(1.2)
A: An' you ga::ve the defendant your telephone
number didn't you?
W: No: I didn't
(0.3)
A: You didn't give it to [him
W: [No:.
(10.2)
A: Dur:ing the:se uh,...

9. A 'slot for audience appreciation' identifies a structural position, post the production of a contrast, in which recipients perform some operation on what they have heard. The results of that operation may, in other contexts than this, be audible; for instance in political speeches this is a slot where the audience applaud (Atkinson, 1984; Heritage and Greatbatch, 1986; interestingly, the length of such applause is about the same as the pauses here in cross-examination, ie. about 6-10 seconds). Of course in cross-examination there is no verbal manifestation, no verbal equivalent of applause, of the audience's (jury's) appreciation of the point in that slot; video recordings of trials might, however, begin to identify some non-vocal manifestations of such appreciations.

References

Atkinson, J. M. (1984), *Our Masters' Voices: The Language and Body Language of Politics*, Methuen, London.

Atkinson, J.M. and Drew, P. (1979), *Order in Court: The Organization of Verbal Interaction in Judicial Settings*, Macmillan, London.

Garfinkel, H. and Sacks, H. (1970), 'On Formal Structures of Practical Actions', in J. D. McKinney and E. A. Tiryakian (eds), *Theoretical Sociology*, Appleton-Century Crofts, New York, pp. 337-366.

Hart, H.L.A. and Honore, A.M. (1959), *Causation in the Law*, Oxford University Press, Oxford.

Heritage, J. (1984), *Garfinkel and Ethnomethodology*, Polity Press, Cambridge.

Heritage, J. and Greatbatch, D. (1986), 'Generating Applause: A Study of Rhetoric and Response at Party Political Conferences', *American Journal of Sociology*, vol. 92, pp. 110-157.

Jefferson, G. (1986), 'On the Interactional Unpackaging of a "Gloss"', *Language in Society*, vol.14, pp.435-466.

Jefferson, G. (1990), 'List Construction as a Task and Interactional Resource', in G.Psathas (ed.), *Interaction Competence*, International Institute for Ethnomethodology and Conversation Analysis and University Press of America, Washington, pp.63-92.

Pomerantz, A. (1984), 'Agreeing and Disagreeing with Assessments: Some Features of Preferred/Dispreferred Turn Shapes', in J. M.Atkinson and J. Heritage (eds), *Structures of Social Action: Studies in Conversation Analysis*, Cambridge University Press, Cambridge, pp. 57-101.

Sacks, H. (1984), 'On Doing "Being Ordinary"', in J. M. Atkinson and J. Heritage (eds), *Structures of Social Action*, Cambridge University Press, Cambridge, pp. 413-429.

Sacks, H. (1987 [1973]), 'On the Preferences for Agreement and Contiguity in Sequences in Conversation', in G. Button and J. R. E. Lee (eds), *Talk and Social Organisation*, Multilingual Matters, Clevedon, England, pp. 54-69.

Sacks, H. (1992), *Lectures on Conversation* (Vol. 1: Fall 1964-Spring 1968), Blackwell, Oxford.

5 The Presentation of Victim and Motive in Discourse: The Case of Police Interrogations and Interviews[1]

ROD WATSON

In 1976, I contributed a sociological paper to Professor Viano's collection, *Victims and Society*, titled "Some Conceptual Issues in the Social Identification of 'Victims' and 'Offenders'". That paper was largely programmatic, trading mainly on illustrative materials, and was intended to introduce an analytic apparatus for examining the concepts 'victim' and 'offender' as descriptions or identifications for persons in ordinary everyday language which are avowed and imputed by society members according to various social conventions and procedures, some of which I briefly outlined in that paper. The conceptual issues to which I referred are not simply issues concerning analysts' concepts; they are issues firmly grounded in society members' own culturally-based conceptual work in identifying 'victims' and 'offenders', and therefore in using those terms.

Since then, I have been trying to "cash the cheque" by developing what I felt to be the promise of such an analytic apparatus for rigorous empirical analysis in applying it to a corpus of data, namely a set of audio and video recordings of actual police interrogations and interviews concerning murder cases. The recordings were made by police and researchers in a North American city as part of the experimental use of recorded interrogations in courtroom proceedings. In all the interrogations excerpted here, the suspect confessed. The recordings were transcribed according to conversation-analytic conventions for the detailed social-interactional analysis of speech-exchange systems (see the 'Data Section' appendix to this paper).

One of my major analytic interests in police interrogations and interviews is in how descriptions of the alleged offender and victim are built up and organized. In particular, I am interested in explicating the ways in which descriptions and identifications can, *inter alia*, serve to display the motivated nature of the alleged offence. (Along with several other sociologists and philosophers, we can note that not all deeds 'require' the specific provision of motive; typically, only those deeds which appear to members to be untoward, puzzling, deviant, bizarre or to comprise some kind of breach seem to be treated as "specially accountable" in this way.) Put another way, my research focus here concerns the way in which language-embedded descriptions of the victim and offender can be selected and organized by the officer, witnesses or (more particularly) the suspect, so that they can powerfully imply or even - though rarely - explicitly avow a motive for the offence. Of course, the "establishing" of motives is not a trivial matter; it has, for instance, great legal implicativeness, especially of course, when the recordings being analyzed have been used in court. In such circumstances, even the fine detail of the descriptions involved is at the very least as important and consequential for the parties to the trial as it is for the analyst.

The "conceptual issues" to which I referred in my earlier paper are, then, not simply conceptual issues for the analyst alone. They are issues concerning society members' own culturally-based commonsensical use and application of concepts such as "victim" and "offender" in given circumstances. A major task of the sociological analyst is, then, to devise an analytic apparatus that explicates speakers' lay conceptual work, and the analysis should be firmly grounded in and address this work. The interrogations and interviews comprise a rich locus of such lay conceptual work, and therefore constitute a particularly suitable case for treatment. The analytic resources I hope to press into service in this paper are drawn largely from the sociological perspectives of ethnomethodology and conversation analysis. (Perhaps the best general introduction to ethnomethodology and conversation analysis is to be found in Cuff and Payne, 1979, chapter 5.) A collection of readings which covers the scope and diversity of ethnomethodological and conversation analytic studies is that of Turner, 1974.

The most immediate observation we can make - and it is an observation amply manifested in the transcribed data excerpts - is that the identifications "victim" and "offender" are rarely used *per se* in the interrogations. Instead, in the account of the offence or the "lead-up" to the account, we get a variety of "other" descriptions of the offender, the victim and indeed for third parties. Suspect C, for instance, chooses amongst the variously furnished descriptions "tough-guy", "member of a gang" and "independent" (Section C, Example C1, lines 113-114). Victims are described as "fags" (Section B, Example B1, line 15) or "faggots" (Section B, Example B2, line 43), "niggers" (Section A, Example A1, line 2 and Section A, Example 2, line 33), and so on, as well as being "described" through their deed, as we shall see below. Third parties are described as "girlfriends", "friends" and the like, and others are described as "uncles" (Excerpt B, Example B2, line 43). However, for members and analysts alike, one way of hearing these identifications or descriptions in an organized way is to map them onto the identifications "victim", "offender (including accessory)" and various "third parties (witnesses, etc.)". This large variety of descriptions tends on the whole to be distributed between the "victim-offender" and such that each description can be heard as transforms of these identifications. The "victim" and "offender" descriptions thereby work as a background scheme of interpretation. However, as we shall see, these identifications and descriptions may also be selected so as to vitiate stark categorical oppositions such as "victim" and "offender". These vitiating elements may be part of an attempt to redefine who is victimized and who offends, and this in turn may well involve reference to the motivated nature of the offense. Indeed, these principles concerning the co-selection of descriptions and identifications and of their organization relative to each other, will be the focal point of this paper.

Membership Categories and their Organization

A major feature of my earlier paper was the reference to membership categories. Terms such as "faggot", "uncle", "wife", "(an) independent", "brother", "victim" and "offender" are all instances of membership categories. Membership categories are ordinary-language equivalence classes for the description and identification of persons - that is, they are commonsense designations which serve to make reference to persons. Sacks (1972 and 1974) has elucidated some conventional procedures which society members use in categorization activities. One procedure comprises what Sacks terms the "economy" rule, namely that a single membership category will, for practical conversational purposes, serve as adequate reference for one or more persons.

As a starting point, we may add to that observation that the explicit introduction of a single membership category is adequate to provide a motive for a given deed. The categorizations "faggot" and "nigger" (when, for instance, mapped onto a "victim" categorization in respect of a given deed) provide cases in point. We can, for instance, predicate motives of sexual and racial hatred respectively on the part of those for whom "faggots" and "niggers" are their avowedly designated categories of victim. Typically, we can impute one motive per membership category *for a given deed*, in order to achieve a "minimum adequate account" for that deed. Thus, in Section A, Example A1, of the data excerpts, the statement "he's a nigger" is taken as adequate to impute a motive, even when a motive such as "hating blacks" is not explicitly provided: reference to the racial membership category allows us, along with other society-members, to "fill-in" that unstated element ourselves.

There is, observably, an additional feature of a statement such as "he's a nigger". Membership categories typically bear more than one "label". The racial category that the suspect labels "nigger" can also be labelled "Afro-American", "Black", "Colored person", "Negro", and so on. Society members have a choice between these various category labels; they encounter, as it were, what Garfinkel terms a "common-sense situation of choice". However, it is clear that these labels are not all equivalent; on the contrary, they may be seen as ranked on a hierarchy (Speier, 1973:188-9) such that "nigger" might ordinarily count as a downranking or downgrading label and "Afro-American" an upranking or upgrading level for the category. These category-labels might also variously be taken as having the qualities of politeness, guardedness, insult, respect, euphemism, etc., which in various ways and to various degrees graft onto and trade upon the upranking and downranking properties.

The selection of a downranked category label can work to achieve a debasing reference or some other subordination. The same analysis applies to the term "fag" or "faggot" relative to, say, the labels "homosexual" or "(a) gay" for the same category, such that a person categorized as a "faggot" might well be seen to be "put down" in contradistinction to the case had he been described as a "gay". Hearers may typically draw inferences about the motivated nature of speakers' selection of one label rather than other candidate labels for a category so as to account for particular deeds committed against incumbents of certain categories of sexual orientation, race, gender, etc. Thus, the selection of a downranking and even a debasing label for a given category may be seen, *mutatis mutandis*, as subject to the same motive which provides, say, for more severe assaults on incumbents of that category. Indeed, in Section A, Example 2, lines 32-3, the suspect's use of the downgrading term "nigger" comes in the very next utterance after the policeman has used the term "colored". The juxtaposition of the two category labels on lines 32-3 is underscored since they occur within the framework of an adjacency pair of utterances, namely a question and answer sequence. (On the adjacency pairing of utterances, see Sacks, 1974.)

The Relational Pairing of Categories

However, whilst the explicit mentioning of one category may be said to comprise a minimum adequate technique for the imputation of motive, we must immediately qualify and complicate this observation by explicating a crucial background understanding used by members in imputing or avowing motive. This understanding involves the kind of cultural knowledge we can call procedural knowledge; in this case the knowledge involves how to turn a one-person problem into a two-person problem [Sacks, 1968:31-40: see the debate between Sacks and various discussants in Hill and Crittenden (1968:31-40).] In short, the invoking of the membership category "Black" (or "nigger", here) projects the relevance of a second category, namely that of "(a) White" - namely the category of which the suspect is observably (for the officer and any onlookers) an incumbent. These two categories, which we may call "Black (person)"-"White (person)" can be taken as an instance of what Sacks (1972) calls a "standardized relational pair of categories", or more simply a "relational pair". Note that in accounting, say, for the murder of a given person, the imputation of motive may characteristically involve the categorization of *two* people - the victim and the offender. It is, of course, through this commonsense procedural apparatus that we can sustain the utterly commonplace observation that the imputation of cross-racial motive involves categorizing both the victim and offender into the appropriate relational pair. It is only when such tacit and unstated reasoning is done that we can impute a racist motive for a given offence though, as I shall indicate below, various complications regarding cross-category motives may be founded upon these category pairs. Garfinkel (1948-9) has apprised us of the immense consequentiality of members' reasoning concerning inter- as opposed to intra-homicides in his study of courtroom trial proceedings; the matters I am here addressing are not "mere talk"; indeed "mere talk" is never merely talk.

A similar analysis can be said to apply to suspect B's provision of the single category "faggot". This in turn might be said to provide for the relevance of the relational pair "heterosexual"-"homosexual" and, given the description of the deed as "murder", to further distribute that category pair onto the "victim" and "offender" pair, to provide a motive such as hatred or phobia of those with other sexual preferences, sexual minorities etc. (There remains the thorny question concerning when category pairs are oppositionally related and when they fit together in terms of complementarity, ie. when the incumbents of the period categories are seen as being opposed to each other (e.g. "assailant" and "defendant") in contradistinction to their fitting together in teamlike ways (e.g. "mother" and "father"). An immense amount depends, of course, on the context in which they are conjoined, e.g. by a deed described as "murder". Some aspects of the issue of complementarity will be addressed below in the section on the membership categorization devices.) Indeed, there seems to be a kind of 'puppetry' to motive-imputation, namely that members seem to produce no greater elaboration or sophistication of motive than that which is perceivedly adequate to make the appropriate category incumbent(s) perform the deed in question. It is through such 'puppetry' that newspaper readers can make inferences from headlines such as "Wife Found Murdered" - implying the reporter's view, at least, that the smart money is on the husband.

The paired distribution of the racial or other identities of the victim and alleged offender is important in other ways too. For example, if someone who is categorized as "(a) white" terms some other person as "(a) nigger", then that term may readily be seen as a "put-down". However, if the speaker is not white but is *also* categorized as a black person, and he calls some other black person a "nigger" then the term may not necessarily be a "put-down". In some local ghetto cultures in the USA, young male blacks may call each other "nigger" as an upranking rather than a downranking label, connoting solidarity, shared category-incumbency and the like. The interpretation of the motivated use of the term "nigger" may, then, differ markedly as between the "white"- "black" and "black"- "black" relational category pairs. The very status of utterances and descriptions is indexical in that it acquires definiteness of sense for society-members through their taking into account the "contextual" features of the discourse, such as the category incumbencies of the parties to the discourse.

Membership Categorization Devices

There is another mode of organization of membership categories besides that of relational pairing - namely that of membership categorization devices. These are "naturally" or conventionally - organized collections of membership categories. Obvious examples of membership categorization devices are "race" (comprising the categories "white", "black", and so on) "gender" ("male", "female"), "family" ("mother", "father", "aunt", etc.); other devices whose categories conventionally "go together" may not have a particularly straightforward label, such as "sexual orientation", ("heterosexual", "homosexual", "bisexual", "asexual"), and "parties to an offense" ("offender", "victim", "witness", etc.) A procedure which is used in connection with these collections or devices is termed by Sacks (1974) the "consistency rule". This procedure has a few maxim-like formulations, but basically it runs: if two or more categories occurring proximally in a conversational sequence can be heard as coming from the same collection or device, then hear them that way. Thus, for instance, suspect C's description of himself, not as a "member of a gang", but as an "independent" (Section C, Example C1, lines 116-7) may be seen as preserving the victim's alleged initial description (Section C, line 113) of him as a "tough guy" as a possible collection or device which incorporates both "member of a gang" and "independent". These categories might then be heard as component categories of the collection "(types of) tough guy". Such is the organizing power associated with the use of the consistency rule that where we get three or more identifications for persons, members can look to see whether one identification counts as a collecting device for the others. The consistency rule formulates one principle for the co-selection of membership categories. A second procedure for the selection of membership categories is that they may be rendered "story-sensitive" or "topic-sensitive". Confessions characteristically manifest a story format and Suspect C's self-categorization as "an independent" is sensitive to the organizing theme and development of his confession - namely, that he acted alone. It remains to be seen how this procedure interacts with the consistency rule in the selection of categories: suffice it for now to observe that suspect C uses each of these procedures in a compatible way.

As can readily be surmised from the above comments, the conventional organization of categories into collections or devices, including rules of application such as consistency rules, can be a locus for the derivation of relational pairs derived from the same device and where the application of the consistency rule comprises a major link between the pair; for instance, the relational pair "straight"-"gay", which we have already discussed, are two categories tied through the consistency rule to the collection "(types of) sexual orientation". Indeed, relational pairs or other cases of proximally-used categories which are perceivedly derived from different devices often seem bizarre in some way, unless some special contextual provision is made for the co-selection. The venerable joke about a Hopi Indian family comprising a mother, father, children, uncles, aunts and an anthropologist is a case in point. Furthermore, we might note in passing that the organization of categories into devices and relational pairs provides the police with a search procedure for tracking down offenders, e.g. to look for members of the family of the victim, starting with the spouse, and so forth.

Additionally, some membership categorization devices have a special property (Sacks, 1972, 1974), that of duplicative organization; that is, they possess a "team-like" quality. The device "family" for instance, divides the population up into members of team-like units, i.e. family units, with conventionally ascribable predicates such as "sticking together", "in-group loyalty", etc. "Members of a gang" may also be seen to have similar team-like properties of "sticking (or acting) together". Indeed, categories such as "member of a gang" may be turned into devices or collections on their own behalf. (For an examination of this issue, see Watson, 1978.) This is conceivably the reason why suspect C disavows that description, for fear of implicating others *via* the property of duplicative organization. Similarly, relational pairs of categories drawn from a duplicatively organized device can also be treated as duplicatively organized, e.g. "mother"-"child", "brother"-"sister", and, consequently as "sticking together", "affording mutual help and support", etc.

Complex Combinational Uses of Membership Categories

Let us now consider the more complicated situation which is found in data Section D, especially lines 6-7, where two conjoined membership categories, "white" and "men", are used in relation to two others, "black" and "sister", the relation being established by the activity-descriptor "going to bed (with)". This construction is complex in that it does not exhibit straightforward compliance with the economy rule; here, one category, say "man", is apparently not taken as referentially adequate. Moreover, whilst the "white"/"men" and "black"/"sister" constructions may be seen to be linked by the consistency rule to the membership categorization device "race", the use of a consistency rule does not readily yield a device which collects the categories "men" (particularly in plural forms) and "sister", especially in view of the apparently sexual nature of the activity provided. Why did the alleged offender not use the "white"/"men"-"black"/"woman" construction, which through the use of the consistency rule would simply collect the categories into the "race" and "gender" devices? How can one analytically account for this complex combinatorial use of membership categories?

Firstly, we can observe that this instance occurs as part of an avowal of motive; it occurs in a stretch of "motive-relevant" talk where the alleged killer (a black male) presents the victim (a black female) ahead of time with the motivated character of his forthcoming deed. The "man" and "sister" categories at least provide some cross-gender elements in the structure, and, indeed, the categorization "sister" is, if anything, the pivotal one.

The "sister" categorization, in combination with the racial categorization "black", serves to reinforce the victim's and offender's co-incumbency of the latter categorization, along with all the implications or predicates this co-incumbency entails. In the offender's reference to a "black sister", we can project two underlying relational pairs of categories, "black-brother"- "black-sister". The category "sister" derives from the device "family", which, as we have seen, is duplicatively organized. Part of this duplicative organization is that individual family units are seen as "sticking together" in team-like ways. Thus, persons relationally paired as "brother" and "sister" may be expected to "stick together" in terms of "in-group loyalty" and the like. When the "sister" categorization is combined with co-incumbency of a *racial* category, such as "black", the palpable effect is to highlight the "sticking together" aspect of such co-incumbency. (On "sticking together" as a category and device-based predicate used in accusations, complaints, excuses and other blame negotiations, see Watson, 1978.) Thus, an emphasis on the implicativeness of co-incumbency of the same racial category may trade on the properties of categories derived from a duplicatively organized device such as "family". Indeed, such combinatorial category uses are so effective at doing this that terms like "black brother" and "black sister" often become culturally institutionalized, "standard format" ways of invoking and intensifying racial or ethnic loyalty.

Derivatively, the invocation of such in-group loyalties also intensifies the potential for highlighting *dis*loyalty, an example in this case evidently being sleeping with males of the racial category "whites". The multiplex relational pairing of the "white man"-"black sister" categorizations does a great deal of highly economical work, then, in imputing motive, for it can preserve a cross-racial element in the motivation of an "offence", even if it occurs between members of the same race. Here, the selection and complex organization of categories does "persuasive work" regarding a deed for which there exists at least three candidate motive-imputations (e.g. financial, sexual and racial).

We are presented with a preferred imputation which preserves and combines elements of two of the motives whilst the financial motive is allegedly disavowed by the offender (line 4). It is very often the case that when a deed is seen as specially accountable, there exist two or more possibly ascribable motives and categorization work is frequently addressed to the selection between competing motives or perhaps to achieving some compatible resolution as between motives; in addition, categorization work is part of the apparatus which is mobilized to persuade interlocutors and others to "see it that way". Another example of more than one motive-ascription possibility is to be seen in Section A, example A2, lines 31-2, where the officer attends to two possibly ascribable motives, i.e., was the victim killed "just because he was colored, period?" or was there a motive addressed to *this specific individual*? Moreover, as we shall see below the avowal or ascription of the motive that *is* selected can also serve to claim moral justification (as seems to be the case in this data excerpt) or mitigation for such deeds.

Victims, Offenders and the Description of Actions

In police interrogations and interviews, we seem typically to get a great many references to actions or deeds and in our data excerpts we get a variety of descriptions of deeds, e.g. "the girl walked up to me an' propositioned me" (lines 109-110, Section C, Example C1), she asks "whether I would like to get laid?" and "propositioned me again", "the girl got you might say kinda pricky", "...an' then she called me a prick: hher no good son of a bitch::an:d she threw what was left of the remainder of the bottle of beer at me" (Example C2, lines 221-4).

One way in which society members make and communicate inferences about such action-descriptions is to treat them as typical manifestations of types of persons. Again, these types of persons are figured up as membership categories and the activities typically associated with these categories are termed "category-bound activities" (Sacks, 1974) - that is, activities that, in the culture, are conventionally tied to a membership category or to a restricted set of categories. One suspect makes fairly explicit reference to category-bound activities when speaking of his victims (Section B, Example B1, lines 12-18) claiming that you can look at a person and tell ("that he's a fag") by his "personal reactions'n stuff". In addition, the same suspect gives us an activity tied to the membership category "hypocrite", i.e. saying that they're doing one thing and going out and doing another (the wrong) thing (Example

B, lines 24-6). Immediately after, the officer transforms Suspect B's claims concerning activities belonging to the category "hypocrite", i.e. "you mean they wear two faces in the house of God". The suspect endorses this. As is quite evident from the suspect's comments, the reference to category-bound activities can also begin to provide for the motivated nature of the offense.

Furthermore, through their category-bound nature, activity-descriptions can stand on behalf of categorizations; they can work implicitly or (more rarely) explicitly attest to the "kind (categorization) of person" in question.

One commonsensical procedure for achieving implicature is for recipients to see whether the action as described by the speaker can be heard as bound to a membership category or to some delimited set of categories, such that one can "work back" to the category from the activity. For example, in the case of Suspect C, the girl allegedly sexually propositioning him, "getting pricky", hurling obscene abuse, not to mention beer, at him, might each and all be seen as the typical actions of a female whom the defense attorney might categorize as a "tramp" or worse, with all the downgrading implications of this category and label. To be sure, there might be seen to be a peculiar power in making such inferences available for recipients to "arrive at their own conclusions" about the girl.

The imputation of a category such as "tramp" might well be seen by the defense as doubly warranted by using as a background scheme of interpretation an attribute conventionally bound to the category "female", namely that women should "wait to be asked", rather than walking up to a man and propositioning him. Activities, then, can be described in ways which render them as category-sensitive. These kinds of category- and activity-based characterological imputations are, of course, frequently and notoriously found in rape trials.

A more or less explicit example of "working back" from some activity to a category is found in data Section B, where the officer, whilst perhaps seeking to mitigate the negative predicates of the category "fag", claims (Section B, Example B1, lines 20-2) that the victim "tried to stay close to God by singing in the churchiz". The suspect artfully responds to this by working back from the activities thus described to the category "hypocrite" (to which such activity could be taken as tied to some alternative definition as a "responsible citizen"). There we have an example of a common-sense situation of choice in which there may be multiple descriptions of persons by virtue of their deeds with consequent differences in motive-imputation.

The observation that activities can conventionally tie to more than one (though still a restricted set) of categories is found in another data excerpt from Section B, Example B3, lines 46-62, where the officer asks whether one of the suspect's victims was "a faggot" too, and the suspect replies "that the victim did a lotta dirty ways dough", and goes on to exemplify this (lines 56-7, 59). Hence, the victim was not homosexual but - working back from "having a lot of dirty ways" to possible categorizations in addition to homosexuals of whom "dirty ways" might also be claimed by ill-intentioned persons - he can find himself tarred by the same brush.

Thus, through the suspect's artful use of the property of category-boundedness, the victim can be presented as heir to the reactions or retribution which such persons might purportedly "deserve". In this sense, the suspect's foregoing talk about homosexuals (not presented in this paper) instructs us what to look for in this non-homosexual's case too. The suspect's tag "though" (line 54) works very nicely as part of a modified denial which can help to preserve this non-homosexual as still being an appropriate victim. A more fully explicated version of the reasoning concerning choice of victim might be as follows:

- Homosexuals are cases of the class of "those who have dirty ways".
- Suspect B deals harshly with homosexuals as having "dirty ways".
- The prospective victim (a non-homosexual) also had "dirty ways".
- Therefore, Suspect B always dealt harshly with him.

Here we have an ostensive element in the suspect's communicative work. He can point to homosexuals as paradigm cases of those who purportedly have "dirty ways" (and perhaps of how he deals with them). Such an ostensive technique is quite efficacious in pointing to what might be an indeterminate or difficult-to-exhaustively specify class or cluster of categories (though here the examples of "getting riled" and "gambling" do valuable work too). Using this technique, the suspect can present his actions as patterned, coherent and accountable rather than quirky, idiosyncratic or the like; he can present his action as a typically motivated response to a typical situation. This example shows how the conventions "underpinning" language uses do not impart a rigid character to members' linguistic or other activities, but instead can be flexibly and creatively applied. It is through these flexibilities that persons who take it upon themselves to purge the world of homosexuals may find themselves with even broader responsibilities.

It is the inter-locking reciprocal nature of category-bound activities which conjoins relational pairs and which together provide a locus for imputing motives. Indeed, one might also observe that activities are not the only predicates conventionally assignable to categories; as this paper indicates, typical *motives* too, may be treated as category-bound. (Indeed, a single categorization may *in principle* provide for a range of "tied" motives.) In some cases, motives may be taken as being tied to all the categories of an entire membership categorization device, particularly where the device is duplicatively organized. Thus, as suggested in the previous section of this paper, one might expect a motive such as "loyalty" to travel across, and to relate, all the categories of the device "gang". This, as we have observed, is doubtless why Suspect C disavows the categorization "member of a gang" so as to avoid implicating others, even if only in the minimal sense of not detracting from the plausibility of the theme of his confession, namely that he committed the offense himself. These are crucial considerations for a speaker wishing to exert control over others' inferences concerning the motivated nature of his/her confession. Thus, the selection of a category might again be said to do "persuasive work" in the face of the possibility of at least two candidate interpretations of what occurred then and during the offence; again we have a practical resolution of a common-sense situation of choice.

Motives, then, do not necessarily tie to single categories; they may also tie to relational pairs or to collections of categories. To be sure, tying a motive to two categories typically helps to "tie down" or specify that motive, to limit its generality. The issue of achieving some definitiveness of sense to a motive is in part what this and the foregoing parts of this paper are about - namely, how are the general communicative resources which involve rather abstract, standardized and anonymous typifications of motives-in-general, actions-in-general, and types-of-persons-in-general put together by speakers in such a way as to provide for what, for all practical purposes, is a specific motive, for a specific deed done by specific people in specific circumstances? Whilst categorizations comprise only one set of resources for the achievement of the practical specification of motive, I believe that especially the previous section of this paper, on complex combinatorial uses of categories, indicates the ways in which such specifications may be embarked upon by members.

Motives and the Moral Order

I have tried to show some of the ways in which motive may be imputed or avowed, either explicitly or by inference. This paper has been informed by the philosophical argument that motives are not elements which exist separately from, or prior to, conduct; nor, as analysts, can we see motives as *causes* of action, especially given the synchronic embeddedness of the motive and the action, the margin of indeterminacy of motive-imputation or the possibility of several "candidate" motives of pertaining to a deed or person (following Goffman's latest volume, we might say the motive and its "animator"). This is certainly not to say that society members do not on occasion (though not always) treat motives as "causing" actions; however, these conceptions should be regarded by analysts as topics for analysis rather than endorsing them, and indeed using them, as heuristic resources. (For some philosophical and sociological objections to the notion of motives as causes, see Louch, 1966:95-9; MacIntyre, 1970; Coulter, 1977.)

Instead, it seems analytically far more well-founded to treat motives as constituent features of the description of deeds and of accounts "surrounding" those descriptions. Motives are so inextricably built into the description of deeds that the imputed motive makes the deed publicly visible "for what it is". In this respect, motives have a *public*, not intrinsically private, opaque or internal nature, since the communicative and cognitive resources deployed in "motive-relevant talk", resources such as membership categorizations, avowals and the like have an eminently public character. These communicative and cognitive resources are shared throughout a society/language community; indeed, the competent use of these resources betokens membership of the community. It is no accident that when one sets out to examine "motives", one invariably ends up by looking at the public, held-in-common resources such as those with which I have been concerned in this paper.

Nor can the descriptions of the deed and its surrounds be regarded as inert phenomena. The avowal or ascription of motive not only comprise activities in themselves, but may also form part of a further activity or chain of activities, namely those activities we gloss as "moral work" - work such as justifying or claiming mitigation for some apparently accountable deed. The invocation of motives is typically part and parcel of the activity of formulating *grounds* or *reasons* for actions. These grounds or reasons may indeed include formulating justifying or excusing conditions, consequently vitiating the tied "all" and "none" allocation of blame as between offender and victim respectively.

A key example can be found in Suspect C's confession, where the suspect's victim, as we have said, allegedly seems to violate the predicates conventionally imputable to the category "(respectable) woman" by twice propositioning the subjects, throwing obscene insults and beer at the suspect, thus potentially invoking various derogatory category possibilities. In these respects, the woman's self-confessed killer can make available the inference that he was provoked in his deed, and moreover, that the victim, who was purportedly looking for a "tough guy", invited and precipitated the deed in certain ways. Consequently, the suspect can attempt to present the motivated nature of his deed in terms of its being a "response" - indeed, in part almost a "reflex" response - to a set of inducements and, eventually, provocations. The inferences that Suspect C makes available concerning the motivated character of his deed comprise a built-in part of the claiming of a significant element of mitigation.

Similarly, twice in his confessions (not transcribed here), Suspect B claims: "He (the victim) did what he had to do and I did what I had to do", i.e. that the victim had envisaged homosexual activity and Suspect B responded to that with "his thing," namely violence. Again, the categorizations and temporal organization of action sequences - not only *what* the initial action was but *who* initiated it - make available various inferences concerning the motivated nature of the offense, together with some claimable element of mitigation.

Hence, the avowal or ascription of motive can comprise part of an attempt to reapportion the quantum of blame such that the offender can divest him/herself of the full blame for the offense and to allocate a part, however small, of that blame to the victim. (For another study of membership categories and their relation to the distributions of blame, see Watson, 1978; and Watson, 1990.) The imputation of motive(s) is part and parcel of the many ways in which society members (if I may take liberties with Jeff Coulter's expression) articulate and apply the logic of the moral order. To impute motives is one way in which we not only make sense, but moral sense, of conduct.

Data Section A

Note: The variously used transcription symbols and conventions used in these data sections broadly parallel those in Schenkein (1978: xi-xvi) and those of Gail Jefferson.

(White male accused of killing a black male)

P = Police Officer, S = Suspect

Example A1

1. P: Why did you shoot at this G...?
2. S: He's a nigger.
3. P: Did you eh were you alone when you er shot at him?

Example A2

31. P: Well then did you know that you were shooting at G...or did you
32. shoot at him just because he was colored, period?
33. S: He's a nigger.
34. P: And that's why you shot him and er.
35. S: That's why I shot him.
36. P: Did you intend to kill him...or?
37. S: Yes...!
38. P: yer.
39. S: Do you think I'd fire at somebody if I didn't intend to
40. kill them?

Data Section B

(Male accused of killing three other males)

Example B1

9. Officer 2: Yih didn' know'm be[fore that
10. Suspect: [Oh ah kno:w
11. (.)
12. Suspect: Yihknow[I know w't]'ee wu:z
13. Officer 2: [O h o h .]
14. Suspect: I c'd look at a pers'n t:ell.
15. Officer 2: I mean didn't yih kne:w 'a wz a:, a fag righ t,
16. Suspect: Yeh you c'd
17. tell bah the puhrs'n'l reaactions 'n stuff. Look at 'm 'n
18. tell.
19. (1.0)

20. Officer 1: Well I understand that uh:: he tried to uh:::::: stay
21. pretty close tih Go:d uh::: by:::singing in the
22. churchiz 'n so forth en : : : uh,
23. ((door squeaking))
24. Suspect: °He's a hyp ocrite.°
25. (2.0)
26. Officer 1: Pard'n?
27. Suspect: He's a hypocrite

Example B2

19. (Toe:) picked che up in the uh (.) wudje say the
20. Thunderbird?
21. Suspect: Yeah. All them hypocrites man.
22. (1.4)
23. Suspect: hypocrites owna sahd a' God. Dass one thing ah cain't
24. say I an not a hypocrite. 'h (1.0) Dey say dey so much
25. diss b't den they go out (.) outside'n do wro:ng de:n.
26. 'h (0.5) °'T's what they do.°
27. Officer 1: You mean they wear two faces uh:: in the house
28. "" God
29. Suspect: Two facces yih know.°
30. they uh::::: ,act one wa: : en uh, °
31. Do de y ohr
32. Officer 1: Yeah.
33. Suspect: un the outside they act inna diffren't way.
34. Y'let ahll yer sin out dehr b't den yih go back outside
35. en (.) c'llect mo:tuh. (0.2) 'n th'l bring it back tih
36. d'house a'God °den dey° (0.4) let it go.
37. Officer 1: A:nd uh:: sometimes feel thet by: walkin:g inoo
38. th't house a'God thet ther purged of their sins uh:: in
39. that manner y'mean uh:
40. Suspect: Not wrilly) you know how it i:s
41. y'know.
42. (1.0)
43. Suspect: Cuz mah oncle 'ee a fiaggot en all th stuff he
44. go through (w'thy his wife you know, (0.9)_e truthf'l
45. yihknow all a'stuff she go through she know w't 'ee is
46. 'n everythi:ng ( ) she don't sa:y nothin °(y'
47. know).° (0.3) She go tuh church ev'ry day ta care a'
48. (th') kiss'n evryt'ing, °( ).° (0.4 'N ah say

	wo::w yihknow, (0.3) 'n den she own th'sahd a'God yih
	know °((0.2)).° B't ah se:g you gotta be thez gotta
	be somethin the way she go through yihknow.
	(0.5)
Officer 1:	We:ll dihyuh think thet uh::: half'v 'er effort'n going

Example B3

	Don't mattuh
	°M-hm,°
	(0.6)
Officer 1:	That guy thet lived nex'door tih you thet uh::: (0.4)
	Mart'n. (0.3) Wuz 'ee a faggot.
	(1.0)
Suspect:	°Hhm:.No.°
	(0.7)
Officer 1:	Huh?
Suspect:	Hm-m,
	(0.6)
Suspect:	Did have a lotta dirty wa:ys, dough.
	(2.2)
Suspect:	Tss-Treated people wro:ng'n stuff yih know he usetih git
	(riled) a whole lotta time yih know.
Officer 1:	W'l [I know-
Suspect:	[Bet own th'ra:cetrack s'n °stuff.°
	(0.1)
Officer 1:	W't he: uh: liked tuh gamble I guess. (did'e?)
	- °He gamble.°
	(0.2)
Officer 1:	'N iz iz wife died a couple a'years ago?
Suspect:	'teh Ah'ohn' know 'about iz wife ah 'ohn' know if he
	married er not.
	(0.8)
Suspect:	Seen s'm pichtez in stuffy'know but ah 'om' know.
	(2.0)

Data Section C

(Male accused of killing a female and then dismembering her)

Example C1

107. P: all right continue
108. S: hhhhn I kept walkin:g (.3) an::d (.8) I tot to the
109. intersection (.2) orf: B an (1.0) when this
110. girl walked up to me ? (.6) an propositioned me.
111. (1.0)
112. P: what did she say: exactly te yer L....
113. you look like ch tough: guy:: (1.2) y. look like the member
114. of a gan:g:
115. (1.2)
116. S: I told'er: I'm: not a member of the gan:g: ? (.) I'm an
117. independent (.3)°hhh (.4) an: she: propositioned me again
118. (1.2)
119. S: I asked her:: ? (.3) if she'd: like to go to a par:ty, (.5)
120. she said yers: (.) °hh[hh
120a. P: [What did she as:k actually say to y.ou:
121. S: °hh[hh
122. P: [ye you can word it(.) use:rr,.(.3)
123. (0.3)
124. S: she [asked me if I would like to get lai:d::
125. P: [(some of the) words:
126. (1.0)
127. P: allright.

Example C2

212. P: all right (.4) con:tinue:on::
213. (.5) (background talking).
214. S: urh:: (1.4) the gir:l: got (.8) might say kind of: (.2)
215. pri:cky: (1.0) an:der[::
216. P: [now tell me exactly what she did
217. S: ( )
218. P: (or: what she said
219. S: [°hhh
220. P: [irs: (.) not goin embarrass us any=
221. S: = she propositioned me agen, (.6) an then she called me
222. eh prick: °hh (.) er no good son:f:a:bitch (.) °hhh an::d
223. she threw:: what was left at (.2) the remain:n:der (.) of
224. th bottle of bee:r at me, (.6) an:d:it struck mein: (.3)
225. the right side of my furhead

226. (.6)
227. P: show me in::(.) in:dicate where: the bottle hit you
228. S: °right about here
229. P: allright

Data Section D

(Police Interview of a Witness regarding a Black male allegedly killing a Black female)

1. Then he turned off the ignition then the one in the back he said
2. "alright who ding whoring around here?" The (S....) said
3. well if you want money, don't have money so the one in the back
4. said we don't want your money, he said we weren't going to be lucky
5. enough to tell what happned and then he said "we disgusted him
6. evertime one of hos black sisters goes to bed with white men and
7. was going to put a stop to it". He asked (a....) again why she
8. went to bed with the white men and she told him she had 3 kids and
9. he said was a God dam liar and punched her in the face and about
10. the body a couple times.

Note

1. I should like to thank the late Professor George Adoff (formerly of the Department of Criminal Justice, New York State College at Buffalo NY, U.S.A.), for his contribution to my analysis of police interrogations and for his provision of various empirical materials. I wish to dedicate this article to his memory. Dr. Christian C.Heath (Department of Sociology, University of Nottingham) has contributed greatly to my analytic work and has provided transcription of a considerable amount of data used in the present paper. Dr. Gail Jefferson kindly transcribed in immense detail one of the interrogations excerpted here. Professor W.W.Sharrock (Department of Sociology, University of Manchester) has furnished very many fruitful observations on the interrogation data. The Homicide Bureau of the Police Department in the (necessarily anonymous) city have offered the researcher every opportunity to gather data. All proper names of persons and places in the transcript have been changed in the interest of confidentiality.

References

Coulter, J. (1977), 'Transparency of Mind: The Availability of Subjective Phenomena', in *Philosophy of the Social Sciences*, vol. 7, pp.321-350. Reprinted with some revisions in J. Coulter (1980), *The Social Construction of Mind*, Macmillan, London.

Cuff, E.C. and G.C.F.Payne (eds) (1979), *Perspectives in Sociology*, George Allen and Unwin, London, reprinted (3rd edition) by Routledge, London, under the authorship of E.C.Cuff, W.W.Sharrock and D.W.Francis (1990).

Garfinkel, H. (1948-9), 'A Research Note on Inter- and Intra-Racial Homicides', *Journal of Social Forces*, vol. 4, pp.369-381.

Goffman, E. (1981), *Forms of Talk*, Basil Blackwell, Oxford.

Hill, R. J. and Crittenden,K.S. (eds) (1968), *Proceedings of the Purdue Symposium on Ethnomethodology*, Institute for the Study of Social Change, Department of Sociology, Purdue University Institute Monograph No.1, Lafayette, IN.

Louch, A.R. (1966), *Explanation and Human Action*, University of California Press, Berkeley, CA.

MacIntyre, A. (1970), 'A Mistake About Causality in the Social Sciences', in B.Wilson (ed.), *Rationality*, Basil Blackwell, Oxford.

Sacks, H. (1972), 'An Initial Investigation of the Usability of Conversational Data for Doing Sociology', in David Sudnow (ed.), *Studies in Social Interaction*, The Free Press, London, pp.31-74.

Sacks, H. (1974), 'On the Analysability of Stories by Children', in R.Turner (ed.), Ethnomethodology, Penguin Books, Harmondsworth, pp.216-232.

Schenkein (ed) (1978), *Studies in the Organisation of Conversational Interaction*, Academic Press, New York.

Speier, M. (1973), *How to observe Face to Face Communication: A Sociological Introduction*, Goodyear, Pacific Palisades, CA.

Turner, R. (1974), *Ethnomethodology*, Penguin Books, Harmondsworth.

Viano, E. C. (1976), *Victims and Society*, Visage Press, Washington, D.C. (second printing, 1981).

Watson, D.R. (1978), 'Categorization, Authorization and Blame-Negotiation in Conversation', *Sociology*, special issue on Language and Practical Reasoning, vol. 12, pp.105-113.

Watson, D.R (1990), 'Some Features of the Elicitation of Confessions in Murder Interrogations', in G.Psathas (ed.), *Interaction Competence*, University Press of America, Lanham, Maryland and London, pp.263-295.

6 Preliminary Notes on Judges' Work: The Judge as a Constituent of Courtroom "Hearings"

MICHAEL LYNCH

Introduction: The Judge as a Constituent of the "Non-ironic" Court

This paper explicates the "interstructural telos" of the court (Robillard, 1974, p. 136), by focusing upon how the judge is an accountable figure in criminal court proceedings.[1] The paper's ethnomethodological approach requires a strict attention to the public observability of constituent activities in a courtroom hearing. A *hearing* is simultaneously organized as sequences of utterances and as analytic renderings of those sequences which implicate the presence and salience of specific parties in the organization of the courtroom speaking round.[2]

My treatment of the judge as a figure within the collaborative production of a courtroom hearing is non-ironic (Robillard, 1974, p. 56) in the sense that I make no use of, for example, Carlen's (1976, p. 12) "method of irony". Nor do I employ Hogarth's (1971) analytic methods for developing social-psychological interpretations of statistical correlations between sentences passed for "the same crimes" by different types of judge. Such accounts describe a behind the scenes judge; where "behind the scenes" can be located "in the judge's head", behind the closed doors of the judge's chambers, or in the judge's social background. The judge I describe is not a secretly or invisibly motivated judge, but a judge who speaks, acts, and overhears what other parties say in the courtroom.

The judge is publicly available in the embodied production of the hearing. This judge is not a social-psychological actor, a dependent locus of sociological variables, or a dramaturgical role in the staging of the hearing.

The judge's analytic status is not exhausted by rational decision making procedures, or by pre-judicial personal and social attitudes. Instead, the judge is a social fact, in Garfinkel's sense (Garfinkel, 1977, 1991; Garfinkel and Wieder, 1992). Garfinkel critically transforms Durkheim's (1938) classic aphorism, "the objective reality of social facts is sociology's fundamental phenomenon", by setting out an ethnomethodological alternative to Durkheim's analytic sociology. The alternative is to examine the regularities of the ordinary society that Durkheim's program objectifies, and to explicate how social order is achieved reflexively, in and through the unrelenting practices of local parties who dwell in a society. It might be said that where Durkheim stresses the relationships between social facts and factors, Garfinkel urges us to investigate the *factories* that produce them. The *social*, for Garfinkel, is not a composite of variables in a regression analysis. It is not specified by measures of socio-economic status, gender, educational attainment, ethnicity, regional background, or any other social factor or combination of factors. Instead, social facts and social factors are uniquely, singularly, and routinely composed *in and through* the concerted production and competent recognition of actions on the 'factory' floor. Such performances *are* social, and their production can be described praxiologically. If it can be said that there are lawful regularities to the organization of social affairs, the initial task is to describe the circumstantial production of such facticity. In the case of the *judge*, the facticity of the judge as a courtroom agency is a public issue for competent co- practitioners. The judge's place in a hearing is more than a role enacted by a person in an institutional setting. The metaphor of role is apt, in the sense that it differentiates the judge's ideal-typical actions from the judge's personality, but it too easily implies that the role of judge is somehow attached to or constructed by an individual actor. It may seem obvious that a judge is a person decorated with symbolic trappings of sovereign and impartial authority (robes, high-backed chairs, an elevated podium, honorary forms of address), a person who performs symbolic functions consistent with a spectacle of justice, but in this study I shall consider the judge as a configuration *in action* that is not, or at least not always, figured or expressed by a robed and bewigged person.

The discussion that follows examines the figure of the judge in Ontario Provincial Court hearings. As a necessary feature of the disclosure of this judge, I shall examine actions produced by other parties to the courtroom hearing. Parties to the hearing include the lawyers, witnesses, and others whose participation contributes to the public accountability of judicial presence:

> ...the publicness of a hearing involves three simultaneous elements. One, it is public because it is a face to face collaborative assembly and therein requires the simultaneous presence of each of the members to one another. Two, it is a speech performative act assembled collaboratively. Three, it must correspond to an authoritative public dialogue larger than the co-present participants, the overlistening of the legal profession (Robillard, 1974, p. 182).

Accordingly, parties are differentially present in the hearing's events as concretely visible speeches and actions and/or as actual or projectable "overlistenings" of those actions. In Ontario Provincial Court criminal proceedings, the parties include the following principal, non-principal,[3] and implicated parties: judge, crown attorney, defense attorney, accused person, lay and police witnesses, court officer, clerk, reporter, present-and-non-present professional overlisteners (including prospective courts of appeal), present and non-present lay spectators (the gallery, the media and their agents). It is important to keep in mind that judicial "overlistening" is not limited to the robed person's sensory processing of others' speeches; rather, judicial "overlistening" provides a set of relevancies when other parties speak and act in the courtroom, regardless of what the judge actually hears. As a party in the criminal court hearing, the judge is perspicuous as *both* a dialogic inhabitant and as an overhearer of the dialogues of others. The judge performs discrete, visible actions in the course of the hearing, while also being an analytical relevance for actions by other parties (including the self-same judge) who explicitly and implicitly orient to a judicial analysis. Judicial overlistening is explicitly relevant to the actions of parties who address the judge with their bodily positioning and gesture, and with the use of such address terms as "Your Honour" and "The Court". In addition, dialogues between other participants (such as lawyers and witnesses) in which the judge does not speak nevertheless implicate the judge as a significant audience who overhears the dialogue in a distinctive, legally binding way. The presence of the judge as an overhearer is thereby made visible in the embodied production of the courtroom hearing.

The Visibility of the Judge

To delineate the figure of the judge in the courtroom hearing requires a competent understanding of the collaborative production of the hearing's events. This is not only a methodological problem for participant observers, but it is also a lively issue for professional participants. Tape recordings of pre-trial discussions between Crown and Defense attorneys provide initial indication of how the projectable actions of a particular judge can become a contingency for a lawyer's presentation of the case, even when the judge is not immediately present:[4]

(1) Longitudinal #17

Defense Counsel and Crown prosecutor are engaged in negotiating a case in which the accused is charged with "indecent assault". The defense counsel has been arguing for a reduction of the charge to "common assault" and the Crown Attorney has been resisting this proposal while offering to accommodate the defense on sentencing.

Def.:	I don't know, see I don't know the judges here.
	(0.4)
Crown:	I think it's Judge Moore this (morning),
	(0.5)
Crown:	and uh, I don- I don't know what he's like on these, I think, I think he won't look upon it as a very serious (incident).
	(3.0)
Def.:	Well, basically, if you read in those facts,
Crown:	Emm hmm.
	(1.0)
Def.:	Ummm,
	(0.8)
Def.:	You know, I- I can't see why: he wouldn't, (want to give a) conditional discharge.

Note how the adversary attorneys project what the particular judge (Judge Moore — a pseudonym) would treat as a serious charge or accept as a reasonable basis for reducing the charges, and note further that such projections feature substantially in the plea negotiations.

(2) Longitudinal #17

Later in the negotiations over the same case, defense counsel tentatively suggests that he will request a private conference with the judge.

Def.:	Now I'm just wondering uh,
	(2.2)
Def.:	you know, like (eh) whether,
	(0.4)

Def.:	(Now, you see,) usually i- i- in Toronto, sometimes (we- we- we get), have a conference with the judge, I'm not sure (what)
	(0.5)
Def.:	you know, even if this even merits it.
Crown:	Uh, they're not too-
	(1.2)
Crown:	They're not too keen on having you come in to talk to them.

Note that when the Crown asserts that the local judges do not encourage conferences, unlike those in Toronto, this acts to foreclose a possible option raised by the Defense.

(3) Longitudinal #3

During negotiations where Defense Counsel proposes dropping a charge of "assault police" to "obstruct police" (a lesser offense that was also charged in connection with the same incident). Crown has been arguing that the offense (involving a woman's actions against an officer who was arresting her husband) is relatively trivial.

Crown:	(A) judge has to look at the eh- you know, the pa- passion involved, the whole scene.
	(0.6)
Crown:	I'd be surprised if (she) got anything worse than a discharge.

Once again, projections about the judge's (or, in this case, possibly *a* judge's) reactions to the details of the case are used in proposals for presenting the case in court.

In each of the above instances, and in many other tape-recorded instances like them, projections of courtroom procedure (criminal charges, materials supplied as evidence, sequential orders of presentation, and procedural options) are tied to the judge's, or a judge's, possible reciprocal reactions. In different instances, the judge's preferences and tendencies are assigned to a particular individual (e.g., "Judge Moore"), treated as a local preference for specific protocols, or ascribed to a disposition to act in a particular way in "cases like this". The attorneys invoke the judge as an organisational principle that locally governs the presentation of the case at hand. Whether or not the attributions about the judge made by the attorneys are accurate, they incorporate the judge into the practical organization of the projected cases, and by so doing they *realize* the judge in their procedures for presenting cases at hand. Therefore, the judge is more than a source of concrete decisions consequent to such presentations.

The possibility that the judge is an analytic relevance in the hearing, which extends beyond the concrete particulars of visible courtroom actions and decisions, imposes considerable difficulty for any attempt to isolate the features of the hearing that implicate the presence of the judge. These analytic difficulties are compounded when a gallery spectator attempts to describe courtroom events. An analysis from the gallery has an indefinite, and uncertain, relation to the intelligibility of court proceedings for the principal parties.[5] Perhaps some comfort can be found in the fact that, unlike, for example, mathematics seminars, courtroom proceedings (or at least major phases of them) are presented for lay audiences, and in the case of jury trials a lay audience enjoys a privileged place in the proceedings. Consequently, while it may be unlikely for a non-lawyer adequately to grasp the legal horizons of judges' work, it is certainly possible to explicate the ordinary horizons of intelligibility for which a judge is also held accountable.

Progressive Characterizations of the Judge as a Presence in the Speaking Round

I shall begin by employing a provisional analytic device designed to make the judge topical. The device consists of a normative scheme for a sequence of actions performed by different speakers in a courtroom hearing. After setting out the scheme, I will present a progression of observations from particular cases, in order to demonstrate how the production of the sequential features of the scheme in actual courtroom circumstances brings into relief organizational practices that are not prefigured by it. Assuming that my scheme alludes to a protocol that parties to a courtroom hearing know, recognize, and rely upon in their work, the failure of the scheme to encompass the situated production of criminal cases will disclose elements of the embodied and temporal production of a case that serve the protocol without being prescribed by it. Initially, I will discuss the theme of "moving the case along"; a theme that formulates a difference between the sequence of a protocol and the temporalization of a case. Specifically, "moving the case along" describes the judge's local efforts to process a case in accordance with the protocol. The protocol's failure to articulate the sequential elements of its 'rational' use in particular cases brings us to a second theme. This is the judge's artful practice of explicating a *reasonable* relationship between a case disposition and the prior testimony. The demonstrability of a reasonable ordering of temporal elements in a hearing's progression is reciprocally available in the way the lawyers devise reasonable arguments for a projectable disposition by the judge.

A Formal Model of Courtroom Proceedings

The following is a schematic outline of a normative order of actions in the Provincial Court disposition of a "guilty plea". The scheme includes a step-by-step order of speaking turns for processing a case. I constructed the outline after witnessing numerous guilty pleas in Toronto-area Municipal Courts. The scheme describes a relatively fixed format for producing a common type of case. For the sake of economy, I am focusing on guilty pleas, rather than trials, bail hearings, and preliminary hearings, because they are less complicated. As should be evident from the outline, guilty pleas are complicated enough. Particular steps in the scheme can be decomposed further into complex subroutines. So, for example, the step comprised of the Clerk's reading of the arraignment routinely begins when the Clerk stands up and recites a series of stock lines. The recitation is more than a rote performance, as it incorporates circumstantial features of the case at hand: the particular name of the accused, a cast of other characters, a chronology of events, relevant legal citations, and various formulations of place.

> Scheme for a guilty plea:
>
> a. Crown calls the number on the docket and the corresponding name of the accused.
>
> b. Accused walks into the court and faces the judge's bench. The accused's Defense Attorney (if the accused is represented by one) walks to a position beside the accused and introduces self to the Court.
>
> c. Crown instructs Clerk to arraign the accused.
>
> d. Clerk reads: Date, street location, "Judicial District of ______", name of accused, "did commit" + charge. Clerk does this for each criminal charge for which the accused is arraigned. Clerk then asks the accused for an "election" of procedure and recites the options: a trial by judge and jury, by judge alone in Superior Court (if an indictable offense), or by a magistrate in Provincial Court.
>
> e. Accused (through the intermediary of Defense Attorney) elects. If accused elects a magistrate's court, accused is then asked by Clerk to enter a plea.
>
> f. Accused (usually via Defense Attorney) pleads guilty or not guilty.
>
> g. If accused pleads guilty, Crown recites the "facts" of the case written on the police "information sheet".
>
> h. Clerk asks accused if "the facts are substantially correct".

i. Defense Attorney answers on behalf of the accused that the facts are correct, that they are "substantially" correct, or that they are correct except for one or more details which the attorney attempts to amend or delete.
j. Judge pronounces 'guilty' (in all but the most unusual of cases).
k. Judge asks both counsel for submissions.
l. Defense attorney submits on behalf of the accused, usually mentioning such matters as the accused's employment record, family situation, criminal record, willingness to make restitution, steps taken to secure treatment for alcohol or psychiatric problems, and items such as recent marriage, enrolment in vocational training, birth of children, etc. to document the Accused's efforts to "straighten up his act". Defense may also submit such documents as pre-sentence reports by probation officers or psychiatric reports on the accused, and may call character witnesses.
m. Judge asks Crown for submission, or instructs Crown that no submission will be necessary in this case.
n. If asked, Crown submits an account summarizing the case and mentioning the criminal record, or lack thereof, concluding with a recommendation for a particular class of sentence (jail term, lengthy jail term, "a stiff fine", suspended sentence, etc.). Crown may also go on record as having no specific submission to make.
o. Judge thanks attorneys for submissions and proceeds to summarize the case, mentioning the facts, the seriousness of the charges, and the demonstrable character of the accused. Judge may speak directly to the accused, often to scold the accused or warn of dire consequences for further offenses. Judge often mentions the difficulties of coming to a decision in the case, and mentions more punitive alternatives that were not chosen ("I was considering a long jail sentence in your case, but ..."). Judge may postpone sentence by requesting further reports by probation officers, or requesting a recess to allow further study of the case. Judge may express approval of the accused's efforts at personal reform and restitution of victims, and may assess the accused as "not a criminal type". Judge pronounces sentence, usually a jail term, fine, suspended sentence, or absolute or conditional discharge with or without a period of probation. If a fine is levied accused may be given an option to pay on an installment plan (if requested immediately following sentence). For a jail sentence, judge may give accused the option of serving an "intermittent sentence" on weekends.
p. Depending upon the sentence passed by Judge, accused is handcuffed and led out of the court by attending police officers, or is instructed to wait for the clerk to process a record of the disposition, and then is directed to present the record (and any fine) to the court bureau.

This outline assigns particular speaking turns to the judge: the judge responds to the submission of facts and pronounces the verdict (j); the judge also requests submissions (k, m) and responds to those submissions (o); and, after having pronounced sentence, the judge responds to any requests by the defense attorney for time to pay or serving the term intermittently. Note that the judge sequentially and substantively responds to the other co-participants in the hearing, and takes an active part in the initiation and closing of particular sequences of action. As Robillard (1974, p. 151) points out, the judge primarily speaks as a recipient to the reading of the facts and the submissions by the attorneys. The judge sometimes intervenes in the speaking round to question the lawyers or 'lecture' the accused, but the judge is free to hear testimony impassively. The judge usually speaks in response to the deliveries of the other parties (except in (k) and (m) when the judge requests deliveries).

The judge's formal place in the hearing is more than a matter of speaking. The Crown, Defense Attorney, Clerk, and Accused address the judge by bowing, and using special terms of address that show deference to "Your Honour". The judge is at times addressed as, "The Court"; a form which makes reference to the judge's sovereign place in, and as, the hearing. The public character of the hearing converges with how the judge "hears" the testimony. In my outline of a guilty plea, the judge is assigned functional properties as one of the principal movers of the action described. The judge's actions are rationalized by reference to the scheme's allocation of speaking-turns, thematic relationships between successive turns, and methods of closing the case.

The Circumstantial Production of Hearings

My scheme does not describe the unforeseen contingencies that arise in a singular case: witnesses may fail to show up, lawyers may arrive late, the docket may be crowded, etc. The difference between the outlined sequence and any actual sequence does not necessarily reveal personal shortcomings or carelessness on the part of the participants; instead, it opens up the question of how a routine guilty plea is collaboratively produced. During the hearings I observed, an array of practical troubles and organizational complications occurred.[6] These included problems of *delay*, *remedying the artifactual features of the procedure*, and *inserts and interruptions*.

Delay:[7] Innumerable delays occurred in the course of the procedures, and the principal participants evidently worked to restore order in the face of them. The judge took a lead role in the local management of temporal order on occasions of delay. Delay thus provided occasions for the display of the judge as a local disciplinarian who not only participated in the hearing, but also took responsibility for the very orderliness of the hearing. A perspicuous instance of a delay is summarized as follows:[8]

> (4) March 2, Peel Court
> A trial involving several Crown witnesses. After the testimony of one witness, the judge called a recess, and parties dispersed from the courtroom for 15-20 minutes. At the resumption of the trial, another witness -- a police constable -- was called by the Crown. The Crown began the examination of the witness and was several questions into the examination when the accused became relevant to the testimony. The officer looked up to identify the accused, and at this time parties noticed that the accused was not present. Defense Counsel then apologised that the accused was outside the court in the hallway and that he had been speaking to him in the hallway during the recess. An officer was sent to summon the accused, and no further comment was made during the interval between the dispatching of the officer and the arrival of the accused to the stand.

The instance points to the relevance of the accused as an embodied presence -- a required body whose evident presence becomes accountable at regular junctures. The discovery of the absent accused made it evident that the accused, though an organizationally required presence, was a locally occasioned presence. More often, missing bodies (of witnesses, lawyers, accused persons) became evident just before hearings began, or at an early point in the proceedings, such as when the Crown would read a number on the docket and a corresponding name, and nobody answered the summons. As the delay following the summons lengthened, the identity of the hearing was transformed by subsequent actions on the part of Crown and judge, as they, for example, would draw up a bench warrant for the missing party before moving on to the next case. Other delays involved the delivery of records to the required readers. Such pauses in the action exhibited the close ordering of the Clerk's work of moving documents around the court and delivering them in coordination with the sequential production of the hearing.

Judges were prominently featured in delay sequences. On occasions when requests for remands were made, the judge typically heard the request and authorized a rescheduled hearing. When momentary delays occurred because of discordances between records and readers, judges used commonplace methods for temporalizing the case; for example, scheduling brief recesses or suggesting minor rescheduling of the order of cases in the docket:

> (5) December 18, Peel Court
> Regarding a police information sheet that the Crown has just discovered is not at hand. The Judge instructed parties to convene again on the case after the noon recess, saying, "I suppose it will show up later in the day. Things have a way of doing that".

The ad-hoc temporal management of the case, and of the day's schedule of cases, was an unremitting feature of the judge's work, as indicated by various spontaneous utterances, gestures, and outbursts during particular hearings. These actions were tied to the detailed requirements for performing a case with the required sets of parties and records. My outline of a guilty plea hearing presumes that required presences are continuously staffed by the parties to a hearing. That presumption fails to describe the work of achieving continuous presence as a hearing unfolds. As circumstantial troubles made clear, the work of assembling the case and managing the temporal exigencies of its coordination was inseparable from the sequence of actions witnessable in any actual occasion of a hearing's production.

Remedying the artifactual features of the procedure: The production of a case often called for remedial measures to contend with the intrusion of court procedures into otherwise "reasonable" ways of going on. For example:

> (6) March 13, Toronto
> A man was charged with failing to appear to a probation officer. He was called, arraigned, and pleaded guilty. He was not represented by a lawyer.
> Crown: Your honor, the accused was arrested- (pause)
> You'll have to bear with me for a while. I have to reconstruct the ((voice trails off)).
> ((Crown arranges information sheet and reads that the accused failed to appear on several dates to the probation officer. A warrant was issued, the accused presented himself for arrest, and has since reported to probation when scheduled)).
> Accused: I'm from St. Mary's ((spoken with a West Indies accent)). I have no idea I was supposed to appear to the probation officer. I appeared as soon as I knew, when the warrant was issued for my arrest.
> Judge: What was the disposition on the substantive offense?
> Crown: Thirty days intermittent.

Judge:	Did you have a lawyer?
Accused:	No, I did not want to pay $500 for a lawyer.
Judge:	Who was the judge?
Crown:	I don't know. ((checks with court officer, court officer murmurs to him, and Crown repeats the Judge's name to the present Judge)).
Judge:	I don't like to convict Mister________.
Crown:	As I said, he was cooperative with the police...
Judge:	He's had one package of trouble- Never mind the Criminal Code- He had one package of trouble, he paid substantially. I'd like to dismiss the charge.
Crown:	I have some doubts about the Crown's ability to ... ((Judge and Crown briefly exchange words to the effect that given the fact that the accused had already plead guilty, the charge could not be withdrawn or dismissed)).
Judge:	I want to dismiss the charge. Enter a plea of not guilty...
Crown:	Strike the plea of guilty and enter not guilty.
Judge:	Charge dismissed.

Delays in the Crown's first few utterances are occasioned by a lack of synonymy between performing the case and reading the appropriate document. In this case, the accused explains that he failed to appear to the probation officer after being released from jail on another offense because he was not aware of the probation requirement. The accused's evident foreign accent supports the credibility of his claim to being ignorant of the probation requirement. The judge queries the accused and Crown attorney about the disposition of the prior offense. The accused tells him that he was not represented by a lawyer, and the Crown and Clerk quietly disclose the name of the judge on the prior case. The prior offense is not mentioned in the present testimony, nor is anything said about the reputation of the judge in the earlier case, but the present judge's solicitation of relevant details, together with his explicit statement that "he paid substantially", may indicate that the prior sentence was a stiff one. The judge goes on to say that the punishment for the prior offense was enough, and that despite the legalities operating at present, the accused has already paid his debt. The judge then attempts to dismiss the case, a procedure that the Crown indicates is foreclosed by the occurrence of the prior guilty plea. In an improvised solution, the judge instructs the Crown to enter a not-guilty plea on behalf of the accused, which then sets up the sequential possibility of the dismissal. Note, that having chosen a specific outcome, the ongoing sequence is aborted as the parties back up in order to install procedural conditions consonant with the selected outcome. This procedural repair demonstrates how the accountable order of the case relies upon locally organized procedures which set up appropriate sequential conditions for the production of an outcome. To mention this does not imply criticism of the particular judge for playing fast and loose with the legal procedures. It would be just as sensible in this case to credit the judge with managing to produce a fair disposition in spite of legalistic requirements.[9] The judge exhibits a normative orientation to relationships between possible pleas and possible dispositions, even though he reverses the temporal relationship between the particular plea and its "appropriate" disposition. The sequential options which are normally part of guilty plea procedures did not in this case determine the manner in which the case was resolved. Instead, the normative-sequential outlines of the case were produced in a post-hoc construction stipulated by a judge who chose righteously to circumvent the procedural implications of a guilty plea.

On other occasions, the sequential production of the case was specifically tied to the judge's response to attorneys' arguments about which next-actions were appropriate. "What to do next" was not solved through the collaborative enactment of a standard procedure. Instead, determinate relations between prior-procedures and next-procedures were established through local assertions about "appropriate" or "legal" courses of action to be followed, such as in the following instance:

> (7) March 13, Toronto
> A case involving two accuseds represented by different lawyers on a charge of "Breaking and Entering".
> The trial resumed after a week-long delay due to a police witness's absence on the first day of the trial a week before. The trial had been interrupted just after the main Crown witness was cross-examined by one of the defense attorneys (Def. 1). The trial resumed with the cross examination of the same witness by the second defense attorney (Def. 2). The Crown then called his police witness, who gave brief testimony on the case, with little of the testimony being of substantive importance for the demonstration of guilt or innocence. The main Crown witness, the victim, had been challenged by the two defense attorneys on numerous contradictions in his testimony. After the Crown announced that he had no further witnesses to call, the following negotiation ensued:
> The defense attorney for Dunlop (Def. 1) made a motion that "there is no credible evidence" to convict the accuseds of breaking and entering, and elaborated this in terms of the testimony of the Crown's main witness. The judge disputed this, and then stated that if the motion Def. 1 had made was for the insufficiency of evidence, then it was not in the proper order, since such a matter as insufficiency

would be dealt with after all of the evidence was heard, and at this point in the trial acquittal could be granted on such grounds. Def. 1 argued that the trial "is not a jury trial, Your Honor is judging on the facts..."

Judge: "This is not a motion for (nonsense)...credibility is not considered for a motion of (nonsense)...".

The judge insisted that such issues had to be dealt with in "their proper place", and he then asked, "You're asking me to say there's no credible evidence?"

Def. 1: "That's correct, there's no evidence in the witness's testimony on a key, nor in the officer's that would be sufficient to convict on break and enter".

Judge: "Are you asking me to consider a plea to an included offense?"

Def. 1: ((uttered something to the effect that this was the Judge's prerogative)).

Judge: "If you're asking for a dismissal, I can't reduce the charge...only on the right motion from you can I ..."

Judge: "Are you moving for dismissal on grounds that there is not correct evidence to convict?"

Defense: "Yes".

The judge then turned to the Crown and asked for a submission. The Crown briefly submitted that the testimony provided grounds to convict, because, by the witness's account, the witness told the accuseds to leave his apartment and they refused.

Def. 1 then argued in reaction to this that the Crown had not heard the testimony entered the week before, because another Crown attorney had handled the case at that time, and he added that the events in question did not turn into a break and enter until after the accuseds had left the premises and the witness decided to charge them for other reasons. The judge then asked for a motion from Def. 2, and the attorney stated that he wished to move in the same manner as did Def. 1. Judge, at an early point in Def.2's utterance cut him off and stated that, as a result of the motion being proposed, Def. 2 was electing to call no evidence. Def. 2 replied that in his understanding he retained an option to call evidence. The judge denied this, saying that there were two options, a motion for "non-suit" or a motion for dismissal on grounds of no evidence (this latter option being, as I take it, part of a final submission). At this point Def. 1 began to rise from his chair in an attempt to reassert his original motion so as to retain the option of calling evidence, but this was quashed by the judge. Def. 1 remained suspended midway through rising from his chair, attempting to protest, but the judge waved him down and insisted that he had already made his motion. Def. 2 then elected for a "non-suit" and the judge addressed the accused Dunlop (Def. l's client), stating, "You acted boorishly..." but he added that there was insufficient evidence to convict. The judge cited the facts that there was no evidence of the key purportedly used to open the apartment door and that there had been previous association between the accuseds and the victim.

Judge: ((to accused)) "You may not have understood his ((victim's)) desire for you to leave. Charge dismissed".

In this instance the judge turned what began as a motion from Def. 1 into a final submission. He asked the Crown for his submission, and then turned to Def. 2, requesting a commitment to the option of motion/submission. When Def. 2 "moved" to do what Def. 1 had done, judge formulated the sequential import of this act as foreclosing any possibility of calling further evidence (that is, he treated the action as a submission occurring after all evidence had been called). Def. 1, having discovered what his move implied in the judge's management of the hearing, attempted to retract the move and transform it into one with different prospective options. By quashing this move, the judge made evident to both counsel the determinative place in the sequence to which their prior actions had taken them. Def. 2 managed to exploit this scenario by changing his move to one that allowed for the subsequent calling of evidence. As it turned out, Def. 1's client <u>was</u> freed from the charge on the grounds of insufficient evidence (as was Def. 2's later), but not before the attorney had been made to suffer the judge's pre-emptive actions. In this case, the judge may have had good legal grounds for his actions, but the point is that, regardless of the distribution of procedural knowledge and ignorance among the judge and the two lawyers, the judge peremptorily achieved a sequence of moves in which the pragmatic import of Def. 1's "motion" did not become apparent to the two lawyers until later, when the judge formulated the options which were currently available. The identities of moves in the sequence, at least so far as the defense attorneys were concerned, were disclosed late in the game through the judge's formulation. Locating the determinative place in the sequence that the motion had taken them was, for a time, a matter of dispute and retrospective attribution among the parties whose actions constituted that sequence. Rather than being an instance of conduct governed by formal sequential procedures, the case appeared to be one in which the sequential context of the particular moves was subject to dispute and local resolution.

Inserts and interruptions: When a case began in the fashion outlined in my formal model of a guilty plea (the accused was called, arraigned, etc.) it did not always, or even often, proceed smoothly to conclusion. In some instances it was discovered retrospectively that "a step" had been left out, such as when a clerk was informed well after the arraignment had been read that the accused had been charged with additional charges. This resulted in a recycling of the arraignment procedure, with the additional charges being read. Other interruptions of ongoing cases occurred when the Crown created opportunities for dealing with other cases scheduled for the same day by interrupting the ongoing case on the floor. Often, at the close of a recess during a trial, one or more remands and guilty pleas (relatively short-duration events) were processed before resuming the trial. On one occasion, the Crown requested an interruption of an ongoing trial because a lawyer for another case scheduled for that day had just entered the courtroom and was briefly available to do business. The interruption was granted by the judge, and the other case was quickly disposed of. These interruptions reflected the court's efforts to process a day of cases. An entire docket of the cases-that-day were relevant to the internal conduct as well as serial processing of particular cases on that day. How much time needed to be taken for any case, the order of cases, the availability of parties differentially over the course of the day, and the more or less pre-scheduled blocks for court time and recesses, were all part of the contingent management of a day in court.[10] The pre-scheduled blocks of time and recess enabled court time to be distributed across types of cases as they were processed. Blocks of time were often opened up at junctures between events, such as at the end of a recess, or at the outset of the morning session. Typically, such junctures were used for opportunistically disposing of cases that were projectively brief; cases in which parties could be instructed beforehand that their case would, for example, be "done-with after the morning recess". The usability of the post-recess opportunities often displaced the temporal relevance of an ongoing trial, as its re-assembly was deferred in light of the opening created by the recess for other cases.

Within any hearing numerous speaking turns were produced as spontaneous actions which were not produced in accordance with the formal requirements of the speaking round. The competent production of these actions involved a sensitivity to the sequential contexts of the hearing and the permissions and opportunities that could be secured for "spontaneous" actions. Judges were especially prominent, not only as arbiters of the order of speeches by other parties, but as overhearers of testimony who could spontaneously enter into the discourse. Their "rights" to do so were non reciprocal. Judges' remarks, which were inserted other than at the formally designated places for articulating a ruling, or responding to requests and submissions by the attorneys, exhibited varieties of relationships to the discourse in which they occurred. Often, judges "picked up" on a cross-examination sequence, asking questions of a witness other than those asked by the examining attorneys, or requesting clarification on matters previously covered in the testimony. On other occasions, judges interjected complaints over the improprieties of the lawyers or witnesses in conducting the hearing. These noted improprieties encompassed such matters as the conduct of question-answer sequences in testimony, protocols of court etiquette, and complaints about the time being taken to process the case.

The Production of the Hearing as the Judge's Work

The previous section elaborated upon how the formal model's applicability to the sequential production of cases is superseded by the locally organized work of the parties in the hearing. The presence of the judge in the speaking round now appears to be more extensive than that of a performance of pre-allocated duties, such as pronouncing guilt or innocence and announcing the sentence disposition for the record. In addition to these assigned tasks in the serial production of the hearing are the innumerable spontaneous actions, which have to do with the ad-hoc management of contingencies in the temporal organization of the hearing. In the sub-sections that follow, the judge's presence in particular cases is described under the headings of "the judge as a 'mover' of the proceedings", and "the judge as a condition for the rational articulation of a sequential orderliness". These topics arise from the formal model's inability to account for the time it takes to do a case, and its irrelevance to the work of demonstrating the rational accountability of the enactment of a hearing in any particular case.

The judge as a 'mover' of the proceedings: although the judge was not the sole mover or even a prime mover of the proceedings, there were many ways in which the judge was exhibited as a contingency in the pacing of the case, as well as a relevancy for the inclusion or exclusion of procedures in the course of the case's progression.[11] "In his own court" the judge in some cases exhibited a despotic authority over the local order of the production. What counted as the protocol in the local magistrate's court was a subject of concern to lawyers in pretrial sessions, and at times the basis for such concern was graphically demonstrated by a judge's admonishments:

(8) January 3, Toronto

The defense attorney is in the course of requesting a remand for the client on the grounds that the former attorney of the client has taken ill, and the present attorney (himself) needs further time to prepare the case. The judge states his understanding of the reason for the request:

Judge: Mister Edwards is ill.
Defense: Mister Edwards is <u>permanently</u> ill.
Judge: Are you acting on behalf of a deity? ... I am aware that he is ill.
Crown: Your Honor, no disrespect was meant by my friend . .

(9) March 13, Toronto
At the beginning of the first case called after the recess, the Crown announced the case number and accused's name. A defense lawyer stood up and possibly said something to the effect that he was the defense counsel. The lawyer turned to face the gallery (turning away from the judge's bench) and looked into the gallery when the accused failed to appear after the summons. Defense counsel kept looking toward the door of the court as a police officer left to retrieve the accused from the hallway. At this point the judge called the lawyer to his attention and complained that "in my court" a defense counsel introduces himself according to a protocol he recited, "Your Honor, I am _____, representing the accused ____ ". The judge further reprimanded the lawyer for not appropriately standing before the judge, and continually facing the judge while waiting for the accused to arrive (defense counsel had taken a few steps toward the railing of the gallery and had leaned toward the gallery). The judge also complained that the accused should be in the court when called, and that it is only through the institution of the system for summonsing persons outside the court by a police officer that they have come to ignore the injunction to be in court when called. He then stated that in the future warrants may be issued if accuseds do not show up in court when called. The defense counsel apologized when the accused appeared, and in subsequent cases that day the 'proper' protocol was rigorously followed and apologies were profusely given for any circumstantial improprieties.[12]

Judges rule over the temporalization of a hearing, by conspicuously monitoring the relevance of the time being taken and the "point" that any line of action demonstrates. There are no formally legislated limits on how many questions can be asked by an attorney during the examination of a witness, yet the overhearing judge and adversary lawyer can collaborate to shut down a line of questions with a courtroom version of heckling. Judges also act on their own to voice complaints to the effect that counsel's questions are coming to no foreseeable point. The license taken by judges to move cases along is evident in the following instances:

(10) March 12, Peel Court
At one point during a preliminary hearing the judge made several marked displays of boredom when the defense counsel was cross-examining a witness. These boredom displays acted as a kind of Greek chorus, to frame the counsel's line of questions as an endless pursuit of petty detail. Counsel had been asking a police witness numerous questions about how he drew up the accused's statement, how the accused was questioned at the police station, how notes were entered in the notebook, etc. Boredom was made visible through the judge's bodily disengagement from the scene of questioning. At one point he leaned back in his chair, and then leaned forward, resting his head on his hands as they lay palm-downward on the desk. When the defense counsel mentioned a statement by a co-accused pertaining to the accused's involvement in an alleged auto theft, the Crown motioned to submit the statement into evidence as an exhibit. The judge responded. "Sure, it won't hurt, but I don't see any reason why it's necessary. The co-accused is not being submitted to trial, and in any event my presence here is academic at this point. I'm already prepared to commit the case to trial". After the remark was delivered, the defense counsel pursued no further questions. The next witness was called, briefly examined by the Crown and was not cross examined by the defense counsel. It was apparent that the judge's remark short circuited the hearing not only by expressing annoyance with the progress of the preliminary trial but, more importantly, alluding to a foregone conclusion that rendered the remainder of the present hearing into an empty exercise.

(11) March 8, Toronto
During a lengthy submission by defense attorney representing an accused who was charged with "assault police" during a protest rally by Palestinian supporters, defense counsel made repeated reference to the peaceable nature of the accused, his lack of a police record, and his intent not to cause trouble at the rally. The counsel then stated that the accused was not a Palestinian refugee, but a Lebanese immigrant, and that such a person would not have been as emotionally frenzied at the protest rally. The judge interrupted and disputed this claim, saying that it was clear that the accused attended the rally and that he carried a placard or flag supporting the Palestinians. Defense counsel attempted to pursue this a bit further, but the judge told him if he did so he'd waste court time. Defense counsel then went on to other arguments, and his voice built up to an impassioned pitch when he claimed that it was an outrage that the case was even brought to trial with the prosecution's case being so weak. The judge cut this off, saying, "I'm not a jury ... this is a trial on fact". I understood this to mean that the theatrics were unnecessary for a magistrate's hearing of the case, that they would do no good to sway his judgement. The remark shut down the impassioned speech and counsel moved quickly to a conclusion.

(12) February 1, Peel Court
During cross examination of a witness, the Judge broke into the defense counsel-witness dialogue to ask several questions of the witness. After the judge finished, defense counsel asked for permission to ask a few more questions. The judge asserted that, "You have no right to ask further questions", but then offered to broker the questions; instructing the counsel to state each question to the judge, who then would decide whether the question was worth passing on to the witness. The questions were asked, and then the judge often pursued them with questions of his own.

(13) February 1, Peel Court
Defense counsel pursued a series of questions on the identification of the accused by the witness. While doing so he raised a number of issues pertaining to the uncertainty of the witness's identification. The judge broke into the cross examination:

Judge: I hope you are not wasting time on this, because the police may have identified the accused.
Defense: I don't know what the police can testify.
Judge: You should ask your client. You did take instructions from him?
Defense: Yes.

These instances demonstrate an active overhearing on the part of judges which is expressed through interventions in the course of testimony. The judge displays an embodied presence to the deliveries of other parties (expressing, among other things, boredom). On the basis of these more obvious interventions it can be conjectured that the judge is pervasively relevant to the design and ordering of testimony, the presentation of arguments and lines of questions. The judge and opposing attorney stand guard over the strategic advantages to concealing the point of a line of questions, or to using a line of questions to discover the point they will have demonstrated (the so-called "fishing expedition").

The Judge as a Condition for the Rational Articulation of a Sequential Orderliness

The general provisions for one action's following another in the production of different types of hearing do not make reference to the work involved in locally demonstrating just how the sequential progression is "reasonably" articulated. This is to say that the negotiation of the projected and historicized course of the hearing is accomplished through an elaborate display of adequate reasons. The judge is both an arbiter and producer of reasons in an interacting assembly of arguments.

In the cases examined for this study, judges almost always gave explanations for their pronouncements on sentence (and in trials, their pronouncements of a verdict). Explanations cited the prior testimony, facts-on-the-record, and submissions by counsels that furnished reasonable grounds for the judgement.[13] Such reasonable justifications were heterogeneous, but for the sake of clarity I will discuss two general classes of reasonable accounts. These accounts were often produced during judicial case summaries prior to delivering the verdict or the sentence. The two classes of justificatory accounts I discuss are "reasons invoking an orderly relationship in the prior testimony", and "reasons invoking the moral character of the accused and/or the offense".

Reasons Invoking an Orderly Relationship in the Prior Testimony

It is sometimes said that court inquiries are peculiar in that the evidence in the vast majority of cases is limited to spoken and written testimony. The predominance of testimonial evidence provides a rich basis for the study of how discourse is endogenously 'analyzed' in terms of what it discloses about speakers' claims and character. As Pollner (1970; 74) observes, judges' summaries make visible the work of selectively crediting or discrediting prior testimony in the service of a present verdict. These summaries not only produced visibly 'rational' accounts of the case, in the face of contested versions of the events in question, they bring into relief the commonsensical as well as legal grounds of judgement. Summaries often trade on subject-object dichotomies for resolving conflicting claims, or dismissing claims by attributing them to perspective, illusion, deception, lies, and bias. Through the application of the naturally-theoretic distinctions and conceptual resources, judges produce case summaries that deploy thematically congruent narratives which account for the charges, document the verdict, and justify the sentence. Through the praxis of "mundane reasoning" (Pollner, 1974; 1987), judges integrate adversary testimony into a congruent and coherent event situation that supports the disposition.

In the cases I examined, judges' summaries used a variety of ways for supporting verdicts and sentences. They did not always, or even often, involve an explicit settling of conflicting claims by crediting and discrediting testimonies in search of the "real world events" in question. Often, a judge would affirm the testimony of witnesses who were held to be credible, while saying nothing about contrary accounts made by other witnesses. "Positive" reasons were thus given in the summaries without explicitly dismissing or discrediting adverse testimony. In other cases involving conflicting accounts of events, the judges summarized "the case" by citing non-contested matters which provided 'enough' to support a verdict.

> (14) January 25, Toronto
> The case involved a charge of "assault bodily harm" which was reduced during the trial to "common assault". The victim claimed she had been punched in the face by a man with whom she had been dancing. She alleged that he punched her after she pulled away from him for attempting to dance too closely. The event was described as occurring at a neighborhood Disco. The accused and a friend of the accused's testified that the accused pushed the woman away after she called him "a dumb Polack", and that while he did so his hand glanced off of her shoulder and struck her lightly on the forehead. The victim claimed that she had not insulted the accused, and that he had struck her face with his fist, causing a red welt on her forehead. There was no medical evidence of any injury and the police were not called until an hour after the event occurred. In summarizing a verdict of guilty, the judge provided the following account: "... there are a number of gaps in all of the evidence. However, I'm satisfied that no matter what interpretation I take, he intended to push her away". Despite the accused's disclaimers about his intentions, the judge noted that he did admit to striking the victim's face in anger, and the judge cited this as sufficient grounds for the verdict. In other words, the accused's testimony which contested the charge was retrospectively turned into an admission, which was minimally congruent with the requirements of the Criminal Code.

In other cases, judicial summaries also showed resourcefulness in transforming claimed "discrepancies" and "weaknesses" in testimony into documents of the credibility of the challenged testimony:

> (15) March 8, Toronto
> During a case mentioned earlier (number (11)) the defense counsel elaborated upon a number of inconsistencies between the testimonies of two police officers called by the Crown. Some of the discrepancies were as follows:
> (a) How many times the accused struck the police officer in question. Defense counsel noted that one police witness said six times and the other said once. Counsel claimed that this was a matter of great importance in the case.
> (b) The flagpole-type object held by the accused. An exhibit of this object was

produced, but Defense claimed that it had been found after the crowd dispersed and that there were "at least fifty" such flags in the protest rally according to witness testimony. One police witness was quoted as having described a different sized and shaped flagpole than was produced for the exhibit.

(c) Whether there was actual contact between the crowd and the police as the police moved the crowd back from the street when the motorcade passed. One police witness was quoted as having said that there was such contact, and another that there was not.

(d) One police officer was quoted as saying that there were no children among the protesters, while the other had said that there were.

After the defense counsel finished his summary, the Judge carefully enunciated a lengthy summary. The summary began with an account of the "numerous discrepancies" mentioned by the defense. The judge asserted that these discrepancies were the "very sort of thing that the court likes to see" when more than one police witness gives testimony some months after a charge is laid. The judge mentioned that three months after the event one expects a certain inconsistency due to the memories of events being "clouded", and that when different police witnesses give identical testimony in all the details of a case, this raises doubt about possible collusion. Therefore, the very discrepancies which the defense counsel upheld as grounds of doubt became grounds of credibility; reasons for attributing an honest if degraded memory of events to the witnesses.[14]

(16) February 1, Peel Court

In a case of driving under the influence of alcohol, a breathalyzer technician was called by the prosecution and testified about the evidence for the accused's intoxication. During the cross examination, the defense attorney questioned the breathalyzer technician about possible selectivity in taking "good samples" of the accused's breath. The witness admitted that when he was taking the breath samples the accused "had difficulty supplying breath". Under further questioning, the witness added that he took several samples, some of which contained insufficient amounts of breath for analysis. Defense counsel asked if there was a reading on the analyser that would allow such an assessment to be made, and the witness replied that there was. The defense counsel then asked if there were readings that were rejected because a reading failed to register, and the witness said, "yes, there were", that several readings were taken and two were accepted; the accepted readings being those that registered above the legal limit of blood-alcohol.[15] In his submission the defense counsel argued that the samples should not be trusted because of the selectivity practiced in the technician's work of certifying the two "good" readings.

When summarizing the case, the judge prefaced his remarks by saying, "...the last witness, Constable Peters [breathalyzer technician] was very honest", and the judge accepted his testimony and breathalyzer results "in total". He then pronounced a verdict of guilty.

In these summaries, judges rationalized verdicts by invoking "discrepancies" between police accounts or between successive measurements not only as tolerable slippages from truth, but as evidence of credible testimony. The judges' summaries implicated commonsense resources which limit the literal applicability of descriptive and logical means for exhibiting discrepancy, contradiction, or other technical breaches in testimony. This is not to say that a monolithic "common sense" rules over the judges' actions, providing them with unambiguous rationales, since what counts as a commonsensical interpretation of events in an adversary environment can be vociferously contested. Numerous arguments occurred between lawyers, and between lawyers and judges, on what a "reasonable man" would infer about the described circumstances. Although this topic deserves closer study, for present purposes I shall only mention that judges' summaries exhibited a hearing of prior testimony which reconstituted assertions and submissions in such a way as to display "reasonable" grounds for the disposition of the case.[16] Clearly, considerable latitude is available to judges to document their decisions with relevant "hearings" of prior testimony, though the resources for doing so are not unlimited and require a degree of ingenuity, and perhaps even honesty.

Reasons Invoking the Moral Character of the Accused and/or the Offense

One of the more colorful behaviors of some judges is the way they deliver impassioned scoldings or "lectures" to accuseds when administering the sanctions of law. It has occasionally been noted (sometimes within court in explicit formulations) that the legal process initiated by the arrest of an accused is itself a form of punishment, regardless of the disposition of the case. A judge's lectures to the accused often constitute a form of punishment administered independently of any punitive disposition through a jail term or fine. Very commonly, these lectures are directed to the accused just before or after the announcement of the verdict or sentence. A few examples of this very common phenomenon follow:

(17) March 8, Toronto
Just before pronouncing sentence on a guilty plea to a charge of "fail to report while released on recognizance", the judge reads accused's criminal record:

Judge: July 7, 1975, "Driving while disqualified", March 10, 1976, "Driving while disqualified", January 23, 1977, "Illegal possession of automobile", April 3, 1978, "Fail to appear". It's quite apparent from that record that orders of the court and the laws of the land do not mean anything to you. When ordered to report you are obliged to report. People like you are largely responsible for chaos in court. What can happen is that Parliament will decide to go back a generation or two and keep accuseds in custody until trial. It's time you learned that . . .

(18) March 8, Toronto
Just prior to sentence on a guilty plea. The accused was charged with "possession of a wallet, under $200". The accused had an extensive criminal record -- three years in the penitentiary for theft related offenses. The defense counsel submitted that the accused "did not know why he took the wallet", and claimed that the accused was largely rehabilitated but had temporarily lapsed into his former habits when tempted with the unattended wallet.
Judge: Mister Pickering [the defense lawyer] says you don't know why you took it. I do. You're a thief. Simple as that. When you decide not to be, then you'll live a productive life. Sentence of three months concurrent.

(19) January 25, Toronto
Just prior to sentence on a guilty plea. The charge was "malicious mischief". The accused admitted to smashing a truck windshield. In his pre-sentence submissions the defense counsel mentioned that the accused was an accomplished artist and that a jail sentence might interfere with the rehabilitative effects of his pursuit of an art career. The judge looked at the record, shook his head and said, "He's an artist all right", and went on to elaborate:
Judge: You're going to end up doing life on the installment plan . . . You're a bad actor. You're a greater menace to society than some poor slob who doesn't have any artistic talent ... You better start taking a good look at yourself ... There's no sense having any artistic talent when you'll be in jail for life on the installment plan ... You of all people should know if you break probation you can get six months in jail.

(20) January 25, Toronto
A guilty plea on the charges of "Misrepresenting to police that dangerous driving had occurred", and "assault police" (the latter charge was reduced to "common assault" at the request of the Crown). Defense counsel argued that on other charges dealt with a month before the accused had followed the plan of his probation: he had stopped drinking, had been seeing a psychiatrist, and was maintaining a job. Defense asked for monetary penalties in lieu of a jail sentence. The judge stated that the nature of the offense "deserves a period of incarceration", and stated further that it was a "question of deterrence". Accused

> was sentenced tọ 30 days on the "failure to appear", and 7 days consecutive on assault.
> Judge: Probation means, don't get into any further trouble... You're not a child anymore, I can see you're not a sweetheart ... have been drinking, you've been bending your elbow, shown a vile temper ... You don't impress me with your rehabilitation. I expect you'll be back here again. You better smarten up and disappoint me.

Such lectures sometimes justify, and at other times compensate for, the disposition of the cases. "Lectures" including vernacular maxims and other earthy references to moral wrongdoing and bad character often occur in conjunction with harsher sentences than those requested by defense attorneys. Note in (18), the identification of the accused as a "thief" provides a concise, if crude, account of the accused's conduct, and it prefaces a more substantial jail sentence than the defense had requested. In (20) the judge makes reference to the visibility of the accused ("I can see you're not a sweetheart"): a noticing documented by the record and, more immediately, by the dishevelled appearance of the man. On some occasions dispositions with a relatively light sentence were accompanied by harsh warnings to the accused that he was being let off easy, and in others by references to an accused as "no villain". The actions of accuseds also were referred to in morally laden vernacular terms which emphasized the seriousness, the distressing character, and the intolerable nature of the offenses to "our community".

The down-to-earth quality of judges' lectures was more than a way of bringing home, in terms the accused could understand, how the offense was reprehensible to the legal authorities. The lectures also invoked a communal morality that justified the disposition above and beyond the technical specifications of the criminal code, the rules of evidence and procedure, and the facts of the case. This communal morality was salient, not as a transcendental basis for court actions, but rather as a resource for embedding the sequential outcome of the hearing within common maxims of moral conduct and vulgar assessments of moral character. The judges thus furnished their conclusive utterances with distinctive references to extra-legal contexts, which were internal features of courtroom justification. The particular moral contexts which were built into case summaries were produced as events in a hearing. They should not be viewed as references to stable circumstances for the administration of justice, but as available ways of enframing the hearing which can be contested, heard without comment, deferred to, agreed to, or otherwise appropriated by other parties to the hearing.

Conclusion

There was no intent in this paper to claim that judges' actions and reasons "reflected" a decision making process. Instead, they were viewed as public constituents of the court hearing. This lesson was driven home during a rare occasion when two colleagues and I were allowed to meet with the judge in his chambers to discuss a case we had been observing from the gallery. Prior to our meeting the judge had pronounced his verdict and given his reasons for it. Before we could begin to ask our questions, the judge laid down a ground rule, saying that he had already given his reasons in court, and therefore it was pointless for us to ask him for the real reasons for his judgement. From one point of view, such a policy puts a severe constraint on a social science inquiry. But, from another point of view, it points to a rich topic of inquiry: the public accountability of judicial actions and reasons as constituents of courtroom hearings.

In this paper, I have maintained focus on judicial actions and reasons as intelligible features in the temporal order of a hearing. To substantiate a picture of the judge as a constituent of the court hearing, I used the device of a guilty plea protocol in order to cast into relief some of the singular ways in which judges entered into the orderly production of cases. In many of these examples, the judge featured as a speaker who took part in the temporal and thematic order of the hearing. As we have seen, judges often take an active, and even controlling part. However, the judge also is a "passive" recipient who hears, or overhears, what other parties say. Indeed, the judge is in many respects a principal recipient for whom the entire proceedings are designed. Following Robillard (1974) it can be said that the judge is an endogenous, teleological feature of an entire system of competency produced by the court assemblage; an assemblage that includes the judge. This competency is implied when lawyers produce lines of interrogation, argue their side of the case, and attempt to expose weaknesses in the adversary case, insofar as they do so with an attunement to the reciprocal dispositions and evaluations of the local court.

In this paper I have not attempted to claim access to a unique vantage point assumed by competent court participants. Perhaps such a vantage point is required for giving an adequate account of the judge's presence to the events of a hearing. I simply do not know. I do believe, however, that a distinctive feature of courtroom hearings, including much of what a judge does or says, is its public accountability. Without denying the fact that not everything relevant to courtroom hearings is made publicly available to a gallery of spectators, there remains much to say about the public display of argumentation, interrogation, and the giving of reasons. The court is not an occasion for 'ordinary' conversation, and yet most of what transpires there is designed to be heard, understood, and evaluated by a lay audience. This paper represents a modest attempt to come to terms with that accountability.

Notes

1. The research for this paper was completed in 1979, while I was supported by a visiting postdoctoral fellowship at the Centre for Criminology, University of Toronto. I am grateful to my former colleagues at the Centre, including Jim Wilkins, Gus Brannigan, Bill Rae, and Candace Brookbank, for making this research possible. The paper originally appeared in 1979, in an unpublished volume, *The Prosecution and the Courts*, edited by James L. Wilkins, Centre of Criminology, University of Toronto. I edited the paper for the present publication, and added a few references, but it is substantially unchanged from the version I drafted in 1979. Consequently, the paper takes little advantage of the work on courtroom activities by Atkinson and Drew (1979), and other ethnomethodologists and conversation analysts who have attended to court processes in the past two decades. After writing this paper, I did not develop the preliminary ideas about judges' work presented in this paper, although I did maintain an interest in pre-trial discussions, and courtroom (and tribunal) interrogations (see Lynch, 1982; Brannigan and Lynch, 1987; Lynch and Bogen, 1996).
2. Robillard (1974, p. 174) remarks with regard to California commitment court proceedings that, "The hearing is a speaking performance!", the "speaking round" and the "hearing round" are one and the same. For competent parties, the analytic sensibility of an overhearer's work is continuous with the public display of what is heard, or might be hearable. By identifying speaking and hearing with the work of parties in the legal setting I do not intend to abstract an organization of "talk" from the embodied context of its occurrence. To an extent, such a reduction will be inevitable whenever I use transcripts and field notes to recover courtroom, or pre-trial, events, and for that reason it is necessary to remind ourselves that a "hearing" is an embodied production in a courtroom, and is not limited to a sensory reception, or cognitive understanding, of spoken word.
3. Robillard (1974 p. 143) elucidates the importance of "non-principal" parties, by

describing the significance of the court reporter, or stenographer:

"Their non-principalness is not to indicate anything but an empirical property of the interstructural telos of the court. As such the non-principalness does not mean that these persons are not feature members of the court. They are. They are structural features of the spatio-temporal transitive transcendentiality of the court. The stenographic record of the transactions is a projectively necessary feature of conducting a court under the auspices of conformance to legal rules where that conduct is reviewable at another place and time by an *a priori* agreed upon grammar of representation and a more or less agreed upon grammar of legal action. The court by having a stenographic record of representations speaks in an agreed upon form of representation, though what is represented may later be challenged, to all further legal interactions involving each individual case. This allows the record to stand by itself for the judgement long after the Judge and the attorneys have forgotten the specifics of an individual case. The record can be then consulted by those involved in future legal actions contingent upon the record and by those charged with administering any rendered judgement as the authoritative presentation of what the court determined and how it arrived at the determination. A hearing as an event being *a priori* its record after its completion requires the presence of the stenographer through the transitivity of being able to be a hearing now only by having as a defined future projectively, in reverse, defines the parameters of the present and *vice versa*."

4. The first three exhibits are transcripts I made from tape recordings of pre-trial discussions in Assistant Crown Attorney offices in a Peel County, Ontario court. I was not present when the tapes were recorded. The tapes were collected by a research team headed by James Wilkins, as part of a "Longitudinal" study of a selection of 100 criminal cases in a particular court jurisdiction. The research was funded by a grant from the Social Sciences and Humanities Research Council of Canada. See Wilkins (1979).
5. Garfinkel (1977, pp. 60 ff.) outlines the "unique adequacy requirement" of methods for studies of naturally organized ordinary activities (also see Garfinkel and Wieder, 1992 and Lynch, 1993, Ch. 7). This requirement is not met in the present study, except insofar as an unspecialized natural language competence is adequate for explicating courtroom events. For an ethnomethodological study of courtroom events that is grounded in a lawyerly competency, see Burns (1996).
6. The methodological use of trouble was pioneered in several of Garfinkel's early studies (c.f., Garfinkel, 1967, p. 54). In those studies an "experimental" procedure was used as a device for producing demonstrations of the "seen but unnoticed" horizons of everyday activities. In the present study, Garfinkel's initiatives are applied to a descriptive interest in the work that produces ordinary settings. It is proposed here trouble in the sequential enactment of procedures provides a momentary exhibit of some of the multitudinous ways in which the

embodied-speech production is exquisitely organized in a collaborative assembly. When the procedures of the court seemingly run like clockwork it can seem plausible that members are following organizational, behavioural, and/or cognitive protocols. But when, for whatever reasons, the temporal organization of the activities becomes conspicuously disconcerted, the resulting struggles to accomplish the procedures provide insight into the organizational requirements for accomplishing a case in court.

7. Additional accounts of "delay" in Peel Regional Provincial Court are provided in Wilkins, Rae and Brookbank (1979), and Wilkins and Kopelman (1979).
8. All of the following excerpts (exhibits 4-20) are reconstructed from field notes taken while attending criminal court hearings in magistrate and superior courts in two Ontario districts: Toronto city courts, and Peel County courts. Peel County is a suburban district about 30 miles from Toronto. I was not permitted to tape record the hearings I attended, and rarely were court transcripts available (except at a high price). After attending the hearings, I would write more extensive reconstructions of the cases. Excerpts 4-20 in this paper are slightly edited reconstructions and notes written in 1978-79. My notes were sketchy, and the dialogues and summaries of judges' and other participants' utterances are approximate, and not verbatim, records of utterances. Although I would have preferred to have had video- or audio-taped records of the hearings, I strongly believe that the records I used are adequate (and perhaps even advantageous) for my analytic purposes in this paper.
9. See Maynard and Manzo (1993) for another instance in which a jury opts to override procedural constraints in a pursuit of justice.
10. Montagnes (1979) provides an ethnographic account of the Crown Attorney's work of temporalizing a list of cases on a court docket into the situated production of cases in court. This work is more than an incidental preoccupation of parties in the courtroom and is a source of a continual order of practices in actual court circumstances.
11. Robillard (1974, p. 149) gives the following account of the judge's work of temporalizing the hearing:

    The judge can demand a pace because he can correspond to the projective horizon of such demanding: he can fulfill the promise of such demanding by moving without hesitation or being by passed by the others to the next phase of a round or to the next case. His demand is a demand of the correspondence of the others to match his performances, a performance that can be matched only if it is actualized.

12. This is a variant of a procedure Pollner (1979) describes under the heading of "self-explicating transactions", only in this case what is self-explicating is a matter of strict adherence to form.
13. I am indebted to James Wilkins for the suggestion that judges' summary remarks are an accessible subject matter for the study of the 'public' display of judges'

reasoning, especially when viewed relative to the prior testimony in court.

14. For a more extensive discussion of memory in testimony, see Lynch and Bogen (1996: Chs. 6&7).
15. For a delightful account of strategies for questioning forensic witnesses, see Oteri et al., 1982.
16. For further discussion of the "reasonable man" in judgements about testimony, see Gluckman (1963), Emerson (1969), and Brannigan and Lynch (1987).

References

Atkinson, J. M. and Drew, P. (1979), *Order in Court: The Organisation of Verbal Interaction in Judicial Settings*, Macmillan, London.

Brannigan,A. and Lynch,M. (1987),'On bearing false witness: Perjury and credibility as interactional accomplishments', *Journal of ContemporaryEthnography*, vol.16, pp.115-146.

Burns, S. (1996), 'Lawyers' work in the Menendez brothers' murder trial', *Issues in Applied Linguistics*, vol.7, pp.19-32.

Carlen, P. (1976), *Magistrates' Justice*, Martin Robertson, London.

Durkheim, E. (1938), *The Rules of Sociological Method*, The Free Press, Glencoe.

Emerson, R. (1969), *Judging Delinquents*, Aldine, Chicago.

Garfinkel, H. (1967), *Studies in Ethnomethodology*, Prentice Hall, Englewood Cliffs, New Jersey.

Garfinkel, H. (1977), 'An introduction for novices to the study of naturally organized ordinary activities', unpublished manuscript, Department of Sociology, UCLA.

Garfinkel, H. (1991), 'Respecification: Evidence for locally produced, naturally accountable phenomena of order, logic, reason, meaning, method, etc. in and as of the essential haecceity of immortal ordinary society (I) — an announcement of studies', in G. Button (ed.), *Ethnomethodology and the Human Sciences*, Cambridge University Press, Cambridge, pp. 10-19.

Garfinkel, H. and Wieder, D.L. (1992), 'Two incommensurable, asymmetrically alternate technologies of social analysis', in G. Watson and R. M. Seiler (eds), *Text in Context: Contributions to Ethnomethodology*, Sage, London, pp. 175-206.

Gluckman, M. (1963), *Order and Rebellion in Tribal Africa*, Free Press, New York.

Hogarth, J. (1971), *Sentencing as a Human Process*, University of Toronto Press, Toronto.

Lynch, M. (1982), 'Closure and disclosure in pre-trial argument', *Human Studies*, Vol. 5, pp. 15-33.

Lynch, M. (1993), *Scientific Practice and Ordinary Action: Ethnomethodology and Social Studies of Science*, Cambridge University Press, Cambridge.

Lynch, M. and Bogen, D. (1996), *The Spectacle of History: Speech, Text, andMemory at the Iran-contra Hearings*, Duke University Press, Durham, North Carolina.

Maynard, D. (1984), *Inside Plea Bargaining: The Language of Negotiation*, Plenum, New York.

Maynard, D. and Manzo, J. (1993), 'On the sociology of justice: Theoretical notes from an actual jury deliberation', *Sociological Theory*, vol. 11, pp. 171-193.

Montagnes, C. (1979), 'Coming apart: Case load management', in J.L. Wilkins (ed.), *The Prosecution and the Courts*, unpublished volume, Centre of Criminology, University of Toronto, pp. 449-524.

Oteri, J.S., Weinberg, M. G.and Pinales, M. S. (1982), 'Cross-examination in drug cases', in B. Barnes and D. Edge (eds), *Science in Context: Readings in the Sociology of Science*, Open University Press, Milton Keynes, pp. 250-59.

Pollner, M. (1970), 'On the Foundations of Mundane Reasoning', Ph.D Dissertation, University of California, Santa Barbara.

Pollner, M. (1974), 'Mundane reasoning', *Philosophy of Social Sciences*, vol. 4, pp. 35-54.

Pollner, M. (1979), 'Explicative Transactions: Making and Managing Meaning in a Traffic Court', in G. Psathas (ed.), *Everyday language: Studies in Ethnomethodology*, Irvington, New York.

Pollner, M. (1987), *Mundane Reason: Reality in Everyday and Sociological Discourse*, Cambridge University Press, Cambridge.

Robillard, A.B. (1974), 'Order of the Selfsame and Hermeneutical Aspects of Decision Making in Judicial Hearings of Petitions for Involuntary Mental Health Hospitalization', Ph.D. Dissertation, University of California, Los Angeles.

Wilkins, J.L. (ed.), *The Prosecution and the Courts*, unpublished volume, Centre of Criminology, University of Toronto.

Wilkins, J.L. and Kopelman, F. (1979), 'The judicial assessment of remand requests', in J.L. Wilkins (ed.), *The Prosecution and the Courts*, unpublished volume, Centre of Criminology, University of Toronto, pp. 203-238.

Wilkins, J.L., Rae, B. and Brookbank, C. (1979), 'Court delay and the remand problem', in J.L. Wilkins (ed.), *The Prosecution and the Courts*, unpublished volume, Centre of Criminology, University of Toronto, pp. 169-202.

PART II
CONTEMPORARY CONTRIBUTIONS

Introduction to Part II

MAX TRAVERS

The studies in this part of the collection were all written after 1980, and illustrate how recent work by ethnomethodologists and conversation analysts has built upon the achievements of earlier studies.

The first paper by Greg Matoesian provides a good example of how ethnomethodological research can provide an alternative perspective on current debates about gender in the criminal justice process. Drawing upon analytic resources from conversation analysis, linguistics, and membership categorization analysis, Matoesian looks in detail at a technique, known by attorneys as "detailing-to-death", which was used in an episode of cross-examination during the Kennedy Smith rape trial. This is, in some ways, the most technical and demanding paper in this collection, but it is again worth noting that it is about what anyone can see in court: a devastating piece of cross-examination that seriously undermined the credibility of the prosecution case.

What is ethnomethodological about this paper is that it shows, precisely, and in great detail, how this was done, through identifying five variants of a device used in cross-examination that Matoesian calls "resumptive repetition". Because it is more than an anecdotal account of this phenomenon, it could, at least in principle, be used to teach trainee advocates some of the craft-skills involved in cross-examination. More generally, it illustrates that the outcome of rape-trials cannot simply be accounted for by "patriarchy", or by a speech-exchange system in which lawyers have the right to ask questions. "Patriarchy" in ethnomethodological terms can be understood as a diverse set of cultural understandings about the relationship between men and women that are widely shared in society, and can become highly consequential in rape trials (Farran, 1992). In this case, the cross-examination drew upon culturally-shared knowledge about the relationship between the categories "women" and "rapists", that would lead us to expect that a woman would not go for a walk in the darkness with someone who had just raped her friend. This kind of exchange may be decisive in determining the outcome of other trials involving rape or sexual assault, and suggests the need for more research on a wider range of cases with different outcomes for defendants.

The second paper we have included by Albert J.Meehan was first published by *Urban Life* (now the *Journal of Contemporary Ethnography*) in 1988, and is an example of how early themes and topics in ethnomethodology have been taken up by later researchers. An early paper by Garfinkel and Bittner (1967), based on a study of an out-patient clinic, proposed a new way of studying official records. Instead of viewing these as providing an unproblematic record of a given phenomenon, researchers could instead consider how records were produced and used in different organizational settings. In this paper, based upon six months observation in two police departments, Meehan shows just how useful this approach can be by examining how the police kept records in dealing with juvenile crime. Like Garfinkel's study of coroners in part 1, this study has implications for how we understand crime statistics, and it is also relevant for the study of police culture and accountability. The "running record" which the police used in decision-making - which includes "the stock of accumulated knowledge about individuals, the places they inhabit, and events that occur within those places" - provides a powerful analytic tool which can be used in any ethnographic study of police work.

The next contribution, a paper by Doug Maynard, and my co-editor John Manzo, which was first published by *Sociological Theory* in 1993, provides a further illustration of how recent research has built upon earlier studies. One of the best known ethnomethodological contributions to studying law is Garfinkel's study of how jurors make decisions. Garfinkel's research was based upon bugging a jury room in which jurors decided responsibility, and the level of damages, in personal injury claims. One point he makes in this paper is that in jury deliberations, the "outcome" takes place before the "decision"; in other words, that jurors decide the fate of a defendant based on common-sense methods of reasoning, and then find grounds to justify this outcome as a properly arrived at legal decision. Maynard and Manzo's paper is a detailed analysis of how a jury reached a decision, based on a video-recording of an actual two and a half hour jury deliberation. This enables them to show how the "outcome" came before the "decision" in this particular case, but also to offer some provocative observations on how "justice" might be studied as an ethnomethodological topic. In contrast to social scientific or philosophical accounts which employ an abstract notion of "justice", Maynard and Manzo treat "justice" as something that "exists empirically - that is, in the talk and actions - of ordinary society". This includes the way in which the members of this jury deliberated on the "justice" of their verdict "in real time" during this episode. This is one example of how researchers can take up Garfinkel's (1988) recommendation to "re-specify" sociological concepts as achieved "phenomena of order".

The next paper by Martha Komter can also be understood in terms of this programme in that it looks at the concepts of "remorse", "redress" and "reform" as these form part of exchanges between the judge and defendant in Dutch criminal trials. Whereas Maynard and Manzo examine the temporal structure of a single episode, Komter draws upon transcriptions derived from audio-taping 31 trials involving violent crime in the Netherlands. This paper is sensitive towards the dilemmas built into a system of criminal justice that invites defendants to express remorse for their actions before they are sentenced. The court requires a public display of remorse in order to legitimate its authority to punish wrong-doing. However, it is difficult for such statements to be believed, since they can always be interpreted as an attempt to reduce an anticipated sentence. In looking at this aspect of criminal trials, in this level of detail, Komter contributes to our understanding of the moral character of the courtroom.

The final paper in the collection is by Stacy Burns, and is a revised version of an earlier unpublished paper, which is sometimes cited by Garfinkel, called "Becoming a Lawyer at Yale Law School". Burns has some measure of celebrity status in ethnomethodology for being the student Garfinkel advised to become a lawyer in order to fulfill what he calls "the unique adequacy requirement of methods": the requirement that one needs to become competent in the skills used in a particular occupation, or technical discipline, in order to study these as an ethnomethodologist. While she was studying law, Burns also obtained permission to tape-record one of her classes, and this paper uses this data to address how students are taught to think and talk like lawyers. The professor teaching this class sought to make students aware of a distinction between an academic understanding of legal rules, and law as it is practised in real-time in particular situations. What Burns calls "the case-specific legal content and task-oriented nature of lawyer's work" is neglected by conventional social scientific accounts, and this paper suggests that future ethnomethodological studies should address this as a topic (see Travers, 1997, for a longer version of this argument).

If one considers the papers in this section as a whole, one can see that there is still considerable scope for further research on law and legal phenomena, and on the situated practices taking places in institutions such as courtrooms, police stations, legal offices and prisons, but also in business corporations, government bureaucracies, and numerous practical contexts in everyday life. Some ethnomethodologists and conversation analysts might want to argue that the value of this research program must ultimately be assessed in terms of its practical value, and that there is potential for the studies contained in this book to be used in the training of police officers and lawyers, through sensitising them to the practical and moral character of their work, and in informing policy initiatives in the courts. Whether or not this is so, these studies also raise important theoretical questions for the academic study of law and legal institutions. Alongside other approaches in sociology and critical jurisprudence, they demonstrate the social, rather than transcendental, nature of law (which is still contested by some legal thinkers). They also pose a phenomenological challenge to the manner in which other social scientists, whether these are positivists, critical theorists or symbolic interactionists, represent and analyze human action. My own view, as a sociologist, is that the studies in this book also have considerable implications beyond law, in that they represent a means of re-connecting sociology to the concerns and relevances of ordinary members of society.

References

Farran, D.(1992), 'A Textual Analysis of Women and Murder', Unpublished Ph.D. Thesis, University of Manchester.

Garfinkel, H. (1988), 'Evidence for Locally Produced Naturally Accountable Phenomena of Order, Logic, Reason, Meaning, Method, etc., in and as of the Essential Quiddity of Immortal Ordinary Society (I of IV): An Announcement of Studies', *Sociological Theory*, vol.6, pp.103-106.

Garfinkel, H. and Bittner,E.(1967), 'Good Organisational Reasons for "Bad" Clinic Records', in H.Garfinkel, *Studies in Ethnomethodology*, Prentice-Hall, Englewood Cliffs, N.J., pp.186-207.

Travers, M. (1997), *The Reality of Law: Work and Talk in a Firm of Criminal Lawyers*, Ashgate:Dartmouth, Aldershot.

7 "I'm sorry we had to meet under these circumstances": Verbal Artistry (and Wizardry) in the Kennedy Smith Rape Trial

GREGORY MATOESIAN

Introduction

Above all else, the art of trial cross-examination prescribes a cardinal rule for impeaching the credibility of witnesses and discrediting their testimony, an infrastructural rule phrased in numerous ways but which basically goes like this: Never ask a question to which you do not know the answer (Tanford, 1983; Bailey, 1985; Mauet, 1992; Carlson and Imwinkelried, 1989). More operationally yet just as prescriptively, law texts advise attorneys to "control" testimony through the use of short, leading questions designed to elicit a single discrete fact to which the witness must agree (Haydock and Sonsteng, 1991; Bergman, 1978). As a corollary to the cardinal rule, attorneys employ such questions to "stretch", expand, and emphasize a piece of evidence over the course of several questions or even several minutes rather than exhausting the topic in a single question or two, a "bit-by-bit" or "detailing-to-death" procedure designed not only to control the witness but to give the jury more time to access and appreciate the significance of a particular point of testimony (Tanford, 1983). In so doing, attorneys may construct a piece of evidence cumulatively over time through a series of questions so that the fact in issue assumes a level of unusual and striking importance. Indeed, as Mauet (1992: 221) summarizes this process in his classic trial text, "Cross-examination is in part the art of slowly making mountains out of molehills".

But just how do attorneys make mountains out of molehills? What precisely does detailing-to-death consist of? And just how does expansion through a series of question/answer sequences control and emphasize the witnesses' testimony, through what organizational logic does it systematically operate? For while the prescriptive recommendations found in law texts are doubtless instructive for trial practice and the law classroom, they nevertheless yield little analytic insight into the concrete details of courtroom performance through which these anecdotal designations are collaboratively and incrementally assembled on line, in real time.

This paper explores the linguistic and descriptive practices for controlling the witness and expanding the impeachment process during adversarial cross-examination. Using transcriptions of video-taped testimony from the Kennedy Smith rape trial, I examine how detailing-to-death unfolds through the poetic structure of trial talk, in particular, how rhythmic patterns of questioning are microcosmically forged through a repetition of grammatical, semantic, and, most prominently, sequential structures. In doing so, I aim to demonstrate how the organization of repetition generates a reflexive interface among grammar, sequencing, and categorization during the social construction of rape's legal facticity. Through an endogenously engineered logic, these poetic rhythms naturalize forms of legal knowledge and structure the epistemological conditions that establish the rationality of actions by situating the behavior of the witness/defendant within a chronologically segmented, sequentially organized, and ultra-detailed matrix of space, time, and motion. As a technique of legal strategy, the "logical" discontinuities portrayed in the unfolding representation of the rape incident constitute a moment-to-moment spatialization of social action that organizes the historical stream of movement between the witness and defendant during the rape incident, an epistemological method in which otherwise disparate phenomena are progressively decomposed into a meticulous array of spatial-motional categories. The defense attorney deploys these techniques of legal discipline to control the witnesses' testimony, to overcome her resistance to the blame implicatures of questioning, and to expand key elements of testimony. Thus rather than viewing questioning practices of control and expansion in prescriptively anecdotal fashion, I hope to demonstrate in concrete detail how they function as methods for making mountains out of molehills and for cumulating doubt through the contextually anchored rhythms of trial talk -- how they create the affective context for interpreting evidence. I begin with a rather brief and more or less selective overview of the characteristics of poetic talk.

Towards a Poetics of Trial Talk

What do we mean by poetic talk? How, in general, does it function? And, much more narrowly, what relevance does it possess for the situated performance of trial interaction, specifically, for the social construction of rape's legal facticity? Linguists such as Roman Jakobson (Jakobson and Pomorska, 1983; Jakobson, 1960) and Deborah Tannen (1987, 1989) have noted a systematic relationship between poetic aspects of literary discourse and talk found in language use in other contexts. Stylistic features of verbal art such as repetition, parallelism, irony, alliteration, and rhythmic patterns at the phonological, morphological, syntactic, and discourse levels occur not only in forms of written poetry but in other genres of language use as well, including everyday conversation and talk in its institutional context. Most generally, poetic discourse refers to those stylistic dimensions of language use that are mobilized with an eye towards fulfilling particular aesthetic and dramatic functions in context -- to a focus on the form or verbal artistry of a message, to the techniques through which language "draws attention to itself" (Jakobson, 1960; see also Sherzer and Woodbury, 1987: 8; Finnegan, 1992).

As a rather simple illustration, consider several classic examples of poetic discourse, all involving repetition and/or parallelistic repetition: the 1950s political slogan, "I like Ike", the famous tongue twister "Peter Piper picked a peck of pickled peppers", and the biblical passage from Psalm 115.[1] In the first example, the rhyme in this trisyllabic political formula achieves its impressive efficiency in the repetition of the gliding vowel /ay/, each repetition of which is, in turn, followed by a single consonantal phoneme -- the voiceless velar stop /k/ in "like" and "Ike" and the voiced lateral /l/ in "like" (Jakobson, 1960: 357). In the second case, the alliterative pattern develops through the repetition of the initial voiceless bilabial /p/ in several words. And last, the rhythm of the biblical passage and the irony encapsulated within it operates through an elaborate parallelistic repetition and contrast of a syntactic frame -- with perfectly balanced clause-initial ellipsis in the second, fourth, and sixth lines -- in combination with the introduction of a different or new element in the identical environment over the course of several sequences: "They have X but cannot Y". As these examples reveal, the most conspicuous feature of poetic discourse, and the one which will preoccupy our interest in trial talk from here on, is repetition (Finnegan, 1977: 90; Hymes, 1981: 42).

The Functions of Repetition in Trial Talk

The above examples also point to some of the numerous functions of repetition during the performance of oral poetry in trial talk, that is to say, its relevance for controlling the witness, for expanding a particular fact of evidence to cumulate a reasonable doubt, in essence, for persuading the jury. But before turning to these generic functions, let me sketch rather briefly a most prominent feature of the trial speech exchange system, because poetic repetition may emerge -- contingently and in key environments -- as a discourse technique designed to manage an evidential stricture found in this institutional context. The constraint is this: the adversarial examination process permits elicitation of evidence only through a series of carefully phrased question and answer sequences, and these speech actions, in turn, are asymmetrically distributed between attorneys and witness -- attorneys ask questions; witnesses answer them (Atkinson and Drew, 1979; Matoesian, 1993). During examination of witnesses, attorneys can neither make statements nor comment on the testimony of witnesses through, for instance, direct displays of skepticism routinely found in everyday conversation, such as “Give me a break” or “Do you expect the jury to believe that?” (or otherwise place an overt evaluation component in their questions). Statements or questions of this sort during trial examination are clearly argumentative and thus procedurally improper because they elicit no new information on the one hand and/or harass the witness on the other, even though, to be sure, they may be appropriate in closing argument.

In light of this discursive protocol, as we will see, attorneys can exploit poetic repetition to comment on or evaluate the testimony of a hostile witness in a strikingly marked fashion without overtly commenting on that evidence. These rhetorical techniques are therefore acutely sensitive to the aforementioned evidentiary strictures and demonstrate how such institutional constraints simultaneously enable linguistic opportunities for creative, improvisational strategies superimposed over the course of question/answer sequences. Because of the capacity to draw attention to itself, poetic repetition may comment covertly on the immediately prior testimony, instruct the jury that the witnesses’ answer is somehow flawed or incredible, and, as an inferential template inscribing cultural knowledge, create an opposing or alternate version of the evidential facts for the jury to consider, even though in a strict legal sense only answers from witnesses and not questions from attorneys constitute evidence.

More generically, like verbal art in other contexts, repetition functions in several overlapping ways during the performance of trial talk (Tannen, 1987). First, it creates semantic relations or links among otherwise disparate, diffuse, and desultory issues of evidence in testimony. In trial examination, repetition provides cohesion not only (or even primarily) between questions and answers or even within a narrative/monologue per se, but also, as we will see, across adjacent question/answer sequences, building broader activity connections from question to question through linear patterns of descriptive detail, creating a cumulative or expansive effect through the rhythmic movement of words, utterances, and ideas. Second and relatedly, repetition foregrounds and accentuates the referential content of talk, and, in the process, triggers affective meanings about rape, rapists, and sexual violence. By virtue of its rhythmic patterns and sound images, repetition merges the emotional with logical processes of cognition to operate as a persuasive sense-making mechanism, and, as this happens, it attempts to sweep the jury along in a trance-like aura of emotional involvement with the questioning attorney (Tannen, 1987, 1989; Atkinson, 1984; Heritage and Greatbatch, 1987). Third and last, repetition permits attorneys to produce utterances in a more efficient and fluid fashion by linking, especially in the case of parallelistic repetition, new information to pre-established structural frames ("they have X but cannot Y") (Tannen, 1987). Attorneys activate and instantiate these structures as rhetorical resources for constructing complex propositional sequences woven out of the tissue of short, controlling -- yes/no -- question formats. On the listening side of the process, repetition similarly aids the jury in the comphrension of talk because, as Tannen (1987) mentions, "semantically less dense" or new information is being presented. In sum, repetition functions in trial talk -- like it does in all talk -- as a type of conversational cement that connects utterances in a powerfully cumulative fashion over the span of discourse space. And it is precisely this quality which weaves together blame implicatures of persuasive force through expansion and control of testimony.

After a brief preliminary observation of the data, this article explores how the defense attorney "carves up" and expands the spatial geography of the historical incident through repetitive patterns of punctilious detail, patterns immanent in and emergent from the moment-to-moment synchronization of verbal action. The repetitive patterns, in turn, mark an incremental progression within the trajectory of a broader activity type: They impeach the witnesses' testimony and impugn her credibility through a molecular constitution of space, motion, and direction. I intend to show how the spatialization of social action is sequentially and grammatically anchored in repetitive rhythms of talk; how the defense attorney organizes the spatial and motional coordinates for navigating the representational pathways of historical action through the poetic dramatization of testimony; and how a finite set of interactional resources assembles the infinitely rich details of this spatialized knowledge. In the process, we can witness how the aesthetic structure of talk merges with the normative function of legal and cultural discourse as a vehicle for persuading the jury.

The paper is divided into three interconnected sections. In the first, I characterize the variant structures of repetition through an in-depth analysis of a single yet lengthy example and show how these function in, through, and across question/answer sequences. As we will see, expansion of testimony and control of the witness involve more than mere syntactic variation of question form. These legal precepts are also embodied in the real-time rhythms of poetic discourse which fragment the witnesses' testimony into tightly segmented episodes of verbal action. In the midst of these sequences, I analyze how spatialized descriptions of ultra-fine detail are mapped onto this conversational domain, and how socially layered intervals of space, time, and motion are systematically transformed into objects of legal relevance through an interaction among sequential, grammatical, and semantic structures, an underlying spatial calculus that not only operates to segment historical knowledge of the case but does so to expand key portions of testimony and to control the witness. In the second part I show how categorization animates the sense and punctuates the significance of discourse strategy, and how it intersects with such strategies to shape our gendered identities into legal prominence. And in the last section I focus on the tense and context of poetic action, specifically how an affective form of tense variation executes distinct impeachment strategies within the defense attorney's narrative.

The Data

On Easter weekend 1991, Patricia Bowman, the stepdaughter of a wealthy industrialist, along with her friends Ann Mercer and Chuck Desiderio spent an evening out at the trendy Au Bar nightclub in Palm Beach, Florida. During the course of the evening -- somewhere around one or two a.m. -- Bowman met William Kennedy Smith, Smith's uncle, Senator Edward Kennedy, and the Senator's son, Patrick. Bowman and Smith danced and talked till the bar closed and then she gave him a ride home to the Kennedy estate at around three a.m. Upon arrival at the estate, Bowman went into the house with Smith and subsequently accompanied him down to the beach, where, a short time later, she claimed that he raped her. Shaken and unable to drive, Bowman called her friend Ann Mercer to come pick her up at the Kennedy estate and drive her home. During the rape trial (in late November and early December 1991 and in which Kennedy Smith was acquitted after only 77 minutes of jury deliberation), Mercer was the first key witness for the prosecution (PA) and testified that she found Bowman crying and hysterical when she first encountered her. According to her testimony during direct examination, Mercer disclosed that Bowman told her Kennedy Smith had raped her, whereupon Mercer then confronted him by saying, "How could you do this to my friend? Where are her shoes?" Defense attorney Roy Black (DA) began his cross-examination of Mercer (AM) by retracing her activities after she arrived at the estate to pick up her friend. The following is a 4 minute and 21 second extract of the beginning of his cross-examination.

Cross-Examination of Ann Mercer by Defense Attorney Roy Black

DA: You say you went to the Kennedy home on the early
morning hours of March thirtieth? is that correct.
(1.5)
AM: Yes.
(0.7)
DA: Your friend says that she was raped? is that right.
(.85)
AM: Yes.
(.)
DA: But what she tells you is that she wants her shoes (.9)
is that correct?
(0.4)
AM: Yes.
(.)
DA: Several times she was worried about her shoes.
(1.6)
AM: Yes.
DA: So you went into the house (.5) is that correct.
(0.8)
AM: Yes.
DA: Into the hou::se (.) where the rapist is (.7) right?
(2.0)

AM: I guess you could say that yes.
DA: It's dark in there.
(1.2)
AM: Yes.
DA: You go through the kitchen right?
(0.6)
AM: Yes.
DA: Into this little hallway.
(.)
AM: Yes.
DA: It's dark in this hallway, isn't it.
(.)
AM: Right.
(.)
DA: You meet up with this <u>man</u> who your friend
says is a rapist isn't that correct.
(1.6)
AM: I was not uhfraid of him (.) no (.) I was
not uhfraid of (him)
[ ]
DA: ( ) That's not my question miss Mercer,
you understand my question? (.) my question
is did you meet this man (.) who your friend says
is the alleged rapist?
(0.6)
AM: Yes.
DA: In this dark hallway is that right.
(1.4)
AM: Yes.
(.)
DA: And you ask him to help him- (.) help- (.)
you ask the rapist to help you find her shoes
(.6) is that correct?
(2.3)
AM: Yes.
(0.5)
DA: And he turns around and goes with you:: (1.5)
uh:::: out of the house is that right?
(0.8)
AM: Yes.
(0.7)
DA: Through the dining room (.) to begin with (.) is

that correct.
(1.8)
AM: Yes.
(.)
DA: It's dark in that house (.) right.
(0.5)
AM: Yes.
(.)
DA: You're walking through the dining room with this
man (0.5) is that correct?
(.)
AM: Yes?
DA: The man who's allegedly a rapist right?
(0.6)
AM: Yes.
DA: You go out the door (.) of the dining room don'chu?
into a little patio area.
(0.8)
AM: Correct.
DA: With this man who's the alleged rapist (.) is that
right.
(.)
AM: That's right.
(0.5)
DA: You go out past the patio and onto the lawn is
that right?
(0.4)
AM: Right.
(0.6)
DA: It's dark out isn't it?
(0.8)
AM: Right.
(0.3)
DA: With this man who's the alleged rapist.
(2.0)
AM: Yes.
(.)
DA: You go acro::ss the lawn with him (.) is that
right.
(0.3)
AM: Yes.
(.)

DA: Towards the beach.
(0.6)
AM: Yes.
(0.5)
DA: As you go across the lawn you get to an
area where there are hedges? (.5) and uh
concrete wall (.) isn't that right?
(0.6)
AM: Yes.
(0.2)
DA: An you're still with this man who's the alleged rapist,
is that right.
[ ]
AM: Yes.
(0.7)
DA: You get to a dark (.) stairway (.) isn't that correct.
(1.1)
AM: Mm::' Yes.
(0.3)
DA: There're no lights in that stairway is there.
(0.8)
AM: No.
(0.4)
DA: You go do::wn the stairway (.) right.
(.)
AM: Right.
(.)
DA: With this man.
(0.4)
AM: Right.
(0.6)
DA: There's a door down at the bottom of the stairway
is that right.
(.)
AM: Right.
(0.6)
DA: You and this man who's the alleged rapist go out
the door (.) is that correct?
(.)
AM: Right.
(0.5)
DA: Out onto the beach.

(0.4)
AM: Right.
(0.5)
DA: And you then spend (.8) uh several minutes looking
for these shoes with this man who's the alleged
rapist? (.) Is that right?
(.)
AM: Right.
(0.9)
DA: Then after uh while you say, well let's forget about
looking for the shoes (.) and let's go back.
(0.4)
AM: Right.
DA: Is that correct?
AM: Right.
(0.6)
DA: You and he go toward the door (.) is that right.
AM: Right.
(0.6)
DA: You entered that doorway.
(1.0)
AM: Right.
(0.9)
DA: Through the stairwell.
(0.6)
AM: Right.
(0.4)
DA: In fact you even told us today he's BEHIND?
you (.) is that right.
(.)
AM: Right.
(0.3)
DA: Going up these stairs this ma::n (.) who's alleged
to be uh rapist is behi::nd you in this dark stairway
is that correct.
(.)
AM: Right.
(.)
DA: The two of you go up the stairway, isn't that right?
(.)
AM: Right.
(0.7)

DA: You get to the top and you start going across the
lawn (.) isn't that correct?
(.)
AM: Right.
(0.7)
DA: And you go into the house with him.
(0.7)
AM: Yes.
(0.3)
DA: And you go into this hall (where) down- (.) towards
the kitchen again is that right.
(0.9)
AM: Yes.
(.)
DA: Where you meet up with your friends.
(0.8)
AM: Yes.
(.)
DA: Now there's one thing you forgot to
tell us in that tuh:::: (.) scenario on direct
examination (0.4) what you said to this man who's
the alleged rapist when you left? (0.8) you forgot
about that didn'chu?
(0.5)
AM: I wasn't asked that sir.
DA: Didn't you tell him you were sorry?
(0.8)
AM: No I did not.
DA: OH- didn't you tell him (.) uh Miss Mercer (.) that
you were sorry:: (.) that you had to meet (.) under
these circumstances.
(1.8)
AM: AH:::: I used those (.) (E-) words=
DA: = I didn't ask you WHY you used them I said
did you sa::::y YOU WERE SORRY (.) YOU HAD
MET HIM (.) UNDER THOSE circumstances.
(0.7)
AM: I did not mea::n I was sorry!
DA: I didn't ask you what you meant!
[ ]
PA: Objection she's not being
allowed to answer the question.

J: Overruled? Please answer the question.
(.)
DA: The question is did you say to this man (.) I'm
sorry we met under these circumstances.
(2.4)
AM: Yes I said that.
(.)
DA: To the man who's supposedly the rapist (.) is
that right.
AM: Yes.
DA: The man who raped your friend (.) right.
AM: Yes.
DA: Your friend who you say is hysterical right.
AM: Yes.
DA: You said (.) I'm sorry we met under these
circumstances.
(1.4)
AM: WHAT I SAI::D AND HOW I SAID IT
[ ]
DA: (Nope-) DID YOU SAY
I'M SORRY WE MET UNDER THESE
CIRCUMSTANCES.
(1.0)
AM: Yes.
[[
PA: Objection argumentative she's not being allowed to
answer the question.
J: Overruled
(0.9)
DA: Is that what you said Miss Mercer?
(0.6)
AM: Yes.
(17.2)
DA: When did you get . . . ((Shift in topic))

Preliminary Observations

Let me begin with several preliminary and rather gross observations about the data. Notice, first off, up to line 208 most of the questions are noticeably short, consisting of only five to ten words, which elicit a "yes" answer to a relatively uncontroversial, factual point in evidence. Second, most of the questions in this rather lengthy series are grammatical yes/no, elipted yes/no, or tag questions. The defense attorney never employs a wh-question, which would allow the witness an opportunity to elaborate the context for her actions and inactions. And when the witness moves to elaborate her answer beyond a simple yes/no (as on lines 040-041), the defense attorney attempts to coerce a yes/no answer in the next turn (on lines 043-046) -- an overt type of negative/positive repair format (with a formal address term in the negative component) designed not only to micromanage a relevant answer in next turn, but, first, to socialize the witness to the institutional order of discourse practices in court, and, second and contemporaneously, to suggest to the jury that she is being evasive or is reluctant to answer the question. Third and in a more speculative vein, while it might have sufficed to say -- simply and succinctly -- that Ann and Will went down to the beach, looked for the victim's shoes, and then came back, the testimony on this topic turns out to have a radically different descriptive trajectory. In purely quantitative terms, beginning from line 018 and finishing at line 208, the testimony encompasses forty-four questions occurring over a time span of three and one-half minutes, a quite belabored pursuit of trivial details -- a detailing-to-death.

How does such a prima facie simple set of propositions, requiring perhaps no more than ten or twenty seconds and perhaps as few as several question/answer sequences to realize efficiently, expand over such a broad span of discourse time and space? Is the locus of this control over the witness rooted primarily in yes/no question structure or in the institutional order of legal hegemony or in their combination? Or is it rooted in something else? I next examine several discourse mechanisms to investigate in more detail what is going on in this exchange.

Resumptive Repetition

One of the most powerful yet subtle strategies of question expansion and control in this spate of cross-examination involves a form of parallelistic repetition or "chain parallelism" (Finnegan, 1977: 101-2), which encompasses a variant activity trajectory of from one turn to several sequences.[2] Beginning with the sequence running from lines 018-024, I want to draw attention to the defense attorney's question on line 018: that the witness "went into the house". After the witnesses' affirmative response, the defense attorney repeats the final phrase of the prior declarative clause ("into the house") as the initial constituent of his next -- elipted -- question on line 021: "Into the hou::se (.) where the rapist is (0.7) right?" I refer to this type of poetic coordination, in its variational formats, as resumptive repetition, occurring in this particular sequence with repetition of the entire adverbial in initial position in the elliptical question. Resumptive repetition modifies, expands, and elaborates the prior clause or phrase intra-sequentially (within a turn), on the one hand, or inter-sequentially (between or among sequences), on the other. It resumes a line of testimony as a grammatically fitted and rhythmically balanced continuation, which occurs through the following syntactic format: [resumptive phrase] + [relative clause].[3] In several variant configurations, the rhythmic repetition is coordinated through anaphoric, clause-initial ellipsis (ellipting the subject/verb) in the resumptive question. By repeating the adverbial or some other final phrase from the prior question in turn initial position in next question, the defense attorney can elliptically synchronize the resumptive turn with that prior question as a continuation.[4] Strictly speaking, only some variations of resumptive repetition combine resumption and repetition, while other variations involve just resumption, on the one hand, and still others consist entirely of repetition, on the other. But practically all the variant configurations constitute a grammatical/sequential continuation of a prior phrase or clause through the [resumptive phrase]+ [relative clause] structure.[5] And all the stylistic variations contingently project a future verbal action within a turn or across adjacent sequences in a discernibly expanded pattern of conversational synchrony. That is, a grammatical structure in an initial question or in an initial constituent of a question creates the context which makes resumptive repetition an immanent possibility later within the same turn or in a next or future question, though, to be sure, that possibility may or may not be realized as a subsequent strategic option.

An even more powerful feature of resumptive repetition is this: it can be exploited recursively in specific linguistic environments to navigate the spatial, ideological, and temporal coordinates of historical action during the representation of testimony. More specifically, the resumptive format functions as the pivotal element in a more expansive activity structure, functioning along several dimensions.[6] First, it operates in a linguistic environment for encoding spatial information about the witness's location and movements relative to the defendant, a process of expanding the historical representation of action through spatial-motional predicates of ultra-fine and progressively discriminating detail. In the process, the spatial expansions generated through grammatical/discourse structure -- through motion verbs, locative phrases, adverbials, and comitative adjuncts anchored within the resumptive framework -- appear as transparent reflections of historical actions during the rape incident. As a result, the discourse space/time continuum in the example may appear longer than the historical space/time Ann Mercer and William Kennedy Smith spent looking for the victim's shoes. Second, resumptive repetition works within the contours of a micro-gendered order which depicts the witnesses' actions as anomalous with category bound expectations governing the relations between women and rapists. The resumptive format foregrounds this ideological categorization in the relative clause to create a powerful impeachment affect. And, last, resumptive repetition interacts with a grammatical system of tense variation that, first, delivers a powerful poetic affect in its own right to the defense attorney's questioning, and, second and just as importantly, contextualizes and recontextualizes distinct impeachment strategies within the testimonial narrative.

The following taxonomy specifies the variant forms of resumptive repetition and the spatial information organized in and around them. After that, I will elaborate how aspects of categorization and tense interact with the resumptive format.

Sequential Resumption

I begin with the prototypic sequential format for resumptive repetition, though the second of these structures is more significant in terms of recursivity. The question/answer pairs in extract (1) on lines 018-021 and extract (2) on lines 073-077 below involve resumptive repetition across two sequences and four turns, a type of noncontiguous repetition over the witness's answer linking a question in a prior sequence to a question in the next sequence. In these cases of phrase iteration, the final phrase of the declarative clause in the first question is either repeated or partially repeated in clause-initial position of the resumptive next question, where the elipted question resumes as a grammatically and sequentially fitted continuation of the prior question.

Extract 1

018 -->DA:		So you went into the house (.5) is that correct.
019		(0.8)
020	AM:	Yes.
021 -->DA:		Into the hou::se (.) where the rapist is (.7) right?
022		(2.0)
023	AM:	I guess you could say that yes.
024	DA:	It's dark in there.
025		(1.2)
026	AM:	Yes.

In line 021 above, the resumptive question repeats the entire adverbial ("into the house") from the immediately prior question on line 018 and continues into a new proposition by conjoining the adverbial to the subject relative: a given/new informational structure consisting of [resumptive frame ("Into the hou::se")]+[relative clause ("where the rapist is")].[7] In this case, resumptive repetition is grammatically synchronized and sequentially continued through clause-initial ellipsis in the resumptive turn and is expanded through the subject relative clause modifying the object noun ("house"). Even more strategically, the resumptive frame foregrounds and thrusts into interpretative prominence the new information embedded in the relative clause. Notice, in particular, that the defense attorney's description does not refer to his client, William Kennedy Smith, but to the "rapist". And it is this substantive categorization which the resumptive structure foregrounds recursively with considerable impeach effect.

The following extract exhibits a similar case in point.

Extract 2

DA: And he turns around and goes with you:: (1.5)
uh:::: out of the house is that right?
(0.8)
AM: Yes.
(0.7)
DA: Through the dining room (.) to begin with (.) is
that correct.
(1.8)
AM: Yes.
(.)
DA: It's dark in that house (.) right.
(0.5)
AM: Yes.
(.)
-->DA: You're walking through the dining room with this
man (0.5) is that correct?
(.)
AM: Yes?
-->DA: The man who's allegedly a rapist right?
(0.6)
AM: Yes.

On line 077, the defense attorney's question partially repeats the animate complement from the final phrase in the previous declarative clause on lines 073-074 to form the initially positioned noun phrase in the resumptive turn. That is to say, the demonstrative "this" is transformed into the article "the" in the resumptive frame ("the man"), elipting the entire main clause as well as the preposition "with" in the process. Yet aside from the dubitative particle "allegedly" embedded in the subject relative, the four-turn design of the sequence and turn shape of the resumptive question -- [resumptive frame]+[relative] -- are organized in the same format as extract (1). And, like extract (1), the resumptive frame highlights the categorial information embedded in the relative clause, that is, reference to the "rapist" category.

In both the above extracts, resumptive repetition cements and expands the textual coherence not only within a turn (as we will see in more detail later) or even between adjacent turns at talk. Stretching across several or more turns, it generates a cohesive link between adjacent sequences as well, a suprasequential -- question-to-question -- connective format occurring as one variant configuration. In a very strategic sense, by linking a current to a prior question through the resumptive format, the defense attorney not only expands the sequence but also produces a double-barrel question that controls the witness's ability to deny the blame implicatures embedded in it, since she has already answered affirmatively to the presupposed information of the prior, feeding question.[8] The witness may agree, for instance, that she "went into the house" but not necessarily to the fact that she went "into the house where the rapist is", especially given the damaging connotations implied by such a reference.[9] Hypothetically, she could have gone into the house where her friend was, or Will Smith was, or Senator Kennedy was (and so on). As it turns out, however, by aligning resumptive repetition within the framework of clause-initial ellipsis in a subsequent question, the defense attorney can produce a burst of short, concise questions that is highly conducive: finely tailored to lead the witness to the desired answer. In extract (1), the witness admits to going "into the house", a description that is expanded in the resumptive turn through the new information, "where the rapist is". When the given information is repeated in initial position of the next question, it sets up a strongly conducive frame for a "yes" answer to the relative component of the resumptive turn and, most significantly, to the new information in it, even though the answer is ambiguous because it could refer to either of the two propositions or both.[10] However, if the witness were to answer "no" in her post-resumptive turn, then this would be tantamount to a recantation not of just the new information in the resumptive frame but of the given information from the previous question as well. And such a disavowal could possibly impeach her credibility on the spot, as it were. In extract (2), the witness admits to "walking through the dining room with this man", the animate complement ("the man") which is partially repeated in the resumptive turn as the presupposed frame for the categorial information in the subject relative ("who's allegedly a rapist"). Here the resumptive turn is even more conducive, more leading, and thereby more controlling, since she has agreed to, first, "walking through the dining room" and, second, doing so "with this man". And the categorial information in the resumptive turn -- "a rapist" --

is an appositive of both "this man" and "the man". In both extracts, the witness has little opportunity to deny the blame implicatures in the resumptive turns because she has answered affirmatively to the information transposed from the respective feeding turns.

Another feature of resumptive repetition is this: it occurs within the broader activity context of organizing the spatial coordinates of historical actions between the witness and the defendant.[11,12] In extract (1), the adverbial, "into the house", functions semantically as a spatial locative (or goal complement) indicating movement into a contained environment. Spatial locatives in adverbial constructions (prepositions like "into") occur typically with motion verbs ("went") to anchor the goal/directional movement in spatial expressions. And with this case marking you can derive, through the place adjunct ("where" functioning semantically as a locative) following the resumptive frame in the next question, the location of a particular person -- in this case "the rapist". When the defense attorney deploys such a locative expression, however, it might well block the possibility of using this form of resumptive repetition again, because if the witness has already entered an environment "where" the rapist is, there is no way she could logically enter a particular place in this manner again, unless, of course, the rapist arrived at some destination prior to her.[13] That such a possibility is indeed foreclosed further suggests a tacit presupposition that she is with (or, minimally, in the process of being with) this particular person. Indeed, as the segment unfolds we can see that all further reference to the rapist occurs in relation to being "with" the witness.

In extract (2), we can witness such a relationship between the witness and rapist in vivid detail. The phrase "with this man" possesses a comitative case marking that indicates accompaniment.[14] Following the points made earlier, the witness does not merely enter a space where the rapist is. Nor does she simply "meet up" with this rapist (as on lines 037-38). Rather, she is actively -- and apparently voluntarily -- doing things with him: "walking through the dining room with this man". When the path locative ("through") + complement ("the dining room") is ordered this way, the defense attorney can expand the proposition through the resumptive format: the [comitative adjunct] + [who-relative].[15] Even more impressively, he can deploy this resumptive format strategically and recursively in either the sequential or intra-sequential environment post each [motion verb] + [spatial expression].[16]

Recursion as an aspect of resumptive repetition derives from the adverbial or comitative adjunct possessing the animate complement in the post motion verb and spatial expression environment.[17] And it is the comitative resumptive repetition -- not the locative resumptive repetition -- which is the powerful one, because this is where the defense attorney hammers out that William Kennedy Smith may not have been a rapist eleven times.

We can also see in these these two extracts and the ensuing ones that the defense attorney mobilizes spatial information in the turns leading up to and following the resumptive format. In the former case, resumptive repetition might be thought of as the sequential climax to a progressive layering or build-up of spatialized facts, a set of facts which with the witness may have little choice but to agree.[18] The witness and defendant traverse a path or series of paths, passing each successive location at some temporal interval, so that each passage through a successive location may (optionally) implicate a state or attribute of that location in the path. Their traversal culminates with the resumptive format. Extract 2 on line 059 begins with the verbs of motion ("turns" and "goes") followed by, respectively, the path directional curve ("around") and source locative ("out") + locative complement ("of the house"). Of special interest here is that the rapist turns "around" and goes with Ann Mercer, as he has to realign his orientational bearings with her movements. She does not go with him. She actively initiates the encounter and the ensuing movements between them.

In the next question on line 064 the path locative + complement ("Through the dining room") is followed by a temporal parenthetic phrase ("to begin with") which recalibrates the representation of passage with the "correct" historical and directional trajectory. Here it appears that the prior representation on line 059, "out of the house", failed to align with the actual flow of historical movement, because prior to this source directional the witness and defendant went "through the dining room", and this step in the historical passage was omitted in the defense attorney's prior question.[19]

What is interesting about such spatial retracement is this: it retroactively engages a missed opportunity for expansion via the spatialization of action. Furthermore, the re-engaged movement salvages an otherwise wasted description of an attribute of the location. Just prior to the resumptive sequence, the question on line 069 elaborates the prior (path) directional, "Through the dining room", by specifying a more exclusive attribute of the locale in which the dining room is situated ("It's dark in that house")[20] -- part of the incremental build-up to the resumptive sequence on line 073-077. Just as impressively, the improvisational repetition of "dark" may modify recursively a successive location in the path of movement (lines 024, 033, 069, 094, 122, and 181) to create a perilous type of imagery -- a type of evil or dangerous symbolism.

More practically, the locative modifier here also reveals a rather subtle interaction between language and the law. Each path of movement through a successive location can be linked to an attribute of that location, recursively linking the "dark" attribute to a new spatio-temporal moment and thereby (technically) avoiding repetition in the process. To illustrate, if the defense attorney employed the location attribute to refer to the state of outside (the house), such as hypothetically, "it's dark outside", after the question on line 059, it would be repetitious with a forthcoming location modifier on line 094 ("It's dark out, isn't it") and hence (potentially) objectionable. But, as it turns out, the recalibrated passage captures the linear trajectory of historical movement in more detail, expands the sequence, and preserves another future opportunity to use a powerful, symbolic location attribute. At the same time, the defense attorney is able to utilize the "dark" modifier as an attribute of the house -- a rather strategic display of how trial participants use language and culture to create meaning in their legal interactions.

To sum up the points in this section: in both cases, grammatical forms function as sequential resources to facilitate resumptive repetition. Both extracts reveal a double-barrel question form that controls and expands the witness's testimony through a grammatically organized and sequentially synchronized continuation through repetition in the resumptive turn. This repetition is neither contiguous with a prior turn nor, strictly speaking, a collaborative effort between the witness and attorney, but rather suprasequential, almost monologic: across sequences of question/answer pairs by the same questioner. But, of course, it only appears monologic. Such an impression conceals the dynamic processes of concerted interaction -- of grammar-in-interaction -- designed to achieve precisely this effect. As is becoming evident, resumptive repetition is part of an organizing mechanism that dissects and expands the representation of historical actions into discretely layered intervals of ultra-detailed density.

Nonrepetitive Resumption

Not all cases of resumption involve repetition. Nor, quite obviously, do all cases of repetition involve resumption. The arrowed questions in extracts 3-5 possess a resumptive format across two or more sequences but occur without phrase repetition in the resumptive turn. Yet even though the questions fail to repeat grammatical elements across contiguous sequences (as in the resumptive format seen in the previous section), they nevertheless repeat in a more macro-text sense: first, by repeating (from previous sequences) the structural design and case marking of the resumptive turn format; and second, by repeating (from previous sequences) the sequential format of expansion and continuation through clause-initial ellipsis in the resumptive question.

Extract 3

080--> DA: You go out the door (.) of the dining room don'chu?
081 into a little patio area.
082 (0.8)

AM: Correct.
--> DA: With this man who's the alleged rapist (.) is that right.
(.)
AM: That's right.

While not containing contiguous repetition from the preceding question, the question on line 084 still incorporates a type of sequential grammaticality because of the [resumptive frame] + [relative] design in the resumptive turn, which is syntactically consistent with and sequentially fitted to the final phrase on line 081(the goal complement "into a little patio area") through clause- initial ellipsis . Although it does not repeat off the immediately prior sequence, the question on line 084 still involves two macro forms of suprasequential repetition: first, semantically, by repeating the comitative adjunct "with this man" from the questions on lines 037-38 and 073-74, and second, syntactically, by repeating the structural design -- [resumptive frame] + [who-relative] --from the prior sequential cluster on lines 073-77. Notice a further measure of rhythmic alignment in this extract. The "don'chu" tag is embedded in the declarative clause, and not in the typical, post-main clause environment, which, with ellipsis of the entire preceding main clause in the resumptive turn, provides a tighter degree of sequential synchrony across the two questions: the comitative adjunct "with this man" in the second question resumes contiguous from the goal directional "into a little patio area" in the first question.

Notice the spatial organization represented in this sequence too. After the motion verb "go", the question on lines 080-81 involves three spatial predicates: the source locative "out the door", the static place locative "of the dining room", and the goal locative "into a little patio area", the latter indicating spatial inclusion in conjunction with the diminutive adjective "little". The question involves a slight spatial expansion compared with extracts 1 and 2 by combining the hierarchally organized source locative ("out the door of the dining room") with the goal locative ("into the dining room") and by elliptically positioning the goal complement in the first question immediately prior to the comitative adjunct of the next question. By expanding the spatial-coordinates of space and movement through these linguistic resources, the defense attorney can expand the amount of time the witness and defendant spent together and the spatial activities they engaged in during the historical incident.

The following extracts exhibit slight variations of nonrepetitive resumption.

Extract 4

089--> DA: You go out past the patio and onto the lawn is
090 that right?
091 (0.4)
092 AM: Right.
093 (0.6)
094 DA: It's dark out isn't it?
095 (0.8)
096 AM: Right.
097 (0.3)
098--> DA: With this man who's the alleged rapist.
099 (2.0)
100 AM: Yes.

Extract 5

122 DA: You get to a dark (.) stairway (.) isn't that correct.
123 (1.1)
124 AM: Mm::'yes.
125 (0.3)
126 DA: There're no lights in that stairway is there.
127 (0.8)
128 AM No.
129 (0.4)
130--> DA: You go do::wn the stairway (.) right.
131 (.)
132 AM: Right.
133 (.)
134--> DA: With this man.
135 (0.4)
136 AM: Right.

In extract 4 on line 098, the defense attorney activates the [resumptive frame] + [relative] format, but this time the resumptive turn is delayed, and is synchronized not with the immediately prior question on line 094 but with the earlier question on line 089: a type of disjunctive yet expanded resumption across three sequences. The resumptive turn is separated from the "go out" question on line 089 by the fourth reference to darkness. In extract 5, the resumptive turn on line 134 constitutes another configuration of resumptive repetition. The resumptive turn is not only grammatically incomplete, elipting the entire main clause in the resumptive turn; it also occurs without overt realization of the relative clause in the post-adverbial position, an intra-turn contraction in the resumptive format.

The spatial organization in these extracts forms rather complex trajectories leading up to the resumptive climax. In extract 4, after the source/path ("out past the patio") and goal ("onto the lawn") directionals, the defense attorney's next -- disjunctive -- question is organized around the "dark out" theme, which is embedded between the feeding and resumptive turns. In extract 5, the witness arrives at a "dark" stairway, a place location which is elaborated a second and third time in the ensuing turns: "There're no lights in that stairway" and "You go do::wn the stairway". In so doing, the defense attorney attaches more than a mere spatial attribute to the location. The vertical adverb "down" also indicates the witness's movement through a dark location with the rapist. In both extracts, linguistic divisions and fault-lines in the social construction of space, direction, and motion expand the sequence building up to the resumptive climax -- projecting, highlighting, while simultaneously delaying, its occurrence.

Intrasequential Resumption

We have seen that resumption may expand sequentially, but there are other variations. The arrowed questions in the following extracts function as sequential contractions in the resumptive format.

Extract 6

DA: You go through the kitchen right?
(0.6)
AM: Yes.
DA: Into this little hallway.
(.)
AM: Yes.
DA: It's dark in this hallway, isn't it.
(.)
AM: Right.
(.)
--> DA: You meet up with this man who your friend
says is a rapist isn't that correct.
(1.6)
AM: I was not uhfraid of him (.) no (.) I was
not uhfraid of (him)

Extract 7

102 DA: You go acro::ss the lawn with him (.) is that
103 right.
104 (0.3)
105 AM: Yes.
106 (.)
107 DA: Towards the beach.
108 (0.6)
109 AM: Yes.
110 (0.5)
111 DA: As you go across the lawn you get to an
112 area where there are hedges? (0.5) and uh
113 concrete wall (.) isn't that right?
114 (0.6)
115 AM: Yes.
116 (0.2)
117--> DA: An you're still with this man who's the alleged rapist,
118 is that right.
119 [ ]
120 AM: Yes.

Extract 8

152--> DA: And you then spend (.8) uh several minutes looking
153 for these shoes with this man who's the alleged
154 rapist? (.) Is that right?
155 (.)
156 AM: Right.
157 (0.9)
158 DA: Then after uh while you say, "Well let's forget about
159 looking for the shoes" (.) and "let's go back".
160 (0.4)
161 AM: Right.

In the above three extracts, the resumptive turns represent a slight variation from the structures we have witnessed previously because they involve neither resumption/repetition from a phrase in the prior turn nor clause initial ellipsis in the resumptive turn but compress the resumption into a single question. Even so, after a main clause the questions still repeat (from previous questions) the resumptive format consisting of the comitative adjunct "with this man" expanded by the subject relative clause "who is the rapist", though technically the resumptive question in extract 6 embeds a parenthetical, "your friend says", in the relative. As we will see in the next section, however, this parenthetical is hardly tangential in the unfolding scheme of things, and foreshadows a matter of immense import in setting up the defense attorney's impeachment strategy.

In extract 9 below, the who-relative is embedded in the subject clause, where it modifies the subject noun rather than the object noun. Moreover, the resumptive turn on line 181 is packaged among several spatialized designations: the vertical directional "up" in the nonfinite clause, the place locative "behind", and the location specification "in this dark stairway" in the predicate.

Extract 9

DA: You and he go toward the door (.) is that right.
AM: Right.
(0.6)
DA: You entered that doorway.
(1.0)
AM: Right.
(0.9)
DA: Through the stairwell.
(0.6)
AM: Right.
(0.4)
DA: In fact you even told us today he's BEHIND?
you (.) is that right.
(.)
AM: Right.
(0.3)
--> DA: Going up these stairs this ma::n (.) who's alleged
to be uh rapist is behi::nd you in this dark stairway
is that correct.
(.)
AM: Right.

In extracts 6, 7, and 9, the spatial organization in these sequences also reveals a prefatory trajectory to the sequential climax in the resumptive turns. In extract 6, the witness traverses a path "through" a location ("the kitchen" on line 027) to reach a specific goal ("into this little hallway" on line 030). On lines 030 and 033, both of the defense attorney's questions modify and elaborate the "hallway" location -- the first consisting of the diminutive adjective "little" on line 030, the second involving the "dark" location attribute on line 033. Through both, the defense attorney suggests that the witness is not only in a "dark" location but in a small, narrow one as well.

And, it is in this dark location that the witness "meets up" with the "rapist". Just to amplify the last point: The rapist does not initiate this encounter with the witness. Nor is their meeting up just an accidental encounter. Indeed, this encounter is intentional; the witness actively planned to "meet up" with the rapist in this "dark", "little" location -- an act of volition on her part.

In extract 7, the witness and defendant once again traverse a path ("across" on line 102) towards some particular goal ("towards the beach" on line 107). On line 111 the path directional "across" is repeated, as the witness and defendant reach two landmarks (the "hedges" and "concrete wall") in route to the ultimate beach destination. While the "dark" location attribute is absent in this sequence, the mere reference to these two landmarks may function in a very similar fashion -- to create inferences pertaining to the witness and defendant in a location where the view is obstructed. Moreover, the resumptive climax to this sequence indicates quite more than the witness is just with the defendant; the temporal adverb on line 117 reveals that she is "still" with him, that she has been with him for some duration of time.

Example 9 constitutes a variant trajectorial configuration and recontextualization of the spatialized movements leading up to the resumptive turn. The sequence begins with the goal directional "toward the door" followed by an entry into that geographical landmark in next turn ("you entered that doorway" on line 168) and a path movement "through the stairwell" in third turn. The question on line 176, however, recontextualizes the spatial trajectory of movement by specifying a horizontal quadrant projected off the witness's body and by mapping this relative egocentric coordinate onto the comitative "with". The witness is not just "with" the defendant. Nor are they just traversing an anchored pathway with a vertical coordinate ("up the stairs"). Instead, the deictic locative "behind" indicates the relative, spatial positioning of their bodies during the movement in this place -- along with the symbolic connotations of this spatial reference in their traversal through a "dark location". Notice further the stress, intonation, and loudness in "behind" in the last two questions and its repetition in the resumptive turn. And, in the resumption, the defense attorney foregrounds the horizontal dimension of positioning bodies in space and grafts this onto path direction, location attribute, and the rapist category to cumulate spatial discontinuities in the historical and textual domains of action.

What emerges in these extracts is a set of interactional, grammatical, and semantic resources for carving up the spatial domain of movement involving the witness and defendant, creating spatial distinctions and expansions of elaborate detail. In this progressive build-up of spatialized facts, the defense attorney navigates the representation of historical action through a linear trajectory of discretely layered movements at successive locations and states of those locations, culminating in the resumptive format. In the midst of these chronological segments, the witness travels through or across a path, towards some destination, reaches, enters, and then leaves it, always accompanied by and/or positioned relative to the defendant, to the "rapist" -- and so on recursively. Along the route the location attribute can be activated at almost any juncture in the motional process to enhance the expansion and thrust into interpretative prominence symbolic formulations that are especially damaging to the prosecution's case. And just as injuriously: by partitioning the historical stream of movement through this meticulous array of short, spatialized facts, the defense attorney leaves the witness in the rather compromising position of having to agree with the damaging inferences contained in and cumulating through each of the questions.

Before turning to the next resumptive format, a brief mention of extract 8 is in order. The resumption here is organized more around the temporal stream of activities between the witness and defendant than the spatial organization of movement: "you then spend (0.8) several minutes looking for these shoes with this man". This constitutes a type of break in the linear trajectory of movement thus far and indicates a recontextualization of spatial organization; it ties the resumptive format to a new set of spatio-temporal coordinates. The witness and defendant have reached a final destination (the beach), completed the task to which their spatialized traversals were directed in the first place ("looking for the victim's shoes"), and redirected their movements back to the origin of their departure ("let's go back") -- with the spatialized shift occurring through the intertextual vehicle of a direct quote.[21] Thus in addition to the time spent with the rapist thus far, the witness, first, has spent some duration of time looking for an ostensibly trivial object with him and, second, is now poised to retrace the spatial coordinates of movement back to the point of origin.

Intra-Turn Resumption with Suprasequential Resumptive Repetition

The questioning format below reveals another instance where the relative clause is embedded in the subject clause and modifies a subject noun.

Extract 10

DA: There's a door down at the bottom of the stairway
is that right.
(.)
AM: Right.
(0.6)

--> DA: You and this man who's the alleged rapist go out
the door (.) is that correct?
(.)
AM: Right.
(0.5)
--> DA: Out onto the beach.
(0.4)
AM: Right.

This sequence, while similar to the previous extracts, forms another variation of resumptive repetition. Like the sequence in extract 9, the relative clause modifies the subject noun phrase and is thus positioned immediately contiguous to it. And like the sequences in extracts 1 and 2, sequential structure is expanded to create a four-part design. But unlike both, the sequence in extract 10 displays a combinatorial logic in which an instance of intra-turn resumption combines with suprasequential repetition to weave a vertically and horizontally expanded pattern: first horizontally through the intrasequential resumptive format of [resumptive frame] + [subject relative clause]; and second vertically through the (partial) repetition and contrast of "out the door" on line 143-44 with the elipted "Out onto the beach" on line 148,[22] a form of resumption continuing with repetition of the spatial preposition "out" in the source (line 143-44) and goal (line 148) directional expressions.

This extract reveals another level of spatial segmentation leading up to the resumptive format. On line 138, the there-existential with the contracted stative verb indicates the existence of the "door", and is followed by the locative expression "down at the bottom of the stairway". Thus prior to any movement in a particular direction or prior to reaching a given landmark (or prior to any reference to a location attribute), the defense attorney can expand the sequence and control the witness through a spatialized fact referring to the mere existence of an object or geographic landmark. I turn next to the final form of resumptive repetition in the example.

Contrastive List Resumption

Two of the most prominent forms of poetic discourse are list and contrast structures, and, when combined, they constitute one of the most powerful rhetorical tools in virtually any type of persuasive discourse. Lists are expansive techniques for producing family resemblances, for creating a conceptual unity among otherwise diverse elements in a perceptual field. They represent a type of incremental repetition that classifies actions through a rhythmically textured and progressively expanded litany of similar items (Atkinson, 1984; Schriffin, 1994). Contrasts are devices for organizing descriptions into a two part, evaluative structure that is often marked -- most canonically and saliently -- with the coordinating conjunction "but" introducing the second proposition or, less frequently, with a concessive adverbial such as "even though" in the first proposition to create a type of antithesis or juxtaposition of opposites: 'if, A then B' is expected to follow logically but only where the latter turns out to be noticeably disjunctive with the former (Smith, 1978; Atkinson, 1984).[23] Together, these rhetorical practices embody a powerful method of linguistic foregrounding through parallelistic repetition of discourse and syntactic structure to contextualize their own interpretation, to transform otherwise disparate elements of evidence into a coherent object of legal knowledge, and to organize that knowledge into a persuasive representational artifact: a stylistic property of language use designed to inter alia emphasize and dramatize referential content of evidence in testimony. As they mutually amplify each other, these emotionally moving and cognitively salient rhythms of talk deliver an incantatory force to the defense attorney's questions, unifying particulars of evidence into a coherent, gestalt-like pattern of ironic affect.

The following extract displays the persuasive power of these devices when they are combined and aligned in a resumptive format.

Extract 11

DA: Now there's one thing you forgot to
tell us in that tuh:::: (.) scenario on direct
examination (0.4) what you said to this man who's
the alleged rapist when you left? (0.8) you forgot
about that didn'chu?
(0.5)
AM: I wasn't asked that sir.
DA: Didn't you tell him you were sorry?
(0.8)
AM: No I did not.
DA: OH- didn't you tell him (.) uh Miss Mercer (.) that
you were sorry:: (.) that you had to meet (.) under
these circumstances.
(1.8)
AM: AH::::: I used those (.) (E-) words=
DA: =I didn't ask you WHY you used them I said
did you sa::::y YOU WERE SORRY (.) YOU HAD
MET HIM (.) UNDER THOSE circumstances.
(0.7)

AM: I did not mea::n I was sorry!
DA: I didn't ask you what you meant!
[ ]
PA: Objection she's not being
allowed to answer the question.
J: Overruled? Please answer the question.
(.)
--> DA: The question is did you say to this man (.) I'm
sorry we met under these circumstances.
(2.4)
AM: Yes I said that.
(.)
--> DA: To the man who's supposedly the rapist (.) is
that right.
AM: Yes.
--> DA: The man who raped your friend (.) right.
AM: Yes.
--> DA: Your friend who you say is hysterical right.
AM: Yes.

The sequence I wish to begin with deals with Ann Mercer's statement to the defendant at the Kennedy estate after the alleged rape incident. In this sequence the defense attorney's question on lines 235-6 includes the adverbial "to this man", which is partially repeated in turn initial position of his ellipted next question: "To the man" + who-relative on line 240. In this instance the repeating adverbial aligns syntactically not only with the defense attorney's question on line 235 but with the witnesses' answer on line 238 -- "Yes I said that" + "To the man ..." -- to generate a densely synchronized and grammatically elipted "bridge" from the question (on line 235) to the answer (on line 238) and then forward to the ensuing question (on line 240): a dual resumptive format, one repeating from the initial question to the resumptive question, the other continuing off the anaphoric demonstrative "that" from the elipted answer to the very same resumptive question.

Moreover, the elipted question on line 240 is the initial component of a three-part repetitive list (the questions on lines 240, 243, and 245), which functions simultaneously as the second part of a contrast off the question on line 235 to generate a contrastive list. The ironic force of the contrastive list incorporates an evaluative algorithm to contextualize a normative clash between expectation and action. That is to say: The direct quote, "I'm sorry we met under these circumstances", exists in contrastive balance with the repetitive list and represents a defense strategy for indicating to the jury that the witness's statement constitutes a surprisingly cordial way of addressing someone who had just raped her "hysterical" friend.[24]

On line 243 the ironic trajectory continues. The noun phrase "The man" occurs in clause initial position, where it, once again, partially and elliptically repeats off the adverbials "to this man" (on line 235) and "To the man" (on line 240) to form the second couplet in the contrastive list triplet. Of special note here is that although this clause initial noun phrase continues resumptively off the prior two adverbials it also resumes, more speculatively perhaps, off the object noun phrase "the rapist" in the subject relative on line 240. I make this claim with the following evidence. First, the noun phrase "The man" on line 243 is co-referential with the noun phrase object "the rapist" in the subject relative on line 240. And, second, the frame variation on line 245 involves a transformation in which the object noun phrase of the prior relative clause (on line 243) becomes the repeated syntactic frame of the ensuing (and final) member of the contrastive list triplet. If this is indeed the case then there may be a more systematic basis for the frame variation on line 245 than what initially appears. The list pattern is coordinated, first, through a repetition, in clause initial position, of the adverbial from phrase final position in the relative -- adverbial to adverbial repetition (lines 235 to 240: "to this man" and "to the man"); and, second, through a repetition, also in clause initial position, of the object noun phrase from phrase final position in the relative -- noun phrase to noun phrase repetition (or grammatical form repetition on lines 240 to 243 to 245: "the rapist" to "the man" to "your friend"). In sum, it is through these grammatical transformations that the criss-crossing resumptive frames form the palpable rhythm of the contrastive list.

It will be instructive to consider this form of resumptive repetition as being organized along the poles of a vertical and horizontal axis. The vertical axis consists of (1) the first pair part of the contrast on line 235 and (2) the second pair part which unfolds incrementally and resumptively as a turn-by-turn progression through the three list questions on lines 240, 243, and 245, the underlying ironic form which can be interpreted as follows: the man is a rapist who raped her friend who is hysterical + but she said "I'm sorry . . ." On the other hand, the horizontal axis consists of the intricately inscripted logic of repetition and variation -- the network of equivalence and contrast relations -- delicately encrusted in each of the individual list members, with each list question itself incorporating an underlying horizontal contrast: a contrastive interface superimposed upon and intersecting with a contrastive list ("The man raped your friend but you said X"; "The man is a rapist, but you said X"; "Your friend is hysterical, but you said X.").

Let me explicate the logic of this criss-crossing network more thoroughly. First, the syntactic frame of the first list question repeats off the adverbial in the initial contrast first part and, along with the relative pronoun ("who") frames the introduction to the categorial information embedded in the subject relative: ". . .the rapist". The syntactic structure of the second list question also consists of a framing structure in which the same elipted adverbial and relative pronoun ("the man" + "who") is repeated as given information to frame the introduction of the new component: "raped your friend". And finally, the syntactic frame of the third and last list question involves a systematic transformation in the initial frame component, a frame variation from the adverbial "(To) the man" to the noun phrase "Your friend", which is repeated from the object noun phrase in immediately prior question to frame the new information in the relative clause ("who is hysterical"). Such a structure, therefore, consists of an overlapping mosaic of repetition/variation relations along the vertical plane of the listing questions, where it exists in a contrastive field with the direct quote on line 235. Second and more speculatively, while not linguistically marked or grammatical realized, each of the list members consists of an underlying contrast format that is organized around a horizontal axis (or intra turn) for a powerful ironic affect.

To summarize the points made thus far. We have witnessed a multiplex and densely synchronized form of resumptive repetition which possesses a powerful projection capacity to extend a course of verbal action over several sequences. This contrastive list incorporates a three- dimensional, cross-rhythmic pattern. It consists of, first, a vertical contrast between the first pair and second pair parts of the contrastive list; second, a horizontal contrast tier in which each of the unfolding list members operates within an underlying contrastive logic; and third an equivalence/contrast network interlaminated in the information structure of each of the questions in the interchange. Of more theoretical note is this: Progressively more given information is elided with each successive list member; each list member appears to include the minimal amount of information needed to anchor the syntactic frame -- a precisely executed interaction among sequential, pragmatic, and grammatical structures in the unfolding list.

Let me turn to the prefatory sequence leading to the resumptive list. As we have seen in extracts 2-10, resumption is the sequential climax to an incremental cumulation of spatialized facts. Extract 11, by contrast, initiates a different sort of ascent to the climactic resolution of the defense attorney's questions, to a puzzle[25] which contextualizes a transition from questioning about the witness's movements with the defendant to her verbal action in the wake of those movements.[26] The puzzle begins on line 209 and refers to the witness's omission of a particular piece of evidence during direct examination: what she said to the alleged rapist prior to leaving the Kennedy estate with the victim. But while the defense attorney refers to the omission as something the victim "forgot" to reveal, his repetition of "forgot" later in the same question fosters the impression that her memory has been intentionally selective on this matter, that she failed to volunteer a perhaps damaging piece of evidence, and that, most generally, she has been evasive. In so doing, he attempts to imply evidence of an impeachable transgression not only by virtue of what she said during the historical incident but also by virtue of her failure to volunteer that evidence during direct and cross examination.

By the same token, the puzzle may build off the meticulous and dense array of spatialized facts just concluded from the prior testimony. The witness, to some extent, has collaborated with the defense attorney in recounting the historical landscape of movement between her and the defendant in minute degrees of detail. But, according to the defense attorney, she omits a most prominent detail pertaining to the end of those movements, which activates the puzzle and projects her selective recall into interpretative salience.

The witness's answer on line 215, "I wasn't asked that sir", displays that she knows the solution to the puzzle while still not providing it, and simultaneously offers a rationale for its omission which is keenly sensitive to the interactional order of the adversary system: The witness is not in the institutionally endowed position of volunteering or proffering evidence; it is the prosecuting or defense attorney's task to elicit that evidence. Yet even though the witness may attempt to deflect the blame implications of the defense attorney's question by denying responsibility for eliciting evidence, this strategy also delays a solution to the puzzle. And by delaying a solution to the puzzle she collaborates with the defense attorney in prolonging it and building up suspense over its contents. Just as injuriously, her failure to provide the solution delivers an opportunity space in next turn for the defense attorney to provide it, which he subsequently does, and as this happens he draws further attention to her selective memory and exposes her actions as hiding evidence of immense import for the trial.[27] The witness fails to volunteer this evidence not only in direct examination and in the cross-examination thus far. She even fails to give an answer after a direct question about evidence that she knows the answer to. In concert with the defense attorney, the witness furnishes a proof that makes her appear to have been evasive in recalling a key point of evidence in the recent and distant testimonial past and that her testimony (and moral character in general) thereby lacks credibility by displaying at this moment a real time instance of evasion-in-process.

On line 216, the defense attorney's next question provides a partial solution to the puzzle: that the witness stated to the defendant that she was "sorry". The witness's answer on line 218, however, constitutes an emphatic denial of this description of her verbal remarks, which serves to escalate the dispute. Indeed, the defense attorney's next question (on line 219) increases the level of precision in describing the witness's historical statement to include a combination of direct and indirect speech: the infinitive "to meet" and demonstrative "these" both indicate present deictic references in direct speech, while the nominal that-clause and corresponding back shift in tense of the verb ("were sorry") and pronoun (second person "you") characterize indirect speech. Moreover, his question is prefaced by a stressed surprise marker ("OH") which suggests an incongruity between, on the one hand, the witness's earlier deposition that she indeed made such a statement along with the indication from her on line 215 that she said "that", and, on the other, her failure to confirm the defense attorney's prior query about making the statement.

The witness's answers on lines 223 and 228 attempt to resolve the dilemma by making a distinction between "what she said" versus "what she meant", and, although not indicated in the transcript, she thus reveals that her words were meant sarcastically not literally.[28] In doing so, she can elaborate the context for her remark to the defendant and frame an alternative set of inferences for the jury to consider based on a linguistic ideology of intentionalist meaning: the meaning of words is reflexively tied to the speaker's declared intention and does not exist independently of them (Duranti, 1992; DuBois, 1992). On the other hand, the defense attorney's response (on lines 224 and 229) symbolizes the epistemological supremacy of what was said, the public, over what was meant, the subjective. According to this view, what the witness said has a meaningful force of its own, and she must deal directly with implications of her utterances. Because control over meaning exists independently of the speaker's avowed intention, she is responsible for her words, the meaning attributed to them, and the implicatures they generate (Duranti, 1992; DuBois, 1992). As a result, the literal force of the utterance "I'm sorry" unleashes a cascade of collective inferences which is less a product of the speaker's subjective state than a collaborative process of assigning meaning and allocating responsibility in speaker/hearer interaction. And in the rape trial context these conventional inferences suggest, as mentioned previously, that the witness's utterance, "I'm sorry", constitutes an anomaly, a surprisingly cordial way of addressing someone who had just raped her "hysterical" friend. Just to amplify the above points: We can gain a transparent appreciation of just how intense this negotiation of meaning is -- for both participants -- by considering the repair organization here. It takes the defense attorney five questions, in which four involve variant repair formats, of increasing levels of referential precision (up to the full direct quote on line 235) to manage a confirmation from the witness, and then only after the judge's ruling on line 233. And it is the last of these question/answer pairs on lines 235-238 that completes the puzzles circuitous trajectory to the resumptive climax -- a journey consisting of the processual and dynamic negotiation among intention, meaning, and responsibility.

One final and more abstract note: while the resumptive list is indeed a climax initiated by the puzzle, at least at a local level, in broader terms it emerges as the point of supreme intensity in a progressively imbricated crescendo of resumptive formats. On the one hand, each resumptive movement and its spatialized prefatory context consists of a minor crescendo (extracts 2-10); on the other hand each is contemporaneously part of a gradual build-up to the major crescendo of the contrastive list (extract 11). As a gestalt totality, the rhythmic pulse of the pattern organizes a succession of spatialized movements to a resumptive climax, each of which, in turn, leads to and culminates in the supreme -- resumptive -- moment of discursive intensity. Seen in this light, the final movement in the crescendi pattern thus begins with the puzzle, which builds a moment of suspense into the testimony thus far and indicates to the jury that the defense attorney has reserved the best point till last. Hence just as each resumptive sequence is a climax to the progressive build-up of spatialized facts, so too the resumptive list is a climax to a progressively imbricated pattern of prior resumptive sequences and is, in turn, thereby part of the broader spatialized pattern.

Categorization and the Moral Order

Our analysis to this point has traded on relatively unexamined assumptions about the damaging implications of the rapist category foregrounded in the relative clause, and it is time to explicate this more thoroughly, for the resumptive pattern is motivated by this category. We can gain some purchase at the outset by considering the witness's "rogue" utterance on line 40, "I was not uhfraid of him . . .", which is a response to the defense attorney's prior question on line 37, "You meet up with this man who . . . is a rapist". Notice, first off, that the question refers to the witness "meeting up with" the rapist, rather than confronting him for raping her friend or merely finding or accidentally encountering him, in a way that will galvanize a parallel allusion with a forthcoming question on line 205: the witness "meets up with" her friends. Second, a not too subtle double-bind ideology is beginning to emerge from the rapist category. Women and rapists co-exist as incumbents in an oppositional (or antagonistic) rather than relational categorial framework, and certain category-bound activities may be conventionally derived from this categorial pair. The defense attorney's logic can be quasi-formalized as follows: On the one hand, if the man is a rapist, do not engage in x, y, and z activities; on the other hand, if the man is not a rapist, you may engage in x, y, and z activities. Ironically, perhaps, the witness's response above may activate (overtly) a further layer of normative expectation to this double-bind equation through a mediating proposition: On the one hand, if the man is a rapist, then be afraid, and if afraid, do not engage in x, y, and z activities; on the other hand, if the man is not a rapist, then be unafraid, and if unafraid, you may engage in x, y, and z activities. Through the witness's contribution, the rapist category naturalizes a normative expectation that women should, in addition to category bound activities, exhibit certain category bound states in relation to rapists, that they should be afraid of them, and if they are not afraid, then why? That women should be afraid of rapists is a normatively accountable matter in the microgendered order. But even by the witness's own admission she is unafraid. Could it be that she is courageous or brave, confronting the rapist for his actions, or that she is merely careless in accidentally encountering him, an unintentional act on her part? The witness's activities with the rapist appear disjunctive, however, with either of these interpretations and document activities of an alternative categorial framework. Put most prosaically, the defense attorney is implying that, if the man were a rapist who had just raped her friend, the witness would be putting herself in danger by walking and talking with him. Moreover, if the man were a rapist she would be putting herself in further danger by walking in the darkness where nobody can see them, and when the darkness does not impede vision it is hedges and a wall. Meeting up with the rapist, looking for the victim's shoes with him, and making specific verbal statements to him constitute category-bound activities that align the witness and defendant more in a relational category, such as the category "co-helpers" engaged in a type of teamwork,[29] than in the antagonistic categorial pair rapists/women. The defendant -- at the behest of the witness[30] -- collaborates with the witness to find the victim's shoes, a type of syllogistic logic in which a man helps women requesting his assistance: (1) Ann helps Patricia; (2) William helps Ann; and therefore (3) William helps Patricia. When category-bound activities and states fail to articulate with an overt category in this fashion, the use of the category can be interpreted as ironic, as saying one thing but meaning something else (Jayyusi 1984).

While the witness attempts to frame a brave interpretation with the "I wasn't uhfraid" answer, there is little opportunity to secure such a reading by meeting up with the rapist to look for the victim's shoes. If she engages in the actions with him, then he is not a rapist, and if she is unafraid, then he is not a rapist. Even if she is afraid, this interpretation is blocked by her actions. In fact, this strategy generates an emerging wave of impeachment strategy: first, by impeaching the credibility of the victim for wanting (or worrying about) her shoes; and second, by impeaching the credibility of the witness, who went looking for the shoes with the rapist. Through this double incongruity, the credibility of the victim is further impeached and the status of her claim cast into further doubt because it appears from the witness's action -- the action of the victim's friend -- that the witness does not believe the man is a rapist.[31] We can also see more clearly that the parenthetical "your friend says" on lines 006 and 037 symbolizes a defense strategy -- a meta-impeachment of the victim through her friend -- by demonstrating that the witness did not act as if William Kennedy Smith were a rapist.

Indeed, the resumptive turn foregrounds categorization work of exceptional significance. But I would be remiss to leave the formulation at this point, for the rapist category embodies more than local impeachment strategies of the defense attorney; that is to say, it encapsulates historical conditions and collective circumstances beyond the context of situated action. The rapist category works by naturalizing ideological assumptions about rapists as strangers jumping out of the bushes rather than a "normal" male who is date or acquaintance, concealing the unique dynamics of this type of sexual assault (Parrot and Bechhofer, 1991; Allison and Wrightsman, 1993). Through a myriad of linguistic and sequential resources, the defense attorney creates a turn-by-turn disjunction between category bound activities/states and the rapist category, drawing attention to the abnormality of rapists, the normality of his client, and the irrationality of the witness's actions if he were a rapist (or the rationality of her actions with a nonrapist). There is no way the witness can do "normal" things with someone who is supposed to be an "abnormal" person. In this way, we can see how social structure is mapped onto categorization work, and how categorization, in turn, is harnessed as an interpretative resource in the constitution of grammatical and sequential structures (see Watson, 1997; Jayyusi, 1984; Matoesian, 1995, 1997).

Tense and Context of Situated Action

In this final section of the paper, I wish to make a brief comment on how a poetic form of tense variation contextualizes distinct impeachment strategies in the testimonial narrative, and how it animates the sense and punctuates the significance of both categorization work and the resumptive pattern. If we look at the questions on lines 024-148, we notice that, even though they refer to matters of historical fact, the defense attorney employs the present tense in recounting the past history of the rape incident as if those events were occurring at the moment of speaking -- a tense form referred to as the historical present, (Schriffen, 1981; Wolfson, 1978, 1979, 1982; Chafe, 1994). The historical present (HP) is a sociolinguistic variable or stylistic variation in the verb/tense system that functions as a dramatic device, the way language reaches beyond referential meaning to create a hypnotic imagery and sense of excitement by drawing past events into the here and now of the present. By making the past appear more vivid and immediate, the defense attorney invites the jury to relive the witness's actions with the defendant and, in doing so, allows the jury the opportunity to evaluate the rationality or irrationality of those actions. Specifically, the witness's movements with this man would be irrational if he were a rapist.

But the HP involves more than the way historical reference acquires the deictic quality of dramatic immediacy or even the way in which language can be manipulated to serve as an internal evaluation device. According to Wolfson, the most significant feature of the HP (or what she refers to as the conversational historical present) is that it alternates with the past tense to organize the narrative into chronological episodes and that this tense variation itself -- in either direction --creates a dramatic effect.[32] With these points in hand, tense variation from past to HP and vice versa functions to contextualize shifts in the defense attorney's impeachment strategy, first from impeaching the credibility of the victim to the witness, and second from impeaching the credibility of the witness through her movements with the defendant to her verbal remarks to him. Turning to line 024 in the transcript, notice that the defense attorney switches from the past to HP in the question, "It's dark in there", which is placed just past the first resumptive sequence. But notice too that at this point his questions occur well past the shift in describing the actions of the victim to those of the witness, so that the tense alternation does not actually coincide with the shift in descriptive context. Indeed, the defense attorney shifts the descriptive context from the victim to the witness on lines 018-023, where it appears that the first resumptive sequence (and the prior contrast) is contextualizing the shift in impeachment strategy rather than the HP. Looking more closely at the data, however, while the resumption appears to shift the descriptive context from the victim to the witness, the product of that shift is not necessarily doing impeachment work of the witness -- at least not at that precise moment.[33] As mentioned previously, that the witness went into the house where the rapist is fails to resolve the question of why she went into the house, for the distinct possibility remains that she was merely unaware of his location, or if she was, she was was going there to confront him. On the other hand, the HP alternation with the past tense on line 024 aligns more closely with the onset of the impeachment process of the witness by contextualizing the movement in a dark location and the genesis of the co-helper categorization -- the process of the witness "meeting up with" the rapist -- and it is this particular information which is crucial to the defense attorney's impeachment strategy.

The defense attorney employs the HP in all the questions[34] up to the puzzle sequence on line 209, where he switches back to the past tense to recontextualize his impeachment strategy from the witness's movements with the rapist to her remark to him. The defense attorney makes the switch to the past tense immediately after the "meet up with her friends", where the alternation, first, bounds the detailing-to-death segment of testimony on the witness's movements and, second, foregrounds the initial ascent to the supreme climax initiated by puzzle sequence. That is, the tense alternation marks the final build-up to the resumptive list and the end of this segment of testimony.

In essence, the HP and alternation between the HP and the past tense adds a further layering of poetic affect to the defense attorney's questioning strategy. The HP animates and highlights key features of testimony for the jury, superimposing a temporal grid onto the spatial pathways of movement. It evaluates that testimony, forming part of the epistemological backdrop for gauging the witness's actions. And by alternating with the past, it segments that testimony into distinct episodes of narrative action, coordinating the context of impeachment strategy from the categorization of physical action to the categorization of talk. But perhaps just as important, the use of the HP illustrates how grammar interacts with the categorial and sequential orders to manage the interactional tasks of trial examination.

Conclusion

In a Court TV commentary on Roy Black's cross-examination of Ann Mercer, a panel of legal experts referred to his impeachment of the witness as a "classic" case of "devastating" cross examination. In this study, I have shown how such an intuitive sense of impeachment strategy emerges as a product of the attorney's skilled deployment of poetic devices, the improvisational wizardry of situated practice in and through which linguistic, sequential, and categorial structures interact to impose a "natural" order on the undifferentiated flux of spatial activity during the historical incident. In the process, I have shown how the linguistic and interactional stylistics of space and time reflexively organize, mediate, and elaborate the historical domain of action to accomplish impeachment work in the realtime context of trial cross-examination. From this vantage point, it is simply not enough to focus on the institutionalized distribution of asymmetrical options, the characteristics of the adversary system, or even the variation in question form as the generating force behind courtroom domination. To capture the dynamics of impeachment strategy, of detailing-to-death and making mountains out of molehills, we must consider the endogenous poetic work -- broader activity patterns unfolding and intersecting from moment-to-moment in the constitution of context -- which integrates both social identities and linguistic variables into a coherent whole and which serves as a vehicle for their imposition.

Notes

1. Psalm 115:
   They have mouths, but cannot speak,
   and eyes, but cannot see.
   They have ears, but cannot hear,
   and noses, but cannot smell.
   They have hands, but cannot feel,
   and feet, but cannot walk.
2. Parrallelism is perhaps the basic principle of poetic utterances and refers to the repetition of the same structural pattern in adjacent phrases, clauses, sentences, and sequences.
3. For an interesting study of participant continuation that occurs in conversation, see Lerner (1994).
4. Resumptive repetition also occurs intra-turn, with slight modification of this format.
5. Extract (5) on line 134 may constitute a slight exception to this, in that the who-relative is elipted.
6. See Heritage and Sorjonen (1994) for an interesting account of the notion of "activity structure".
7. For a thorough review of information structure in discourse see Lovejoy and Lance (1991).
8. By breaking apart his sentences the defense attorney gets the witness to give two affirmative answers to what is in fact only a single question.
9. Compare her hedged "I guess" answer on line 023 with her direct "yes" on line 020. Also notice her problematic answer on line 040-41.
10. "She went into the house" or "the rapist is in the house".
11. Though the resumptive repetition in extract (11) is not organized around spatialized information.
12. The forthcoming analysis is not meant to compete with more complex linguistic studies on the encoding of spatial information, the linguistic features associated with this encoding, and the ramifications for the theory of linguistic relativity. My aim is much more modest: to analyze the interactional work this information accomplishes for impeaching testimony in the trial context. For excellent studies of the former sort, much of which I draw on here, see Levinson (1992, 1994, 1996); Brown and Levinson (1993); Bloom et al. (1996); Bennett (1975).
13. He does say, however, "You went into the X [location] with this man, the man

who . . .".

14. This comitative adjunct also functions in a locative sense by indicating the witness's position relative to the rapist; it answers the "where" locative question in, "Where is Ann?" with "Ann is where the rapist is" (Lyons, 1977: 693).
15. The resumptive sequences and turns consist of the following structures: (1) [verb of motion] + [resumptive adverbial + relative clause], as in extracts (1) and (11); and (2) [verb of motion] + [adverbial] + [resumptive comitative adjunct + relative clause], in the other extracts.
16. However, in at least one instance the resumptive format occurs prior to the motion verb and spatial expression (as on line 143-144), though this type of positioning only occurs within a coordinate structure (that is, the compound subject, "You and this man who . . .") and this appears to have consequences for repetition and resumptive options across sequences.
17. As we will observe in more detail, "where the rapist is" is not as important as "who is the rapist" and the latter can only be derived from the animate complement in the adverbial or comitative adjunct. More clearly now, the locative resumptive repetition in extract 1 is the only case in this entire example where the resumptive format occurs without the animate complement ("the/this man") but occurs with the goal complement ("into the house") instead.
18. Another way to think about this is that the resumptive format may function like a "chorus" or refrain and the witness's answer seems to be saying "amen" to the "alleged" element in the defense attorney's detailed discourse rather than imparting any new information per se.
19. Notice also how the path directional links resumptive repetition to spatial-motional predicates: the first question in the resumptive format -- the feeding question on line 073 -- includes a repetition of "through the dining room" from line 064.
20. Consisting, in extract 2, of the dummy prop "it", stative verb "is", adjective, topological preposition "in" for indicating spatial inclusion, and locative complement "that house" (or the deictic adverb "there" on line 024 in extract 1).
21. Limitations of space do not permit me to go into the interactional and ideological work transacted through direct quotes. See Chafe (1994), Lucy (1993) and Matoesian (1997) for overviews.
22. Ellipsis here may involve the sentence "You go out the door and onto the beach", where the subject-verb ("You go") and the prepositional complement ("the door") are omitted.
23. Although contrasts do not have to be linguistically realized to register an ironic effect.
24. The direct quote includes the verb of saying plus quotative complement, occurring with characteristic differences in tense, number, intonation, demonstratives etc.
25. Even though animated through an embedded resumption, the question appears

functionally geared more to the suspense of the puzzle and its final -- partially repeated solution -- on line 235.

26. Or more accurately perhaps the puzzle represents a transformation from the flow of events in the historical incident to a contemporary puzzle of direct and cross examination.
27. What is just as interesting about this is the following: By not providing a solution to the puzzle which incorporates a combined justification and admission, such as hypothetically, "I sarcastically said I was sorry", the witness puts herself in the sequentially disadvantaged position of having to admit to the prior issue of merely having uttered "I'm sorry". By either rejecting or attempting to justify the issue as an isolated strategy she is vulnerable to question on the prior issue of admitting to making the statement, which is, of course, precisely what the defense attorney wants because he can then invite inferences based on the literal force of the utterance alone. On the other hand, if the witness had combined an admission with justification, then this would consist of, to some extent, what she intended by her remarks, and the puzzle was organized around initially what she said. As it turns out, however, by not beating him to the punch as it were she winds up on the defensive -- attempting to produce justifications in a blame relevant environment -- in a struggle with the defense attorney over elaborating the context of her remarks. At this point all she succeeds in accomplishing is creating a further puzzle of her own: "I didn't mean I was sorry" and "I used those words", both of which still leave open the question of her precise meaning. She never provides a solution, just a further puzzle and an allusion, while the defense attorney provides a specific candidate solution with its attendant inferences based on her utterance.
28. The first item raised by the prosecuting attorney during redirect examination of Ann Mercer dealt with the intended meaning of "I'm sorry", and as the witness indicated there her remarks were intended to be sarcastic.
29. Or are even friends, in a parallel allusion with the "meet up with your friends".
30. On line 053 "You ask the rapist to help you find her shoes".
31. Moreover, this may operate as a thoroughly unveiled allusion that the witness's actions with the defendant were similar to those of the victim.
32. See the debate or misunderstanding between Schriffin and Wolfson in the citations listed above for a discussion on the different functions of the HP.
33. Parenthetically, this first instance of resumptive repetition does not possess the spatialized prefatory component as in extracts 2-10, and now we can perhaps speculate why. In this case the resumptive sequence does not function as a climactic resolution to the progressive build up of spatialized facts but functions instead to recontextualize the defense narrative from describing the victim's actions to those of the witness.
34. On line 209, however, the defense attorney uses the HP progressive in the declarative clause, which indicates durative aspect.

References

Allison, J. and Wrightsman, L. (1993), *Rape: The Misunderstood Crime*, Sage, Newbury Park.

Atkinson, J. M. (1984), *Our Master's Voices*, Methuen, London.

Atkinson, J. M. and Drew, P. (1979), *Order in Court*, Humanities Press, New York.

Bailey, F. L. (1985), *To Be a Trial Lawyer*, John Wiley, New York.

Bechhofer,L. and Parrot,A. (1991), 'What is Acquaintance Rape?', in A.Parrot and L.Bechhofer (eds), *Acquaintance Rape: The Hidden Crime*, Andrea Parrot and Laurie Bechhofer, John Wiley, New York, pp. 9-25.

Bennett, D. (1975), *Spatial and Temporal Uses of English Prepositions: An Essay in Stratificational Semantics*, Longman, New York.

Bergman, P. (1978), 'A Practical Approach to Cross-Examination: Safety First', *UCLA Law Review*, vol.25, pp.547-576.

Bloom, P., Peterson, M., Nadel, L. and Garrett, M. (eds) (1996), *Language and Space*, MIT Press, Cambridge.

Brown, P. and Levinson, S. (1993), 'Uphill and Downhill in Tzeltal', *Journal of Linguistic Anthropology*, vol.3, pp. 46-74.

Carlson, R. and Imwinkelried, E. (1989), *Dynamics of Trial Practice*, West Publishing, St.Paul.

Chafe, W. (1994), *Discourse, Consciousness, and Time*, University of Chicago Press, Chicago.

Du Bois, J. (1992), 'Meaning Without Intention: Lessons from Divination', in J.Hill and J.Irvine (eds), *Responsibility and Evidence in Oral Discourse*, Cambridge University Press, New York, pp.48-71.

Duranti, A. (1992), 'Intentions, Self, and Responsibility: An Essay in Samoan Ethnopragmatics', in J.Hill and J.Irvine (eds), *Responsibility and Evidence in Oral Discourse*, Cambridge University Press, New York, pp.24-47.

Finnegan, R. (1977), *Oral Poetry*, Cambridge University Press, New York.

Finnegan, R. (1992), *Oral Traditions and the Verbal Arts*, Routledge, New York.

Gumperz, J. and Levinson, S. (eds), *Rethinking Linguistic Relativity*, Cambridge University Press, New York, pp.177-202.

Haydock, R. and Sonsteng, J. (1990), *Trial Theories, Tactics, and Techniques*, West Publishing, St.Paul.

Heritage, J. and Greatbatch, D. (1986), 'Generating Applause: A Study of Rhetoric and Response at Party Political Conferences', *American Journal of Sociology*, vol.92, pp.110-157.

Heritage, J. and Sorjonen, M. (1994), 'Constituting and Maintaining Activities Across Sequences: And-Prefacing as a Feature of Question Design', *Language in Society*, vol.23, pp.1-29.

Hymes, D. (1981), *'In Vain I Tried to Tell You': Essays in Native American Ethnopoetics*, University of Pennsylvania Press, Philadelphia.

Jakobson, R. (1960), 'Concluding Statement: Linguistics and Poetics', in T.Sebeok (ed.), *Style in Language*, MIT Press, Cambridge, pp.350-377.

Jakobson, R. and Pomorska, K. (1988), *Dialogues*, MIT Press, Cambridge.

Jayyusi, L. (1984), *Categorization and the Moral Order*, Routledge & Kegan Paul, Boston.

Lerner, G. (1994), 'Responsive List Construction: A Conversational Resource for Accomplishing Multifaceted Social Action', *Journal of Language and Social Psychology*, vol. 13, pp. 20-33.

Levinson, S. (1992), 'Primer for the Field Investigation of Spatial Description and Conception', *Pragmatics*,vol. 2, pp. 5-47.

Levinson, S. (1996), 'Relativity in Spatial Conception and Description', in J.Gumperz and S.Levinson (eds), *Rethinking Linguistic Relativity*, Cambridge University Press, New York, pp.177-202.

Levinson, S. and Haviland, J. (1994), 'Introduction: Spatial Conceptualization in Mayan Languages', *Linguistics*, vol. 32, pp.613-622.

Lovejoy, K. and Lance, D. (1991), 'Information Management and Cohesion in the Study of Written Discourse', *Linguistics and Education*, vol. 3, pp. 251-273.

Lucy, J. (ed.) (1993), *Reflexive Language*, Cambridge University Press, New York.

Lyons, J. (1977), *Semantics Vol. 2*, Cambridge University Press, New York.

Matoesian, G. (1993), *Reproducing Rape: Domination through Talk in the Courtroom*, University of Chicago Press, Chicago.

Matoesian,G. (1995),'Language, Law, and Society: Policy Implications of the Kennedy Smith Rape Trial', *Law and Society Review*, vol. 29, pp. 669-701.

Matoesian,G. (forthcoming), 'You Were Interested in Him as a Person? Rhythms of Domination in the Kennedy Smith Rape Trial', *Law and Social Inquiry*.

Mauet, T. (1992), *Fundamentals of Trial Techniques*, Little, Brown and Co., Boston.

Schiffrin, D. (1981), 'Tense Variation in Narrative', *Language*, vol.57, pp. 45-62.

Schiffrin, D. (1994), 'Making a List', *Discourse Processes*, vol.17, pp.377-406.

Sherzer, J. and Woodbury, A. (1987), in J. Sherzer and A. Woodbury (eds), 'Introduction', in *Native American Discourse: Poetics and Rhetoric*, Cambridge University Press, New York, pp.1-16.

Smith, D. (1978), 'K is Mentally Ill: The Anatomy of a Factual Account', *Sociology*, vol. 12, pp. 23-53.

Tanford, J. A. (1983), *The Trial Process*, The Michie Co., Charlottesville, VA.

Tannen, D. (1987), 'Repetition in Conversation: Towards a Poetics of Talk', *Language*, vol.63, pp. 574-605.

Tannen,D. (1989), *Talking Voices*, Cambridge University Press, New York.

Watson, D.R. (forthcoming), 'Some General Reflections on "Categorization" and "Sequence" in the Analysis of Conversation', in S.Hester and P. Eglin (eds), *Membership Categorization*, University Press of America, Lanham, MD.

Wolfson, N. (1978), 'A Feature of Performed Narrative: The Conversational Historical Present', *Language in Society*, vol. 7, pp. 215-237.

Wolfson, N. (1982), *CHP: The Conversational Historical Present in American English Narrative*, Foris Publications, Dordrecht.
Wolfson, S. (1979), 'The Conversational Historical Present Alternation', *Language*, vol.55, pp. 168-182.

8 Record-Keeping Practices in the Policing of Juveniles

ALBERT J. MEEHAN

"People-processing organizations" (Hasenfeld, 1972) are by necessity involved in information collection and processing through written and oral records that are brought to bear upon decisions about how individual clients are to be treated. However, records used to make decisions are also used to evaluate the productivity of staff and the organization as a whole (Seidman and Couzens, 1974; Manning, 1977). The dual character of records is particularly evident in policing, where institutional demands and expectations make accounting for acts a fundamental consideration (Pepinsky, 1976). In this respect police record work must serve at the same time organizational orders in the provision and control of services for their "clients", and administrators and outsiders such as the courts and the public in their attempts to monitor members of the organization. These conflicting organizational demands affect the sort of records kept, the type of information created in records, and the practical management of records by police patrol officers.

This article focuses on these organizational tensions as they affect and are expressing police "record work". By this concept I intend to emphasize two interrelated processes relevant to police record keeping: First, record work highlights the processes affecting how patrol officers *produce* a variety of work- and organization-relevant records. Particularly central here are the ways in which the projected organizational uses and longer-term "careers" of records shape their forms and content. Second, record work references the ways in which police officers *interpret* and infer the meaning, import, and "accuracy" of the various sorts of records they rely upon in carrying out their routine activities. As many officers note, "The record can tell you some things but not others". Describing the process whereby local background knowledge is brought to bear to determine what particular records can "tell you" comprises a second component of record work.

Research Sites and Data Collection

The data used in this discussion are drawn from a one-year field study of the police handling of juveniles in two adjoining suburban police departments.[1] This study was part of a larger three-year federally funded project examining the relevance of national standards for the police handling of juveniles in four police departments. I had primary responsibility for the project's relationship with two suburban departments and spent a total of 250 hours on ride alongs in these communities with patrol and youth bureau personnel.

Observation of record-keeping practices provided a major focus for research. I spent two weeks in the records room of each department learning the system, discussing record-keeping procedures with administrative personnel, and collecting arrest and contact records from the previous two years. Over a period of six months I spent an average of four days per week in the field. I recorded field notes of the ride alongs and interviews with administrative personnel directly after leaving the field setting. After this period of active field research, I met more occasionally with police task forces and individual officers in each department during the next four months to discuss the project's findings and to draft recommendations for the department.

The police departments I observed served two small suburban towns located outside a large northeastern city. Grandville's population is almost twice that of Hargrove's (49,000 as opposed to 26,000), although both occupy five square miles. The residents of both towns are predominately white-collar professionals, although proportionately more blue-collar workers reside in Grandville than in Hargrove. In Grandville there are more multiple-family dwellings and apartment buildings. Both towns have public housing projects that are perceived as sources of problems with young people. Very few members of racial minorities reside in either community. Each town has one high school and several middle and grammar schools. The towns have a town manager form of government, accountable to elected boards of selectmen. The selectmen exercise control over the police departments in ways equivalent to the police commissions found in larger cities.

The Grandville police department has approximately 80 sworn officers. Two detectives serve as the juvenile officers, investigating cases involving juveniles in addition to an adult caseload (the latter constituting about 35% of their caseload). One works the day shift and the other works the evening shift. These detectives are expected to patrol, especially during the evening, but do not respond to routine calls for service involving juveniles unless additional assistançe is needed or requested by patrol officers.

The Hargrove police department has approximately 60 sworn officers. Three officers (two patrol officers and a detective) serve as the department's juvenile unit. The patrol officers split their time between working the day and evening shifts, while the detective works only days. In contrast to Grandville, these officers only handle cases involving juveniles. In both towns, whenever a juvenile is arrested a juvenile officer is called to process the booking and notify parents.

Record Work in the Policing of Juveniles

Each level of police response to an incident (i.e., communications, patrol, detectives) may produce some *paper trace* of that incident. Some of these paper traces are official documents, some are more "informal documents", and others are personal records.[2]

Police officers in both Grandville and Hargrove work with a variety of official forms, including incident/arrest reports, officers' patrol logs, and dispatchers' incident cards. Officers know or assume that the use of official documents routinely extends beyond the individual who produces them. Although it is not possible to specify exactly who might use that document next, or when, or for what purpose, members of the organization can anticipate potential uses and project routine careers for an official document. Police distinguish between two general types of such projected careers: external and internal. That is, whereas some records are assumed to be accessible and primarily of interest to external agents (i.e., the courts, the mayor's office), others are assumed likely to be seen and used only or primarily by co-workers. The projection of external as opposed to internal uses of a record, and vice versa, fundamentally shapes the form and content of the resulting documents.

Other paper traces have no formal organizational status and take the form of individual or personal records. Primary examples of such records include an officer's pad, scraps of paper assembled during the course of an investigation, and, in some instances, personal jottings on or additions to official forms. This type of paper trace is a personal system of work-relevant records and an essential source of information immediately available to that individual officer.

Despite the pervasiveness of such written records, much information is "recorded" without leaving paper traces.[3] Patrol officers acquire a particularly rich stock of local work-relevant knowledge that is an essential and often utilized source of information (Bittner, 1967; Rubenstein, 1973). Such information has a "factual" and authoritative status and for all practical purposes constitutes a record. Each officer accumulates such a stock of knowledge through his or her work experiences and develops his or her own "mental dossier" (Cicourel, 1968: 668), which augments the generalized occupational knowledge of the police subculture. In addition, officers share information, and these occasions for revealing information are important interactional events. These interactional exchanges, which I call the "running record", can be conceptually distinguished from both organizational and personal written records, and provide important resources in police decision making.

While creating or producing records makes up one major component of police record work, officer practices for making sense or finding the meaning of the records produced by others proved a second critical component. For officers rarely take a record at "face value", viewing it nonproblematically as a set of objective "facts". Rather, when faced with a formal written account, officers will invoke their mental dossiers and the running record to interpret the significance of the written record for their policing. In effect, officers "read between the lines", treating the record as the product of a set of known decision-making and record-producing practices. Under these circumstances the reading of a record is reflexively informed by an understanding of the work relevancies involved in its production and of the anticipated uses guiding this production.[4]

Organizational Records and Projected External Careers

Records that organizational members assume to be available for *external* consumption (whether on a routine basis or whenever special accounting is required outside the organization) are accorded a projected external career. In policing such records include arrest reports, which are routinely forwarded to court to be used by the prosecution and defense attorneys, and traffic accident and certain other incident reports (i.e., thefts), which are routinely sent or made available to insurance companies for claims purposes.

Records with projected external careers have what Garfinkel and Bittner (1967) call contractual as opposed to actuarial uses. An actuarial use of a record seeks to derive a statistical profile. On the other hand, a record may be read as evidence of a contract between the organization and the person served; in the case of medical clinic records, Garfinkel and Bittner (1967: 199) observe, "the contents of clinic folders are assembled with regard for the possibility that the relationship may have to be portrayed as having been in accord with expectations of sanctionable performances by clinicians and patients".

Similarly, in the police context, arrest reports are assembled in ways that portray the actions taken by the police as standing in a "correct" or sanctionable relation with court honored standards of law enforcement. This assembling process may involve the selection, recasting, and, on occasion, even fabrication of "the facts" and the sequence in which they occurred. These dimensions of police record work in construction an arrest report can be examined by analyzing in close detail the following extended field observations. These field notes describe the decisional contingencies of responding to an emergent street situation, and then turn to the processes by which the arrest report framed this incident in anticipation of its likely contractual uses in the court setting.

> A call reporting youths throwing bottles was dispatched to the adjoining sector car. A second call for the same location was then dispatched reporting a possible assault in progress. The officer I was riding with (Bill Brady) was patrolling the sector dividing line, three blocks away from the address, and decided to check it out. Turning up the street where the incident had been reported, the officer stopped and rolled his window down. The sounds of glass breaking, a loud pounding noise, and people yelling could be heard. Speaking toward the direction of these sounds, the officer observed two youths walk out of a driveway, get into their car and leave the scene. The officer turned his spotlight into the driveway, where there were three youths, one of whom had a tire iron in his hand. When the light came on, they immediately ran. The officer leaped out of the car and chased them down the street and into a backyard about seven houses away. At this point, three other patrol cars arrived as Brady reappeared with one youth handcuffed. This youth was then placed in a nearby patrol car.
>
> After this, Brady said to me, "Come on, let's see what they were doing up there. I heard glass breaking". The driveway and yard were searched, but no broken glass was found. Upon leaving the yard, a citizen who had been nearby said that a window on a van down the street was broken. The van was examined and the window was cracked but still intact. "That must be it", said Brady, and he took down the license plate number. He then asked the citizen if he knew the owner, but he did not. No victim of an assault was located at the scene either, although another citizen stated to us that someone was definitely getting beaten up in this backyard.
>
> At this point a detective on the scene discussed the incident with Brady. The

> detective stated that incident was "obviously" drug related: someone reneged on a drug deal and they were settling the score. According to his "street information", the arrested youth and his friends are "known" pushers dealing to this side of town: "No one will come forward on this assault, Brady, but you can bet it was drug related". Brady agreed with his assessment and thanked him for the information.
>
> Brady parked in a parking lot several blocks away to write the report that had to be filed at the station. He then said, "I'm sure you know I'm gonna have to fudge this one. I violated a lot of procedure back there by not calling in what I was doing or taking my radio with me. But by the time I could have done any of that, those kids would have been gone. There was no way I could have waited for the sector car on the arrest".

In this situation, as in many police incidents, everything happens very quickly. In coming upon and handling this situation, the officer brought to bear a stock of background knowledge to determine what was happening. The officer pursued the youths on the grounds that the available cues on arrival (yelling, glass breaking, the youths running when he saw them) were inferably the signs of illegal actions. By contrast, Brady did not pursue the youths who were observed walking out of the driveway where the trouble was to be "discovered". Yet their presence leaving the driveway led him to examine it more carefully and thereby locate the other three youths who began running. As Brady mentioned later, "You know they were in the wrong because they blew out of there so fast". Those actions were framed in the context of receiving a call about youths breaking bottles, and a second call for the same location reporting a more serious problem (an assault). (Generally, a second dispatch to a location is assumed by officers to be indicative of more trouble.) Although at this point he did not know what the illegality was, let alone whether anything illegal actually occurred, Brady followed the standard patrol practice of responding immediately and worrying about the law and organizational procedure afterward.

This incident also displayed the use of an officer's stock of knowledge. When the detective told Brady that the person arrested was a known pusher, the incident was provided with an interpretive frame (i.e., a drug vendetta), which made it meaningful in a way that it would not have been otherwise. This interpretive frame resolved ambiguities such as the failure of the van owner to come forward at the scene and the failure to locate someone on the scene who had been beaten as reported by the dispatcher and citizen.

Moreover, for Brady and the detective the incident as originally encountered posed less a legal than a practical problem: drug deals on this side of town may be entering a violent phase, increasing the need to monitor the neighborhood and persons within it. The information shared at the scene identified drug activity and violence as the real problem and established the interpretation of the incident relevant "for us as police officers".

How the event is reconstructed for the arrest report is another matter: Brady wrote his report and gave it to me saying, "You probably won't recognize this as what you saw, but that's the way it has to be". The report stated,

> At 23:05, while on routine patrol, I responded to a call at 27 Rogers Road for youths drinking, throwing bottles, and yelling. When I arrived at the above address, I observed three youths walking down the street yelling and screaming loudly. I further observed the above suspect, Gerald McGee, with a tire iron in his hand, take the iron and smash the right rear window of a Ford van, registration number BK-7538. When the youths saw me, all three began to run down Rigers Road. I pursued them to 84 Rogers Road, where they ran into the back yard and the suspect dropped the tire iron. There I apprehended Gerald McGee, aged eighteen, advised him of his rights, and placed him in cruiser number 353, in which he was transported to the station. He is charged with malicious damage to property and being a disorderly person.

The official report on this incident bears a strained resemblance to what I witnessed. The events as they unfolded are retrospectively fitted and, where necessary, clearly altered to create the elements of what the law defines as an offense. That the youths were "guilty" was established for all practical purposes when they ran away, and this action provided the officer's grounds for pursuit and arrest. To prove guilt in court, however, requires the reconstruction and transformation of what happened into "facts" that will appear to confirm with proper legal procedure. The account is assembled with a set of "facts" that have been inferred from the behavior of the suspect, which do not in themselves constitute illegal conduct (e.g. running), a set of "facts" indicating evidence that can be produced in court (i.e., the tire iron). And a set of "facts" that are lies (i.e., Brady did not observe the three youths screaming and yelling, nor did he observe McGee break the window).

The process of inferring what happened, and of proving what happened in accordance with the rules of law, is clearly problematic to the officer. Those very inference procedures for acting in the first place are ironically constrained in the official report. Officers see themselves as having few choices in such instances and present such dishonesty as an inevitable occupational hazard and a matter of simple survival (Manning, 1977: 179;

Van Maanen, 1978: 119). As Brady commented during the ride back to the station with his report,

> I said when I came on the job that I'd never fudge a report. I heard about it in school (the academy) and all that but I said "not me". But when it comes right down to it, it's got to be done, otherwise you're liable for false arrest. You know they were in the wrong because they blew out of there so fast. And you can't let them run away like that because then they think they have control, that the cops won't do anything. But when you get in court, if you don't say you saw it, you might as well forget it.

The "drug vendetta" interpretation of the incident was also invoked to explain the subsequent fate of the case in court. The car owner was identified and summoned to court, but testified that the window had been broken two weeks prior to the incident. Indeed, this testimony served to verify the police interpretation. After the case was dismissed, the detective commented, "This is typical in drug cases. They won't testify against each other, they'll settle their scores out of court".

Organizational Records and Projected Internal Careers

Records with envisioned uses primarily or exclusively within an organizational setting may be associated with some projected internal career. Policing juveniles created three types of such records in the two departments studied: (1) the dispatcher's incident cards; (2) patrol officers' log sheets; and (3) field interrogation/observation (FIO) cards.[5] Because the Grandville department did not utilize FIO cards during the period of my field research,[6] a direct comparison of the uses of this document is not possible. Hence, the following analyses will examine only record work practices involving log sheets and incident cards.

Patrol Logs

Accounting for how time is spent on patrol is an age-old problem in policing (Rubenstein, 1973), and the "log" has been an administrative solution to this problem. The patrol log is one example of an internal record that has actuarial uses for the department. Each officer maintains a log sheet for every shift, summarizing activities such as calls for service, patrol area checks, traffic citations , and medical assists. For patrol officers, keeping the log is, first and foremost, a matter of displaying their "activity", performance, and productivity for review by superiors and administrators.[7]

While on patrol, "keeping the log" represents yet another demand on officer time that requires its own forms of creative management. That is, although all calls to which the officer is dispatched will be entered on the log (primarily because the dispatched call has an additional source of verification at headquarters), the problem for the administrator is how to hold officers accountable for how time is spent between calls. The "solution" to this problem of accountability from the patrol officer's standpoint involves manipulating "on-view" entries, that is, entries of activity initiated by an officer. There is considerable discretion in defining what constitutes an on-view activity and what entries one "needs" to make for the evening. In the police vernacular, patrol logs for a tour of duty are commonly referred to as "cheat sheets" or "my lies". Instead of recording all "on-view" activities in a manner parallel to the logging of all call responses, only those necessary to fill the time gaps between calls are recorded. Indeed, on evenings on which the officer has a large number of calls for service, there is no need to fill these gaps, even though other work that could be entered onto the log is done (i.e., assisted motorists, wrote parking tickets, conducted area checks). One evening an officer who responded to ten calls for service remarked, "No need to cheat the sheet tonight. I'm already looking like a rate buster!" Indeed, one must "appropriately" manipulate the logs to avoid making coworkers look bad and increasing the administration's expectation of productivity.

One common strategy for managing the logs is "banking" some on-views. For example, areas announced at roll call, especially ones in which citizens have complained that kids are drinking and smoking dope, are ready made "on-view entries". Indeed, officers will record area checks at these locations, even though the checks were done at different times or never checked at all. The log need only show that officers are doing something between calls.

Another tactic is to stretch the definition of an on-view entry. For example, one slow evening we were having coffee at the local coffee shop when a lost motorist asked for directions (this type of service is often rendered during a shift). At the end of the shift, while filling out the log, the officer recalled the encounter and entered it into his log as "assist motorist", a category normally reserved for helping cars that are broken down.

Log entries can also be "traded". One evening an officer stopped a car in another officer's sector for running a stop light. We were meeting this other officer to relieve the boredom of a slow night. The first officer commented, "It was such a blatant and dangerous violation I couldn't let it pass, even though it's an embarrassment to George; I shouldn't be doing this". However, George saw us (he was on his way to meet us) and pulled over. After a quick apology and explanation about the "asshole" motorist who ran the red light, the officer stated, "It's all yours, George". George chuckled, "Great, I need some of this activity". George completed the traffic stop (i.e., he notified the dispatcher of his location, called in the license plate numbers, and issued the citation) and thereby received credit for an "on-view" that had corroborated documentation at headquarters.

Because log entries are known to be the basis upon which a patrol officer's productivity will be judged by higher-ups, one might expect that officers would record all possible incidents, and perhaps even fabricate log entries, at least for those sorts of incidents for which no other record existed. Yet patrol officers are generally constrained from entering everything possible on their logs by at least two considerations: (1) officers assume they would be held accountable by administrator for higher levels of activity in the future; (2) the apparent incidence of "trouble" in the community would increase, possible leading to community and political questioning of the department's efforts.

Patrol logs in general can be treated in actuarial ways to assemble an account of the productivity not only of individual officers but also of the department as a whole. Indeed, police administrators have their own concerns with the actuarial summaries that can be produced from log entries, and upon occasion will issue directives to change log-entry practices in order to make certain problems appear and disappear in the actuarial sense. Budget requests for additional funds, for example, often rely upon statistics derived from the logs as an important source for "proving" the department's need; but given administrative directives, those log entries may not in fact have been assembled independently of making such a budgetary showing.

All in all, both patrol officers and police administrators are fully cognizant of the contingent, organizationally propelled character of log entries and of their doubtful correspondence with actual events. To take these records at face value is to draw a naive picture of police activity. Indeed, several officers advised me not to base any research on "these things", chuckling as they filled in the evening's activities.

Incident Cards

In these jurisdictions, the first paper trace in the organizational processing of an incident is the dispatcher's *incident card*. The front of the card records the time of call, the nature of the complaint, the location of the problem, the name and address of complainant (if available), the responding officer(s), and the disposition of the call. The card is time stamped at the time of the phone call, when the dispatch is made, when the officer arrives on the scene, and when the call is cleared.

Incident cards serve a number of routine management functions: they provide a record of the response time of the organization, as well as a quick count of calls for service for which a car is dispatched during the shift. But incident cards also provide critical information for actively working cases. Often this work-relevant information is not that "officially" recorded on the card. As both departments require responding officers to review and sign the incident cards they have investigated during or at the end of the shift, officers may take the opportunity to write additional comments on the backs of the cards. The opportunity to write something on the backs of incident cards is not to be minimized, especially when officers are not filing any other report. If nothing is written on the back of the card, it suggests that nothing about the call is "reportable" from the viewpoint of the officer; that is, it is a "routine" call for this type of problem.

The backs of the cards may contain a short description of "what happened", a name (sometimes a witness or possible suspect), or a "fact", such as the size of a window found broken on the scene. For this reason, they are reviewed daily by the detective bureau (which includes the juvenile officers). Detectives, administrators, and other patrol officers use these comments in follow-up investigations of incidents. As one officer observed, "Especially if the incident didn't require a report, this is the only information you have to go on short of tracking down the guy and asking him about it". During an investigation of widespread vandalism, for example, a juvenile officer reviewed incident cards covering a period of about three weeks to see if there were any pattern or additional information responding patrol officers may have noted. While reviewing these cards the officer commented,

> The front of the card tells you nothing. You'd have to read a lot into it to figure out what happened on the call, and even then you may not know. But if the guy writes something on the back of the card, you have a better idea about what went on and you know it means something to him if he took the time to put it down.

In a sense, the front of the incident card serves the administration's schema for accountability and control, whereas the back of the card may contain work-relevant information for any interested party within the organization. Put differently, the front of the card contains information on processing time, sector car assigned, and offense category, whereas the back of the card can provide information for "making sense" of the formal information on the front. Indeed, information will be recorded on the backs of cards exactly for this purpose:

> One evening a patrol officer entered the detective bureau and asked the juvenile officer if he had heard about the car fire. The juvenile officer said no. The patrol officer then reported that he had responded to an incident where a small fire had been started under a car. Upon arrival, he observed two juveniles (both age 12). One juvenile was under the car and another was standing by the car. The two admitted to the officer that they started the fire but it was an "accident". They reported that some crackerjacks (a cap similar to those put into toy guns) had sparked and began burning the leaves under the car. The officer knew one of the youths (who was related to a doctor in town) and obtained the name of the other. The officer warned them about the danger of playing under the car, how the fire could have let to an explosion, and then sent them on their way. It was unclear whether the caps could have started the fire, but there was no other evidence (e.g. matches) to suggest otherwise. The patrol officer asked the juvenile officer if something else should be done about the incident since there was no complainant. The juvenile officer said "let it go" since there was no complaint, and suggested to the officer that he talk to the parent. The juvenile officer then instructed the patrol officer to put the juveniles' names on the back of the dispatch card and that if something else came of it, he (the juvenile officer) could follow it up with a report.

In this instance, the juvenile officer would know what the names on the back of the card "meant" in relation to the event reported on the front. Specifically, the names identify the juveniles as "suspects" (whereas names could also indicate witnesses) and index the officer's report of the incident. Thus, while no "official" report is filed, an official report could be generated from the incident card in the event that the car owner complained (or something else occurred). It is not the case that this type of record is hidden from the public and therefore is for police use only. Rather, it is because this type of record is never used by the public (e.g., courts, attorneys, insurance companies), that it becomes a place to note information *for the police*.

Although juvenile officers rely heavily upon incident cards, reviewing them daily for information that has no "official" report status yet might be consequential for their work, incident cards are not limited to such internal uses. For summary information from the shift's composite of incident cards is transferred to the department blotter by the officer in charge during or at the end of the shift. The daily blotter, summarizing calls for service and arrest activity, is one of the most public police records, available by law to any member of the public upon request and routinely used by the local newspaper to monitor police activities. In this sense incident cards, while central if unremarkable internal records, are also crucial for the construction of a record that has possible external relevance and contractual uses. The projected external career of incidents that get recorded on the blotter thus shapes both the handling of incident cards and the process of entering information from such card on the blotter.

Incident cards can be managed in different ways at different points in the police response to keep certain information off the blotter. The dispatcher can simply not fill out a card. In one instance dispatch received repeated calls about youth drinking over several nights from one neighborhood. The dispatcher concluded that neighbors had organized a "call in" program to get the police to patrol the area more frequently and stopped filling out incident cards on such calls.

At the patrol level, I was told that "on occasion" I may see incident cards ripped up by patrol officers to keep incidents off the blotter. And although I never directly observed an instance of this, almost every officer whom I asked to discuss the ins and outs of the blotter recounted how at one time or another they had ripped up cards to "bury" minor incidents (e.g. drinking) "as a favor" to the persons involved or even to another officer. The most serious instance of burying a case was reported by an officer who had investigated the sexual assault of a girl by her boyfriend. Both the girl and the boy were the children of two prominent politicians who were friends of the police chief. He had destroyed the incident cards "as a favor to the chief" but showed me several detailed incident reports documenting his investment, which he kept in his own personal file.

A more common practice for managing the blotter involves defining the nature of the incident. The officer in charge, who transfers information into the blotter from these cards, has considerable discretion in redefining the nature of the incident for the blotter. For example, a 15-year-old juvenile who had considerable "mental problems" had taken his parents' auto without permission, driven onto the lawn of his ex-girlfriend's house, and sped recklessly through residential areas. The youth reported to his parents (who had informed the police) that he was contemplating suicide. When he was finally apprehended, he was released to his parents, who promised to call the youth's psychiatrist. When it came time to enter the incident card, which had initially been coded "stolen auto: using without permission", the officer in charge commented to the responding officer, "If we call it a stolen auto, that's not technically true because the parents won't press charges. If we call it a mental case, it'll have the address here and embarrass the parents. Why don't we just call it 'trouble with son'?" This decision reflects a sensitivity to possible legal implications for the organization as well as to the personal circumstances of the parents and youth.

When records have a projected external career, they will be primarily accountable to formal legal and organizational expectations and will be taken at face value. Indeed, they are designed to fulfill these expectations. The attention given to the contractual use of arrest reports is evidenced by the review they are given by a patrol officer's superiors, who will require an officer to rewrite an arrest report in order to "cover one's ass" and/or make the charge "stick in court" (Manning, 1977: 191; Van Maanen, 1978: 126-127). Although such a record can be used internally and interpreted "between the lines", this possible interpretation does not define its production. Similarly, records with internal careers differ greatly in form and content. Although these could be used externally, it is questionable what use could be made of them by outsiders as they do not provide an "objective" account to be taken at face value. Rather, they depend upon an interpretive "between the lines" reading and access to the organizational routines and expectations that define their production and are presupposed in such a reading.

Personal Resources: Individual Records

"Official" forms of the organization are not the only written documents that are important records. Personal records, such as officers' pads as well as other "scraps of paper" that are invariable produced over the course of an investigation, are also important sources of information. The officer relies upon these to construct official reports or to trigger his or her memory about individuals and incidents.

For example, the juvenile officer in Hargrove kept a file of all active and closed cases he generated during the month. He offered this explanation of a piece of paper in this file containing only a date and a phone number: "[This is] a situation where four kids in a family whose parents are never home have been seen running around the neighborhood at all hours of the night. The neighbors have been complaining. These kids will be a neglect case soon enough". Although the officer did not file an official report on the incident, he did count it at the end of the month as a neglect case in his official departmental report, which is forwarded to the state. Of interest is how the event is and is not a "case" just yet: officially on record, there is nothing to suggest that the situation exists; yet unofficially, the details of the reported event and the elements of it as a possible case in the future are available and triggered by the notes on the piece of paper.

It is not uncommon to find notes on desks and in the case files of officers. Indeed, they are typically used to construct the "official" report, a copy of which is usually attached in the file. The meaning of these pieces of paper necessarily relies upon the individual officer's interpretation and recounting of the original context of its production. Thus, making sense of them depends upon having direct access either to the event or to the officer's account of the event. However, such accounts, as in the above example, stand as quite "factual" and real matters to the officer. In this sense such personal records, despite their lack of official basis, their brevity, and their often idiosyncratic nature, have significant organizational relevance.

The organizational relevance of such personal records is illustrated by the use of the officer's pad in the court context. While the pad provides a source of information for the officer's own use (in preparing reports, etc.), some officers anticipate its use in courts and the potential challenges it might encounter. In this sense, the pad can have both internal and external career, and entries into it may be made with both possibilities in mind:

> Whatever entries you make are memory joggers. You see, everyone has their own system, their own code and you can look at this (pointing to the pad) and not know what any of it means. Now some guys will use it on the stand (in court), but that can be dangerous once you pull it out, the defense can look at it because now it is part of the record in court at the point. That's why you develop little tricks. For example, never write the same way, don't make entries in the same direction, move from one page to the other writing on different sides of the page. You know why? See my elastic band here? That's a marker that I use so that the attorney, if he takes the book, can only go forward, not backward into the book. If you write in different directions, he has to flip the book around trying to make sense of it all, and he looks quite foolish up there, aside from the fact that it's mostly unintelligible to begin with. So it's useless to him. So you develop these techniques. Of course, when I go on the stand I like to be prepared so I don't have to use it. At this point the officer began to recite a litany of times, dates, and

> facts about an incident and said, "If you asked me about that three days ago, I couldn't tell you all of that, but it's all here in the book".

Police administrators have long realized the value of officers maintaining their own records. Thus, officers in Grandville were required to carry a pad that the department issued to them. The use of pads was common in both jurisdictions. A new officer assigned to the juvenile bureau showed me his pad, which contained the names of all juveniles he encountered during the first three months of this assignment. This included not only suspects and victims but anyone he encountered in patrol. He justified this practice on the grounds that he needed to know the "population".

The pad is used to document past experiences with youths who have been "given a break" or to assemble information about situations that may require police attention in the future.

> One evening, while an officer was observing a car whose owners were suspected of dealing drugs in a park, several obviously intoxicated female youths were leaving the park after it officially closed. The officers stopped them and asked, "What was the attraction in the park?" To which they replied, "Nothing, we just like the park after dark". He put their names in his book, next to the name of the park, the date, and the van plate number. As he was doing this, one of them asked, "Oh, are you putting this down somewhere, like will our parents find out?" "No" the officer said "it goes no further than here. You can be in the park until ten, the next time you're in there after ten you'll be arrested for trespassing".

Although it goes no further than the book, this information is nonetheless "on record". And the officer's concern is with the association of the girls with the car (i.e. "They may be using drugs, or are being used by the drug dealer"), not with the violation of the local ordinance of which he informed them.

Personal Resources: The Running Record and the Mental Dossier

Whereas the courts, the public, and social researchers have relied upon written accounts for information about crime and the police, the police themselves in their routine activities overwhelmingly use verbal exchanges as their critical sources of information. In talk with one another, whether in more formal reports or in fleeting exchanges, officers learn about recent events and individuals as well as about continuing departmental lore. In such common conversational activities as bitching, bantering, complaining, and telling "combat stories" officers assemble, disseminate and hence create a stock of knowledge about local individuals and situations to which I will refer as the *running record.*

The running record is an oral history of persons, places, and incidents constructed by virtue of the police officer's access to the everyday activities of individuals. The stock of accumulated knowledge about individuals, the places they inhabit, and events that occur within those places constitutes the running record. The running record also includes the ongoing monitoring of events within the department, as the politics of the work environment often has an impact upon the work of officers.

The running record can be conceptually distinguished from an officer's "mental dossier", the term used by Cicourel (1968) to refer to the personal recollection of events or persons. The running record is a collaboratively produced and shared reporting of persons and events. Whereas the mental dossier is particularly important for recalling events, the running record is an occasion for revealing selected aspects of one's mental dossier on an individual, place, or event. In doing so officers share with one another their knowledge, display their expertise with respect to the situation, and effectively present themselves as trustworthy coworkers.

Officers do not share all they know, reveal all their expertise, or care to present themselves as trustworthy all the time. Cliques within the department, whether following patrol/detective, "brass"-front line, or even internal union divisions, all contribute to this. Clearly, information sharing is shaped by political alliances and personal disagreements among officers. Thus, by withholding participation in the running record, officers can reveal their colleagues to be incompetent, not trustworthy, or ignorant of the ways to police the streets. Indeed, the running record attains its legitimacy and authority by virtue of participant's decisions in the first place to share information in an environment in which information is invaluable but not usually shared. Thus, although a written record attains its legitimacy because it is impersonally produced and read (i.e., is available to "anyone"; Wheeler, 1969), the running record is valued exactly because it is not available to just anyone.

In the following example, two officers discuss an arrest that had occurred one hour into the evening shift. Neither officer was personally involved in the arrest. Yet one can see how the running record on "Kirkin" is a collaboratively produced history of this youth's prior encounters with the police:

Sgt: Who was that they arrested?
Off: Barry Kirkin.
Sgt: For what?
Off: Driving under [driving under the influence of alcohol].
Sgt: Good ol' Barry, this will mean his license again I'm sure.
Off: He's lucky e didn't kill anybody. There were a lot of kids running around the project at that time.
Sgt: Did he give them a hard time?
Off: No, he was more upset at himself once he realized what might have happened. He was looking like he might try punching a hole in the wall.
Sgt: He should be upset, he just got his license back.
Off: Yeah, he had the green paper. He was coming back from a cousin's wedding. He must have really been crocked. He's not a bad kid though.
Sgt: I know, the parents are just as nice as can be.
Off: Yeah I know them. His mother is a good person.
Sgt: Yeah, they're both nice people. But Barry, I don't know where he went wrong.
Off: Well, he's got that problem.
Sgt: He's got *problems*. It's not just the booze that's doing it to him. Anyone who would jump head first into an empty swimming pool has got more than just a booze problem.
Off: Broke his neck then, didn't he?
Sgt: Yeah, but he's never quite straightened out.
Off: You had him a while back didn't you?
Sgt: January 9 [this is June]. He was quite upset at us then, not himself. Maybe this time he will learn something.
Off: Well, he won't be driving. What do you think will happen to him?
Sgt: This time, they may put him in a special court program for fifteen days. Then he'll be put on probation.

The officers assess the current arrest in light of previous arrests (including the exact date of the last arrest), the youth's demeanor toward the police, his family circumstances, and the apparent incongruence between a good family and a youth with problems. His problems, as manifested by diving into the empty swimming pool, reflect more than just alcohol. Furthermore, his behavior is not explained by "family problems", as the parents are nice people. Rather, Kirkin becomes known on the running records as just plain crazy.[8]

The running record is also evoked at key points in decision making. In the following example an officer discusses with another officer a 16-year-old juvenile apprehended for shooting fire rockets from a "doctored" highway flare over the roof of a supermarket:

> Off 2: What's his name?
> Off 1: Paul Brisbane. You know him?
> Off 2: Lives up on Prescott Road?
> Off 1: Yeah there are several Brisbanes up around there. Wasn't his brother the peepster [peeping Tom]?
> Off 2: Yeah, if it's the same family, the address sounds right.
> Off 1: I was going to bring him to the station, but he came over to the car voluntarily. I don't know, maybe I should just bring him home. How are the parents, cooperative?
> Off 2: Yeah, they were the last time.
> Off 1: Okay, we'll drive up there then.

The youth was brought home and released to his parents with a warning to stay out of trouble.

Here the running record is used to assess the viability of handling the situation by taking the juvenile home. Taking a juvenile home always involves anticipating parental reaction: Are the parents going to challenge the officer and side with their child, or will they believe the officer? Officers openly acknowledge that parental cooperation is important in their handling of juveniles. Offices stated that they would arrest juveniles whose parents had reputations for challenging the police. By making these parents come to the station, the police can define the situation on their own turf, and the degradation ceremony of processing the arrest and release to the parents gives the police more control. This information about parents and their reputations is gleaned from the running record. As one officer simply states, "The word gets around".

The running record, in combination with officers' mental dossiers, is also used to assess the meaning and relevance of the information provided in written records or by other officers. The following examples illustrate this process.

Knowledge of the Person

Officers "test" a report's account against their own prior experiences with the person involved; reports that do not mesh with knowledge of that person are treated more skeptically. For example, one evening the juvenile officer was processing Deveau, a juvenile just arrested for drinking in public with whom he had several previous contacts. This juvenile was considered "trouble", and his name was well known in the department.[9] Upon reading the report, which stated that the youth had been observed drinking beer in the park with his girlfriend and had refused to leave the area, the juvenile officer commented, "It didn't sound like something that kid would do; he isn't that dumb to refuse to leave the area when the officer gives him the chance".

The juvenile officer then spoke to the youth, who said he was making out with his girlfriend and had been harassed by the police. During this exchange the officer stood close to the juvenile, and later commented that the youth didn't smell like he had been drinking but had probably taken some drug. The juvenile officer then contacted the arresting officer, who stated that he came upon Deveau and his girlfriend making out (i.e., kissing) while he was responding to a call about youths dumping barrels in the park:

> So I told them they had to leave because the park closes at ten, and Deveau, acting like a big man, says they're not going to because they're not doing anything. Then next to the bench they're on, there is somebody's empty bottles of beer in a six-pack. But some of the bottles have beer in them too. I don't think it was their beer though. Deveau grabs one of these beers, opens the top, and says, "This ain't mine, but I want it anyway", and takes a sip. So I said, "Screw you", and placed him under arrest.

This account confirmed the juvenile officer's initial suspicion that the report was incongruous with his knowledge of the arrested youth.

Knowledge of the Reporting Officer

Among their colleagues, police officers are known for their specialties. An officer's pattern of law enforcement is typified by coworkers, and these patterns are brought to bear upon the reading of a report generated by that officer. "Some guys are into traffic cites (moving violations); not me", reported one officer. "I'm into house breaks", reported another; "I like to stop suspicious cars acting funny in neighborhoods. Pinched some thieves last week...[I] leave the drinking [arrests] to somebody else". Some officers tolerated no drinking whatsoever, and would arrest regardless of the persons involved (to the surprise of some other officers). One sergeant was described as "a no-bullshit- arrest-type officer; if he arrests you, you really had to be doing something wrong!" Another officer was known to his colleagues as a nice guy but a "hothead", who was easily ticked off and made bad arrests.

Records are read in light of such knowledge of the officer involved, a practice that enables officers to reconcile incongruities. For example, if a juvenile not known on the running record as a "troublemaker" is arrested for disorderly conduct by the "hothead", the officer's reputation tends to inform the reading given the incident and to mitigate the guilt attributed to the youth.

In the following example, the juvenile officer met with the parents of one youth who had been arrested with a friend for breaking and entering and larceny earlier in the shift. The officer's report stated that the youths were observed climbing out of the school window and that one of the youths had in his possession the microscope and audio tapes that were taken from the building.

> The mother kept asking,"Which boy had the stolen objects in his possession?". The juvenile officer could not answer that question except to say, "According to the report both youths were observed coming out of the building. Regardless of who had the objects, ma'am, he was trespassing in the building". The juvenile officer then left the bureau and went to the dispatcher and requested that the arresting officer come into the station. While at dispatch he commented, "This case stinks, it sounds like a dump job to me. Paul [the arresting officer] is not that sloppy". The arresting officer came into the juvenile bureau and, after asking the parents to describe their son, reported that the other youth had the objects in his hands. After the parents left, the juvenile office instructed the officer to write this "fact" into the report. The arresting officer then stated apologetically, "Look Pete, I just came on duty when I got a call to go up to the school. Riley [the veteran day officer, who was just finishing his shift] stumbled into these two coming out of the building. So he grabs them and dumps them on me saying, 'Arrest these two, I'm going home'. So I didn't get all the information. I don't know if their kid had the stuff or not. But I could see you were in a tight situation". The juvenile officer thanked him for his help and commented to me after the officer left, "I could tell it was a dump job by the time of day [i.e., shift change] and the fact that Paul is very thorough. We do favors like this, but sometimes it could cause trouble".

The juvenile officer's between-the-lines reading of the report takes into account his knowledge of that officer's reputation and aspects of the organization (i.e., shift change) that clearly had an impact on the official record of the incident. Interestingly, when challenged by the parent (i.e. an outsider), he sticks to a face value reading of the report, even though he is certain that the incident could not have happened in that way. He thereby preserves the organization's "front", without exposing the complexities of the "backstage".

Conclusion

For many purposes official records are assumed to stand as nonproblematic, objective accounts of events. This view decontexts such records, treating them simplistically as merely accounts of those events, and ignoring the practical organizational and personal circumstances within which they are produced. But records can also be understood as products of the organizational context within which they are generated, including those schemes of accountability enforced in that context. In this case the accounts that records render are seen as part of the very same organizational circumstances they are describing. As Buckholdt and Gubrium have emphasized (1983: 249-250), "All accounting schemes produce descriptions that, while they are about clients and what is being done to and for them, are embedded in and reflect practical organizational concerns and realities". In this respect records document (or can be read as a documenting) not simply the events and incidents they presumably merely describe, but these very organizational concerns are realities.

In a number of ways, the police recognize and are sensitive to the organizational qualities of their own records and record-keeping practices. Officers are only too aware that in producing records they are creating documents of their own performance as well as of those whom they encounter. As competent organizational actors, they then routinely take care to shape these records in ways that will promote the evaluations of this performance that they desire. In this way, police officers orient as record keepers to the prospective uses of the documents they produce, uses that have their locus both within and without the police department itself.

One implication is that an understanding of the police use of records is indispensable to an interpretation of what any particular record "really" means. This implication holds not only for researchers trying to analyze police records, as Kitsuse and Cicourel (1963) insisted some years ago, but also for police officers themselves when attempting to use and understand the meaning of records in their own routine work.

A second and related implication is that a complete and rich understanding of police work requires attention to the ways in which officers author, use, and read documents. It is not merely that records happen to reflect a range of practical and organizational concerns other than or in addition to "correspondence to what happened". Rather, these concerns explicitly inform and infuse the ways in which police code and decode their records. Indeed, the skillfully deployed knowledge of the organizationally embedded nature of records to write and read documents comprises an important dimension of their competence as organizational actors. This article has sought to make this knowledge and these skills visible.

Notes

1. This research was funded by a grant from the Office of Juvenile Justice and Delinquency Prevention. Access to the police departments was negotiated by full-time project staff, including myself. All of the data collected are subject to a confidentiality requirement ensuring the anonymity of all participants. Consequently, names of persons and places have been changed.
2. Although the types of records produced by the police differed slightly in Grandville and Hargrove, I will for the most part ignore these differences in the analyses that follow (but see note 5). For these variations did not fundamentally affect the relationship between the form and content of records and their projected organizational career.
3. Although the written record has attained prominence in American society, nonwritten records can still serve as a primary basis for decision making. Yet written records possess a number of characteristics that differentiate them as a type of information from "informal" communication. After Wheeler (1969: 5), these characteristics include

   "-a legitimacy and authority usually lacking in more informal types of communication;
   -a permanence that is generally lacking in informal communication;
   -a physical transferability that can create a career for the record;
   -a capacity for facelessness that is missing from interpersonal communication; and
   -a combinatorial capacity in which records from different sources can create a composite profile independent from the original purposes for collection".
4. Although the data and arguments presented here deal specifically with police record-keeping practices vis-a-vis juveniles, there are strong grounds for suggesting that similar tendencies mark much police work with adults. First, I necessarily observed a number of police encounters with adults while on ride alongs with patrol officers in Grandville and Hargrove, since only juvenile officers deal more or less exclusively with youth. Many of the record-keeping concerns and practices were similar to those typical of juvenile cases. Second,

in prior field research on the policing of juveniles in two larger jurisdictions, and in subsequent study of police handling of the mentally ill in Madison, Wisconsin, I observed processes similar to those described here.

5. Field interrogation/observation cards (FIO) are used in the Hargrove department for recording the suspicious, but not necessarily illegal, activities of a person whom officers interrogate or observe in the field. These cards document contact for which, in the normal scheme of paperwork, officers would not be required, or do not have the desire, to write a more lengthy incident report. Those FIOs involving juveniles are routinely forwarded to the juvenile bureau. In this way, the FIOs are used to record many contacts between patrol officers and juveniles when no other record with a possible external career is routinely created.
6. Although the Grandville department did not utilize FIOs during the period of my research, they had been in use five years prior to this time. Approximately one year after my field work, the department reinstated the use of FIO cards. The Grandville juvenile officers did have a "contact" card system. While FIO cards allow the Hargrove police to maintain information on all contacts, whether or not they involved illegal activity, contact cards in Grandville are generated when an official report involving a juvenile is filed (e.g., incident/arrest report). Nevertheless, the cards provided a place to record information such as distinguishing physical features, school, marital status, current offense, and the disposition of the offense by the courts and penciled in notes about a particular juvenile (e.g., "subject is retarded"). In this way, the contact cards serve an important intelligence function. They are filed alphabetically, allowing the juvenile officers to have their own record of all contacts with the juvenile during the past several years. An important use of the contact card was to maintain a record of how many "breaks" a juvenile had been given by the department (i.e., cases in which the juvenile was arrested and formally booked, then released with a warning without forwarding the case to court).
7. As Rubenstein (1973: 44) notes for the Philadelphia police, log entries are read and evaluated for how much "activity" an officer has generated during a particular shift. In Philadelphia the major categories of "activity" include such proactive interventions as "meters" (parking-meter tickets), "parkers" (illegal parking), and "movers" (motor-vehicle code violations). As Rubenstein (1973: 44) argues,

   > "Activity" is the internal product of police work. It is the statistical measure which the sergeant uses to judge the productivity of his men, the lieutenant uses to assure himself that the sergeant is properly directing his men, the captain to assure himself that the sergeant is properly directing his men, the captain to assure his superiors that he is capably administering his district, the department administrators to assure the public that their tax dollars are not being squandered.
8. Later that evening Kirkin tried to commit suicide in his cell, an action that

confirmed this assessment. Indeed, one of these officers referred to "crazy Kirkin" while instructing a younger officer in techniques for properly searching a prisoner to avoid such problems.

9. For a police officer, the more often a name is mentioned in the context of police work, the more memorable and significant it becomes. Some officers write down the name of every person they encounter; others pride themselves in just knowing names and the "family" history. One officer, upon stopping a group of juveniles trespassing on town property, asked each to identify himself. He later commented, "I recognized some of the names, but not as *offenders*". Recognizing the name supplies additional information for assessing the report's credibility even if the officer has never had contact with that person. Consequently, names of known trouble makers have a special status independent of any personal experience.

References

Bittner, E. (1967), 'The police on skid-row: a study of peace keeping', *American Sociological Review*, vol. 32, pp. 699-715.

Buckholdt, D. and Gubrium,J. (1983), 'Practicing accountability in human service institutions', *Urban Life*, vol.12, pp. 249-268.

Cicourel, A. (1968), *The Social Organization of Juvenile Justice*, John Wiley, New York.

Garfinkel, H. and Bittner,E. (1967), 'Good organizational reasons for "bad" clinic records', in H. Garfinkel (ed.), *Studies in Ethnomethodology*, Prentice-Hall, Englewood Cliffs, N.J., pp. 186-207.

Hasenfeld, Y. (1972), 'People processing organization: an exchange approach', *American Sociological Review*, vol. 37, pp. 256-263.

Kitsuse, J.I. and Cicourel,A.V. (1963), 'A note on the use of official statistics', *Social Problems*, vol. 11, pp. 131-139.

Manning, P. (1977), *Police Work: The Social Organization of Policing*, MIT Press, Cambridge, MA.

Meehan, A. J. (1983), 'For the record: interactional and organizational practices for producing police records on juveniles', Ph.D. dissertation, Boston University.

Pepinsky, H. (1976), 'Police patrolman's offense reporting behavior', *Journal of Research in Crime and Delinquency*, vol. 13 , pp. 33-47.

Rubenstein, J. (1973), *City Police*, Farrar, Starus, Giroux, New York.

Seidman, D. and Couzens, M. (1974), 'Getting the crime rate down: political pressure and crime reporting', *Law and Society Review*, vol. 8, pp. 457-493.

Van Maanen, J. (1978),'Kinsmen in repose: occupational perspectives of patrolmen', in P. Manning and J. Van Maanen (eds), *Policing: A View from the Street*, Goodyear, Santa Monica, CA.

Wheeler, S. (1969), *On Record: Files and Dossiers in American Life*, Russell Sage, New York.

9 Justice as a Phenomenon of Order: Notes on the Organization of a Jury Deliberation

DOUGLAS W. MAYNARD AND JOHN F. MANZO

This paper concerns a jury and how it develops and uses a notion of "justice" in the course of deciding whether to convict or acquit a criminal defendant. Because "justice", as a concern for a person's due allotment of benefits and burdens, has such a venerable history in law, philosophy, psychology, sociology, and other disciplines, we wish to review its traditional treatment, at least within the social sciences. Our approach to the topic is very different. It may help develop a proper theoretical understanding of justice in sociology, but only if our enterprise is understood in relation to the traditional treatment and on its own terms. In relation to the tradition, we argue that sociology has not yet found justice as a real social phenomenon, but only presumptively invoked the concept as an abstraction and as a guide to empirical investigation. On its own terms, our investigation is an attempt to recover justice as a "phenomenon of order" (Garfinkel, 1988). Thus, as a meaningful and usable concept in a situation where members engage in the practicalities of making a decision, justice exists in the concreteness of their locally produced and naturally organized actions.

In sociology, an *explicit* concern with justice, roughly translated as "fairness" or "equity", traverses various sub-areas ranging from social psychology to the sociology of law and studies of courtroom decision-making. As well, justice is an *implicit* theme in other areas where theories of inequality motivate the understanding and investigation of social phenomena such as stratification (Rytina, 1986). Whatever the approach, and however explicit or implicit, scholars characteristically employ or impute some model of justice in evaluating, or seeing how others evaluate, the fairness or equality of some specific social system.

Several of such models predominate. Distributive justice refers to the apportionment of scarce goods, such as wealth. Procedural justice concerns the means whereby parties resolve conflicts of various kinds. Finally, there is the distinction, dating at least to Aristotle and articulated sociologically in Weber's famous discussion of bureaucracy, between formal and substantive justice. Formal justice is embodied in the principle of equality before the law and is no "respecter of persons", dictating that parties' background and circumstances are relevant in decision-making only to the extent that they pertain to something that legal or other rules specify. Substantive justice is sensitive to the abstractness, inflexibility, and consequent distance of legal and other rules from particularities in concrete cases, and aims to make allocations on the basis of social values and all that can be known about an individual case.

Thus, with regard to both distributive justice (e.g. Blau, 1964; Homans, 1961, 1974) and procedural justice (e.g. Deutsch, 1975; Leventhal, 1980; Thibaut and Walker, 1975), researchers examine how subjects, by evaluating the relative disparity of what they receive as compared to what they deserve, attribute justice to a situation. This can involve power and control over decision-making (a concern with procedure) or the content of the decision itself (distributive matters). With regard to formal justice, students of criminal sentencing use it as standard in determining whether defendants are convicted and punished for who they are as much as for what they have done. The supposition is that defendants should be treated according to the legal seriousness of their offenses and without regard to age, race, socioeconomic status, gender or other "extra-legal" attributes (see the discussion in Maynard, 1984: Chapter 7). Scholars concerned with substantive justice, on the other hand, have concentrated on plea negotiation, arguing that it embodies the attempt to tailor general laws and the penalties they stipulate to the specifics of acts, persons and circumstances (Newman, 1966; Rosett and Cressey, 1976).

To repeat, the pattern across these diverse subfields and studies is for social scientists to impute some model of justice and to measure either actors' conformity with it or their use of such a model in perceiving a situation to be just or unjust. We can draw an analogy between "justice" and "rationality" here. Both Schutz (1943) and Garfinkel (1967) have argued that rationality has a plethora of meanings (e.g. reasonable, deliberate, planned, logical, etc.), any of which investigators can use as a template to assess how rational human action is. In traditional game theory, for instance, Von Neumann and Morgenstern (1947) define rationality as behaving, in actual conditions of choice, according to pre-established criteria. In Schutz's (1943) and Garfinkel's (1967) view, approaches like this neglect how actors perform rationally in everyday life, where they seldom, if ever, follow some abstract definition or template. Rather, they behave in line with typifications, "recipes", or pieces of commonsense knowledge, as undergirded by presuppositions to the effect that such knowledge is mutually shared and required for application to concrete choices. When people use typifications properly, it acts as a claim of rationality for which they expect to receive confirmation and ratification. Moreover, according to such commonsense reasoning and "everyday rationality", --i.e., from within their ordinary interactive and discursive experiences--participants search for the ways in which their choices will accord with a retrospective interpretation of the outcomes such choices produce as having a rational history. In other words, there is an orientation to rationality among the members of society, but it cannot be separated from their temporal activities of now adducing a plethora of criteria for some loosely adumbrated decision and later, under the auspices of the realized decision, selectively reviewing and even recasting the criteria that produced it. In performing this way, members again anticipate upholding others and being supported themselves. This perspective implies that, beyond being an object of professional theoretical conceptualization and a means for specifying testable hypotheses, rationality is a phenomenon for society's members to administer. Sociological analysis could therefore concentrate on such member-produced practical orientations to and displays of rationality.

Parallel to rationality, justice has been a model and resource for sociological inquiry. Either social psychologists study justice judgments, hypothesizing that persons' perceptions of justice are determined by varying attributions of cause and responsibility in concrete situations (e.g. Cohen, 1982:119), or students of criminal justice use formal and substantive criteria as metrics for determining how equitable the processing of defendants is. Accordingly, in traditional social science, justice is something of an <u>archetype</u> for both members and professionals and therefore phenomenally as elusive as the collective sentiments on which it is based. A different approach, as we have said, is to treat justice as a "phenomenon of order" (Garfinkel, 1988), which, to the extent that it is sociologically real, exists empirically in the workings--that is, in the talk and actions--of ordinary society. The ordinary society here is a jury, and we analyze how its members strategically introduce and develop "justice" as a procedural part of determining the fate of a criminal defendant.[1]

Background

Our approach follows Garfinkel's (1967:113) study of the "actual practices" of deliberation in investigating naturally-occurring (rather than experimentally-controlled) interactional phenomena that traditional investigations of legal and other decision-making processes have largely ignored. We wish our ethnomethodological approach to make two theoretical contributions to the sociological understanding of justice. First, the overwhelming bulk of jury research examines the effects of social structural variables (gender, age, class, race) on deliberative outcomes. This is because of a preoccupation with causal analysis and a presupposition that social organization inheres mostly in the hypothesized relation between externally-based matters and some momentary interactive product, such as a decision for guilt or innocence. Our strategy, by contrast, is to analyze the deliberative process to capture that real social organization which is intrinsic to conversational and other aspects of the interaction. It may be that social structural statuses of one sort or another can eventually be mapped onto the practices we identify (for discussion, see Maynard, 1988:317; Schegloff, 1987; West and Zimmerman, 1985). However, the immediate invocation of social structural or other variables clearly obviates appreciation of forms of practical action that lie in constitutive particulars and details of actual deliberative proceedings.

Stated slightly differently, our concern is captured by Pomerantz and Atkinson (1984:287), who point out that "ethnomethodological research sets out to describe how human behaviour works, rather than to explain why some particular type of behavior occurs". It can be added that the how question might precede the why question, in that outcomes which are similar when separated from the paths of their production, may be embedded in quite different forms of social organization that constitute these paths. Causal analysis, then, might benefit from investigations that treat outcomes as aspects of real rather than hypothesized social organizational relationships. Concern with real, situated relationships, however, is not to be equated with simply identifying or describing the particularities of a decision (cf. Pomerantz and Atkinson, 1984:295-6). It is meant to capture and analyze those methods and practices of decision-making that infuse those particularities as organizational activities (Garfinkel, 1988).

Secondly, in line with the discussion of rationality above, we dispense with the notion that justice can be a template according to which deliberative outcomes could be measured for fit. Instead, we will explicate the use of "justice" as part of the temporally-situated, in-course, commonsense, lively, and contingent determinations of jury members. In concrete terms, this means we wish to be analytically responsive to matters to which other scholars have already at least pointed but not incorporated in the theoretical understanding of deliberative phenomena. For instance, jurors often apparently enter the jury room with a more or less firm position regarding the guilt of the defendant. As the deliberation proceeds, some of them may find, in and through their own and others' talk, just that argument which articulates the position to which they hold. Or, because of the way a particular argument resonates with commonsense understandings, they may change positions, and then provide a narrative recasting that fits with instructions about legally relevant criteria for their choice. Or, they may feel strongly about a position that is contrary to the majority opinion, with protest give in for purposes of a unanimous vote, and then yield to others' persuasion as to why such a course is morally and legally permissible.[2] Our analysis aims to capture just such phenomena, and the role of "justice" as part of them.

In a way, then, this study would seem to fulfill Furby's (1986:179) call for research on how adults define justice, and "what falls within people's understanding of the domain of justice and what falls outside it". However, for interrelated empirical and theoretical reasons, the attempt to see how jurors define justice poses difficulties, if by that is meant how they stipulate its abstract properties. The jurors here never do provide such a definition in their deliberations. Instead of using a definition, they employ the term in discrete conversational contexts, and it is their activities in these contexts that are determinative of its meaning. In this respect, the jurors appear like the pre-Socratic Greeks who, Havelock (1978:37) argues, never conceptually designated the term. Yet, they were aware of and identified justice as a rule of propriety or procedure "embedded in action".[3] The parallel between the early Greeks and the jury can be deepened if we consider that the former comprised an oral society and the latter, as well, accomplishes its deliberative task through primarily oral means. According to Havelock (1978:43), the demands of memorizing cultural information in such societies are unfriendly to the expression of principle in abstract terms, whereas these demands are hospitable to information that is "represented as doings":

> In short, in order to frame a legal directive, a situation is conceived and stated, cast in the form of an event or an action by a given agent, not in the form of a general principle within which a given case might fall (Havelock, 1978:43).

Faced neither with a legal literary tradition (Galanter, 1990:256), nor with reading about the case, nor rendering a verdict through written arguments, jurors, in a fashion something like the early Greeks, may be following a disputatious form that is intrinsic to orality. In the deliberation we examine, the jurors do not define justice and then see whether the facts of the case and a decision based on those facts can fit their definition. Rather, in the course of posing puzzles, articulating the law, casting individual ratiocinations into narrative form, and persuading one another of proper procedure and outcome, "justice" emerges as something to be "done" as they solve their puzzles, attempt to follow the law, work collaboratively to ponder the case, and ultimately arrive at a unanimous decision. Empirically in the deliberation, then, justice is also a propriety embedded in action rather than a principle (Havelock, 1978:181) whereby jurors handle the facts of a specific individual's confrontation with the law. Such a phenomenon is consistent with Pitkin's (1972) discussion of how to approach justice, in Wittgensteinian fashion, in terms of its use rather than its definition. Plato, says Pitkin (1972:305-6) "offers an ideal static picture of justice achieved; we do not see justice at work". In our investigation, it is in "working" and practical terms, not ideal and abstract ones, that justice emerges and becomes a prominent feature of the deliberative process.

Data

The jury deliberation for this study was videotaped by Professor Steve Hertzberg of the University of Wisconsin Law School, who made the tape available to us. Hertzberg's work occurred in collaboration with the Public Television Service's Frontline series, which showed a reduced and edited version of the deliberation in a one-hour program called "Inside the Jury Room".[4] The original deliberation lasted approximately two and one-half hours, and our research involves a videotape of nearly the entire deliberation. The case was a real one that was tried in a county courthouse of a major midwestern city. Just as the case was real, the jury, rather than being "mock", was the actual set of citizens who deliberated the case and decided its outcome. Thus, the deliberation was neither a simulation nor a scripted recreation. In the analysis below, jurors are identified by numbers, according to how they were sitting around a table in this configuration (the foreman is Juror 1):

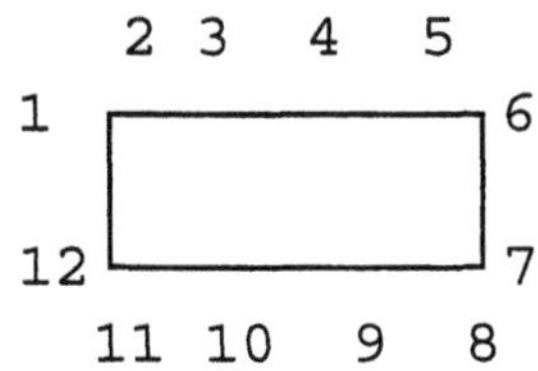

In this case, the defendant, whom we call "Larry", was tried for owning a gun. Larry had spent time in prison for a bank robbery twenty years prior to his present arrest. This was a felony violation, and it is illegal for ex-felons to own guns in the state where Larry lived. When Larry inquired about registering the gun at the police department, he was asked to produce the gun. He went home and returned with the gun, and was arrested. According to the defense, the gun was purchased to comply with a requirement set forth in a mail-order "detective school" to which Larry had applied as a means for securing employment. The jury was instructed to determine, beyond a reasonable doubt, three things: whether the defendant had been on parole when the violation occurred, whether the defendant had been in possession of a hand gun, and whether the defendant knew that he had been in possession of a hand gun. If they found that these things were true, that was to be grounds for conviction. We refer to these three matters as the jurors' "hardline" or as legal criteria for guilt. During the deliberation, the jury took three ballots, with the first producing a ten-to-two vote, the second an eleven-to-one, and the third a unanimous vote for acquittal.

We approach the deliberation as a procedural, formal interactional occurrence that, as we have said, participants organize not because they are "influenced" by exogenous factors (e.g. their sociodemographic backgrounds and conceptions of "justice") but through practical ways in which they structure the evidence they see and hear in such a way as to fit a "rational" outcome, in the ethnomethodological sense described above. Our approach is to let the data "present themselves", and so we derived no propositions beforehand as to what the deliberation would, should, or could contain as particular constitutive elements. In a way, we "discovered" justice as an analytic phenomenon because the jury members seem to discover it as a way of handling puzzles and contradictions in the case before them. Thus, our goal is not, as in conventional content or discourse analysis, to calibrate pieces of talk and interaction into *a priori* categories. The aim is to represent the jurors' own manner of organizing their perceptions, decisions, and deliberations.

This is, to be sure, a "single case" study. While single cases have unique contours and tenors, they are nevertheless composed formally. As Sacks (1984:21) has observed, "Social activities--actual, singular sequences of them--are methodical occurrences. That is, their description consists of the description of sets of formal procedures persons". However, such description, and our inductive approach, is not oriented to idiographic ends. It is analysis in the fullest sense of the word, being a determination of the components of a complex phenomenon. Of course, no analysis of a social event such as the deliberation can involve all its elements, but with an appropriately limited investigatory scope, can consider some class of phenomena that emerge and bear a relationship to other aspects of the event. Our focus on how jurors discover, specify, and exhibit the rational basis for their decision through articulating their senses of justice touches on orderly procedures that are also under detailed investigation (e.g. Manzo, 1988; 1991). At points in this paper, we make reference to these other features of the deliberation. Our overall goal is to build something like a "natural history" of the deliberation by recovering the practical ways in which the jurors arrive at an accountable decision or one that they regard as capable of being justified in terms of their folk legal conceptions.

Our concern with justice fits with this "natural history" orientation, in that we will be tracing the ways in which jurors' use of the concept of justice develops over the course of the deliberations. That it develops over the course is their phenomenon, not ours. We shall attempt to show that they prepare the way for using this concept and then do use it in patterned ways that are, with other discourse patterns and strategies, co-constitutive of the deliberation as a collaboratively-structured event.

Examination

For purposes of presentation, we will show five stages in the use of the justice concept. These stages roughly follow the chronology of the deliberation, but these stages are heuristic only and by no means to be considered as part of our findings. The stages are a means for identifying points at which the concept of justice or its converse, injustice, arises or potentially arises as part of the reasoning practices the jurors employ. The five stages are (1) posing a puzzle or dilemma; (2) maintaining the hardline; (3) referencing justice; (4) referencing the knowledge of the defendant, and (5) convincing the last "holdout".

Posing a Puzzle or Dilemma

At the very beginning of the deliberation, each of the jurors makes what we would call an opening statement. In these statements, a number of the jurors pose a dilemma; according to the criteria they have been given, they think the defendant is guilty. Upon admitting that, they immediately set up a contrast, which is often a "but" statement. Jurors 3, 6, and 10, who speak in succession, but not immediately after one another, are representative.

(1A)
J3: Okay I feel that the defendant is guilty uh on all three accusations
technically. But I guess I feel that we should also take into
consideration the fact that he does have a reading disability, as
well as some other disabilities. I'm not trying to play on your
sympathies or whatever but it is something that I have to consider
and right now I haven't determined whether I should name the
defendant guilty or innocent...

(1B)
J6: I think that the way I feel is that it's true, all the counts have
been met. By the law, the man is-- he doesn't have a case, he fits
all three criteria, but I think there are some imp- there are some
important points. From our standpoint I don't think any of us
as citizens have to sit around and, regardless of who it is, and
say the law is absolutely right because somebody made it for
every individual. I think it's a tough position to be in to say, I am
a judge of the law. But I think that's what the jury system is for,
it gives the people a chance in some instances to make some type
of statement toward a specific law as applied to a specific case.
And y'know I think there are cases where it's not clear and I
think in this case, there's a lot of questions which have yet to be
answered that we need to talk about.

(1C)
J10: I agree that Mr. Rex is guilty based on the law. I believe that
the law is good. I believe that the idea that there can be an
exception made because of a particular defendant is what we
have to deal with here.

All three jurors start by noting the defendant's guilt according to the criteria they have been given (that he had been on parole, was in possession of a gun, and knew he had the gun). Then, after acknowledging this, each one introduces a contrasting position. Juror 3 (1A: line 2) and juror 6 (1B: line 3) do this with the marker "but". Juror 3 suggests that the defendant's reading disability be considered. Juror 6 proposes that "the law" must come under scrutiny and that there are "a lot of questions" that they "need to talk about" (1B:lines 12-13). Juror 10 (1C: lines 1-2) notes her belief in the law as "good" and next says she believes an "exception" is what they must "deal with" (1C: lines 2-4). The contrast being developed here does not question the facts of the case, which are left intact. Instead, the jurors seek some way out of doing what these facts dictate according to law. Thus, the use of contrast is a primary organizing principle or formal aspect of these opening statements, despite at least slight differences in what each juror offers as the second part of the contrast. It is not enough for the jurors to assert the need for an exception, however; they do not here claim that the defendant is innocent. Thus, the puzzle or dilemma they exhibit is in recognizing both the factual guilt of the defendant and the exceptional nature of this case. What next transpires is their looking for a way of making the exception legally justifiable and accountable.

One further feature of these statements is that the jurors appear to be struggling with the role and identity of the jury. This is evident in how juror 3 (1A: line 2) and juror 10 (1C: line 3) invoke the collective "we" and thereby propose what the duty of the jurors is. Juror 6 is more expansive on this topic, in characterizing their role as citizens to be a "judge of the law" (1B: lines 4-8) and suggesting "that's what the jury system is for" (line 8). This struggle to define the jury and its role is apparent in another juror's opening statement, which embeds the formal contrastive principle. Juror 12 starts by minimizing the importance of the defendant's "mental abilities and reading level" (lines 1- 2 below). This may be responsive to juror 3 in excerpt 1A (line 1) above, who first mentions the defendant's disabilities.

(2)

1. J12: I feel that the um defendant's mental abilities and reading level
2. level are not the crucial issues here. Uh I feel that he, he meets
3. the criteria for us to find guilt. But I think ((clears throat))
4. we have a very philosophical argument on our hands, in terms of
5. are we obligated as a jury to follow the letter of the law and
6. find him guilty? Or are we obligated as a jury to use our special

7. level of conscience uh as the defense lawyer said--otherwise it
8. you know it could be decided by a computer--um and acquit him
9. because of perhaps an injustice that has been done to him,
10. the-- the arrest.

Juror 12 nevertheless induces a contrast, parallel to juror 6's, between following the letter of the law and using the jury's distinctive role. She develops this contrast by depicting a verdict according to the three criteria as "decided by a computer" (lines 7-8), whereas, using their "special level of conscience" (lines 6-7), the jury could acquit him because of the possibility of an "injustice" having been "done to him" (lines 8-9). This excerpt, then, contains the first reference to justice, although this occurs in an indirect fashion, through juror 12's invocation of justice's converse, "injustice".

Subsequent to this, juror 12 develops a related contrast, between being non-emotional in following the law and using their conscience:

(3)
11. J12: y'know on one hand we are supposed to remain nonemotional
12. and nonsympathetic and just follow the letter of the law, is
13. what we've been instructed to do. But I wonder if there's a
14. special place for a jury to use um y'know our-- as people as
15. human beings we have a level of being able to to think and uh
16. use our conscience to say that even though the defendant has
17. met all of the criteria to establish guilt, can we as a jury say
18. given all these facts uh there is still a place for us to with
19. reason and not with emotion or sympathy with reason still
20. there is still a purpose or a reason to acquit him. And you
21. know as I was thinking about this I think it comes down to
22. questions like what is a jury and what is a jury for, what is our
23. purpose here.

Juror 12 marks the contrast by prefacing the acknowledgment of guilt (lines 16-17) with an "even though" phrase (line 16), and then asks if there isn't a "place" and a way "with reason" for the jury "as human beings" to acquit (lines 17-20). And she further poses a question of what the "purpose" of the jury is (lines 19-21).

So far, then, justice is being invoked as a lack, or a negative, that needs to be set right. Indeed during a subsequent portion of her opening statement, juror 12 says, "...on a simple level it would be very easy to say he is guilty, but we all feel I think that an injustice has been done to this man through his arrest". Thus, it is now not only that a dilemma has been posed, a contrast between following the letter of the law, which in this scheme seems to demand finding guilt, and making an exception. Making an exception would correct an injustice. Moreover, on behalf of the others, juror 12 has now explicitly formulated a quest for the place that would represent where the jury could exercise its special role. Toward the end of her opening statement (not excerpted here), juror 12 expands on what the place would be. She once more concedes that the defendant is guilty according to the law, and then asks, "do we rise above that somehow is there a place for us to then say even though he meets the law you know we cannot in good conscience find him guilty". Thus, to follow the metaphor of a "place" where the jury can reasonably acquit the defendant, it is perhaps to be found by "rising above" the law. Thus, throughout the opening statements of those who favor acquittal, there is evidence of an orientation to a formal "rules, but ..." contrast, and a search for a solution to the puzzle that this contrast evokes.

Maintaining the Hard Line

Juror 12's proposing how the jurors "all feel" (that an injustice has been done) is a device that has elsewhere been described as "speaking on behalf of" (Sacks, 1966; lecture 9; cf. Maynard, 1986: 269). Not everyone on the panel exhibits agreement with the assertion, however, nor accepts the idea of going beyond the judge's instructions and rising above the law. Two jurors consistently maintain a "hard line", by urging that the group should adhere to the rules they have been provided. Juror 4 in excerpt (4) is one of these, and the following is a portion of his opening statement:

(4)

J4 I feel that the plaintiff, the city has found him uh guilty beyond a reasonable doubt to the three points that we are to discuss. What the sympathetic point of view would be, what his intent was, or what he did not intend to do, and that's not for us to reason over. Ours are the three main points which we have to find beyond a reasonable doubt and I believe that we did ... anything after that is up to the judge as far as the sentencing ... Our three points have been in my mind established beyond a reasonable doubt.

Juror 1, the foreman, and the last to produce an opening statement, is the other "hardliner".

(5)

J1: My personal opinion, uh I think differs from a lot of the ones
that I've heard around the table here and in that be-- that --
our instructions were to decide whether beyond a reasonable
doubt is he guilty of this crime. I think those three elements have
been met then yes he is guilty of this crime. All the reasoning that
I've heard around this table for each person's decision as to how
they're leaning has been speculation which we were all instructed
not to use speculation. We have to use the testimony, and uh my
opinion is that even though there might be facts in this case
that weren't brought out that we weren't allowed to hear or made
aware of, uh we can't assume those facts, we can only use to make
our decision what was testified in court. Uh physical evidence and
testimony as evidence. We can't use what we think his mental
ability is or what we think he understood or what he didn't
understand or what we think he knows or what he doesn't know.
We can't use that. We have to use what was brought out, the
statements that were made in the courtroom and were allowed.
I think the scope of a jury is to decide guilt and innocence not
to be a presiding judge and uh so I think uh I have to follow the
letter of the law.

In countering prior arguments and announcing himself as favoring conviction, J1 reminds the jurors of their instructions concerning reasonable doubt and the "three elements" (lines 3-5), and charges that the other jurors are using "speculation" (line 7-8), which they were instructed to avoid. Furthermore, the jury is only to use testimony and evidence (lines 12-13); its role is not to be the "presiding" judge (lines 17-19). Thus, juror 1 displays a concern "to follow the letter of the law".

In short, the contrasts uniformly displayed in the statements of jurors 3, 6, 10, 12, and others do not appear in those of jurors 4 and 1. Moreover, rather than joining the quest for some way or place to transcend the hardline, the latter two jurors embrace it in a way that their instructions have provided. Formally, their argument involves invoking the relevance of the jury's instructions, taking only physical evidence and testimony into consideration, and consigning other determinations to the realm of sympathy or speculation about "extenuating circumstances" whose significance is in the purview of the judge to decide. Consequently, in the talk of jurors 1 and 4, the desire for further deliberation appears minimal, whereas the other jurors do explicitly invoke a "need to talk" (excerpt 1, line 20). Or, by raising questions and initiating a search, they implicitly suggest that further deliberation is necessary.

In summary, two positions have emerged in the jurors' opening statements. The majority holds the first position, which allows for the reasonableness of applying the law while taking into account special circumstances, encouraging the discovery of an accountable alternative to following the law, and exhorting the jury to fulfill its special role by finding this alternative. A minority adheres to the second position, which involves following the legal criteria, viewing the evidence and testimony, finding the defendant guilty, and leaving the consideration of special circumstances to the judge. Observing the hardline already provides the minority with an accountable position. Thus, where the majority seeks an expansive version of the jury's role, the minority proposes a narrow one.

The Discovery of Justice

If members of the minority do not wish more talk, they nonetheless engage in further bolstering of their perspective. Thus, juror 1 takes on the argument that an "injustice" has been done to the defendant:

(6)

J1: From what I gather everybody is afrai-- is afraid of doing an
injustice to this man and uh uh, I don't think by uh our
decision, that either way we're going to do an injustice to this
man. My personal opinion is that he's met the three points and--
and I feel that if we would acquit him we'd be doing him an
injustice. Uh I think that it's the judge-- judge's job to uh uh
see to it that this man either gets the required training to uh
help et cetera, sentence whatever it may be. I think it's his job
an uh uh by that I don't think that we're doing him also doing him
an injustice to convict him uh I don't feel an injustice either way,
and uh maybe moreso one way than the other but I think we're

here to decide the law, not to be the judge and that's my stand I
guess. I don't think we should decide his-- his uh intent or his
y'know what he understood or what he couldn't understand an'
everything I think that's, although some of you are experts in your
respective fields, uh I can appreciate that but uh I don't I think--
that's beyond our scope.

At first, this juror suggests that acquitting the defendant would be doing him an injustice (lines 5-6) but, after once more going over the judge's role (line 6-9), professes that the issue of injustice is essentially irrelevant (lines 10-11). He next rehearses the point that the role of the jury is "decide the law, not to be the judge" (lines 11-12). This means that considering the subjective issues of the defendant's intent (line 13) and understanding (line 14) is "beyond their scope" (line 17).

Juror 6 immediately counters juror 1, especially with regard to what the role of the jury is. At lines 2-7 below, he claims that the jury has more of a duty than simply to determine whether the three criteria have been met. In this context, he makes the first reference so far in the deliberation to the concept of justice.

(7)

J6: I disagree with that. I totally disagree. I'm not saying I'm making
this decision but I think we have more capabilities than to say one
two three, these are met on a very simple level, cut and dry,
guilty. I don't think that we as JURors that is necessarily our
role. We are here to do more than that, we're here to sit and talk
about he-- the whole case as it is not just to accept everything
that is put in front of us. If we do I don't think there is any
argument. We can argue about semantics about the words in this
case what is possess mean what does know mean what does felon
mean we could argue about this from now until, you know until
we no longer exist in this particular world. But we're here to do
a justice to someone and my point is the way I'm trying to
decide in my own mind, has justice been done here. I don't care
WHAT the law says, has justice been done?

Juror 6 also seems to avow the futility of arguing "semantics", or the meaning of fact-characterizations such as whether the defendant possessed a firearm, whether he "knew" he possessed a firearm, and whether he was a "felon" (lines 8-11). Using the "but" marker at line 11, he then asserts a contrast; here it is between "accepting everything that is put in front of us", where that would mean there is no argument (lines 7-8) presumably with the three criteria, and the proposed task of the jury "to do a justice to someone" (lines 11-12). In their opening statements, jurors who favored acquittal had posed the divergence from following the rules as a puzzle, in terms of its accountability. That is, they broached a search for some grounds upon which perhaps to find the defendant not guilty, but did not find those grounds except in the sense of correcting an injustice. In this excerpt, "justice" is offered as a solution to that puzzle. Indeed, in raising the question as to whether justice has been done (lines 13-14), juror 6 raises the possibility that not following the letter of the law and making an exception would, in a positive sense, be "doing justice". It is as if the place for transcending the law or the "hard line" is where justice resides.

We have given an interpretation of juror 6s's talk, but evidence for our interpretation derives from the immediately subsequent turn of juror 2, who formulates (Garfinkel and Sacks, 1970) the sense to be made from that talk (lines 1-7 below). Juror 2 proposes that juror 6 is "pulling back from looking at the instructions" (lines 3-4), which juror 6 seems to confirm with his own version of what he is doing (line 5).

(8)
1. J2: Okay there's a couple o' things I wanna say that are governing
2. the way I'm thinking now and it's uh, it's a good time to bring
3. it up y'know because you are pulling back from looking at the
4. instructions and--
5. J6: I'm not at this point I'm not arguing the instructions.
6. J2: Right that's why I'm saying you're pulling back from just
7. looking at the instructions and taking into a larger frame of
8. is this justice. Okay and uh a couple thoughts on that. I look
9. at the defendant and I think is he a threat to society, and if
10. what we decide here if we decide that he's guilty is that just?
11. And a couple things I wanna point out. He originally went to the
12. store and was fascinated by an antique gun. I think that says
13. something. You can-- everyone in this can take that to mean uh
14. whatever. I think it means something to this case. Again what if,
15. is he a threat to society and also if he is dangers to society
16. why would the detective tell him, allow him to bring the gun in,
17. transport it on a public bus, y'know and uh ask him and request

for him to bring it down to uh to his office if he felt that he
was a dangerous felon?

Then, in line 6, juror 2 agrees with juror 6 and further characterizes the latter as distancing himself from the instructions by invoking the "frame" of justice. With regard to justice, juror 2 also has a "couple of thoughts" (line 8), and asks whether the defendant is a threat to society and whether finding him guilty is just (lines 9-10). With the rest of his turn, he suggests ways in which the defendant would appear as unthreatening--he was fascinated by an antique gun (lines 11-12) and the "detective" asked the defendant to bring this gun in on a "public bus" (lines 16-17). It seems, therefore, that juror 2 uses the concept of justice to "pull back" from the official criteria of guilty, in the way that he has characterized juror 6 as doing, in order to examine the relevance of convicting a man who is arguably harmless.

"Justice", in short, is a resource for those jurors who have sought a solution to the dilemma of following the rules versus making an exception. For ten out of the 12 jurors, justice can be invoked to account for how they can transcend the law and consider other issues surrounding the case. But what of the two jurors who have expressed a commitment to following the instructions and three criteria for finding guilt? We might predict that because "justice" is being *contrasted* to following the three criteria, they would be likely to disavow the relevance of the concept, at least in the way the majority employs it. To be sure, we have already seen how juror 1 has argued that at least the question of doing an injustice to the defendant is irrelevant. Furthermore, the instructions have provided the legal accountability of these two jurors' position, and thus they need no other recourse for voting to convict. In fact, as the deliberations continue, the two holdouts do eventually agree to form a unanimous decision, and they continue to hold to their formal position in which following the official criteria is paramount.

Referencing the Knowledge of the Defendant

One of the two holdouts for conviction does change his mind about the conviction, but he does not do so on the grounds of doing justice. We will examine his arguments to demonstrate two interrelated points. First, while jurors may arrive at a unanimous decision, they do not have to do so on unanimous grounds. Second, the concept of justice is not used uniformly in this deliberation. Juror 1, who is the one who changes his mind, does so within the framework of the three criteria that had been provided to the jury; he does so, in other words, by adhering to what we have called the hardline. We saw, in excerpt (5), how he asserted the essential irrelevance of the concept of justice or at least "injustice" to the determination of guilt or innocence. Accordingly, while he changes his mind to favor a *verdict* of innocence, he does not alter his attitude with regard to the irrelevance of justice and injustice in arriving at that verdict. Before we inspect the talk wherein he explains his change of vote, we need to summarize an argument of a juror to whom he refers in this explanation. At several points in the deliberation, various jurors had expressed wonderment concerning the issue of whether the defendant "knew" that he possessed a firearm. In addressing this issue, juror 5 contrasted how an ordinary adult might go out and buy a gun with the way that Larry bought a gun in order to fulfill the requirements of a detective course as advertised in a magazine. After he articulated this contrast, the following exchange occurred:

(9)
1. J1: Are you saying that all he was attempting to buy, what was
2. represented by a picture in a handbook?
3. J5: I think that's true.

Thus an understanding of juror 5's argument was that the defendant had not purchased a gun per se but rather an element--a "visual image", juror 5 later says--in the "global detective course".

Shortly after this discussion, the jury panel took a ballot. Eleven members voted for acquittal and one voted to convict. It soon became apparent that the remaining "holdout" was juror 4, while, as already mentioned, it was juror 1 who changed his vote:

(10)
1. J1: I now I've changed my mind. I uh I have somethin' to say and
2. an' I kind of uh my few comments I made and it's started to
3. make me think. And uh I believe that what you said y'know uh
4. uh taking into account his mental ability and everything that
5. it's just possible he purchased an item of his course. And
6. now those first two points you could uh uh define them y'know.
7. Uh it says that he had ta know that he possessed a gun. He
8. mighta knew he possessed a piece of his course. Uh and an'

when you brought that up at made me think. And maybe he just
was simply following instructions, had no uh relationship like
you or I or anybody else does in this room between a gun and
bang bang. Uh y'know uh uh I'm sure at his age he's watched a
lot of tv and uh uh whatever you see detective movies on on
shows on tv and every detective has a gun. His detective book,
he's now gonna be a detective, I'm gonna be a detective I'm
gonna be a standup citizen and be a detective and the course
says something about a gun he's gonna do everything he can to
do it right and and I'm not sure that acquitting him is doing
him justice, uhm I I personally don't feel it is. But I can see
your point I can see a reason for somewhat of a doubt however
minor it may be. Go ahead.

After announcing his change of mind and projecting that he has "something to say" on this (line 1), J1 provides a justification that incorporates the argument J5 had made (lines 3-12) and substantiates this reasoning further by hypothesizing how watching detective movies might inform Larry's reading of the detective book (lines 12-18). Even if J1 has decided to vote with the majority, however, he clearly disaffiliates from their position in regard to justice (lines 18-19). His "somewhat of a doubt" comes from seeing juror 5's "point" (lines 19-21). At this juncture, J1 allows J6 to talk ("go ahead", line 19). In taking his turn, J6 purports that an acquittal does not mean that the "justice system" will abandon the defendant; indeed, the defendant's parole officer would have better insight into Larry. While J1 then acknowledges that he can see "a little bit of what you're saying", he still disassociates from the relevance of justice. He concludes his narrative by returning to the question of whether the defendant really did know what he was doing:

(11)

J1: Did he know that that uh y'know uh a gun was purchased or did
he purchase an item of his course? Uh so it-- that's my reason
for changing my mind.

In short, juror 1 manages to change his vote while retaining the primacy of the hardline or the judge's instructions, and he orients to these instructions as the way to render his vote accountable. The facts of the case, then, have been altered to the extent that the defendant is seen as not knowing that he purchased a "gun" per se.

Convincing the Last Holdout

Juror 1, therefore, reconciles enough with the majority to vote for acquittal, but differentiates himself in terms of the grounds for so doing. Juror 4's eventual vote is similar. How he comes to vote with the majority is a complex phenomenon in its own right, and here we can only provide a brief sketch. Having been a "hardliner" all along, when he indicates that he will in fact vote with the majority, he suggests that it is because he does not want to be the one to "holdup eleven people that are very strong in their feelings". Thus, J4 says, "I will change and vote along with you to give a unanimous vote, but I will never feel right about it. I feel it was pushed by the jury on psychological and other feelings that I do not agree with. But I will go along with a unanimous verdict".

While the jury is willing to accept his vote, they are bothered by J4's affect and his claim of being coerced. Accordingly, in a variety of ways, they proceed in attempts to convince this juror of the validity of his vote. For example, they engage in what we call "testifying" (Manzo, 1988, 1991) which consists of three facets. First, the testifier declares some commonality with others in the group and with the reality of the situation they face, including their legal mandate and the facts of the case. Second, the testifier notes some personal experience that brought about a change of attitude in relation to the mandate. Finally, the testifier contends that his or her decision is legally-accountably correct. These procedures are evident in the testifying of both juror 1, the other hardliner, and juror 10, who has favored acquittal on the grounds of doing justice. Responding to J4, their turns occur in tandem with each other, and we will take them up in order.

(12)
1. J1: I wanna tell ya the reason. I-- I walked into this room feeling
2. exactly like you do. Maybe even more so. Exactly like you do.
3. And some certain degree of me still feels that way. Okay, but the
4. only, how should I say it uh I take this situation, this second
5. item. Second item. Now I-- now I'm using, my making my
6. decision purely by these three items. I don't care what was said in
7. here today, I'm still tryin' to rationale with these three items And
8. uh I'm applying them to my six-year-old son, which is in the first

grade, which is pretty near to what we're talkin' about here. Uh now he could easily be led to purchase something-- Now i-- I'm relating this with toys, every kid watches TV, sees the commercials on TV. I think they-- there's a lot of shows y'know that are nothing but uh half hour commercials, they don't have a concept, they don't know what they're buying. All they know is, they're buying a name. And that's why when we started talking and mentioning that he bought a picture and it's possible son of a gun it is possible, it's-- it's sorta-- it rang a bell, it-- damn, it just could be, y'know it-- it uh it's possible, okay? I'm not saying it is, that it was out and out what went on. I'm not saying that it wasn't. But what I am saying is that, it could be. Okay.

The components of testifying here are as follows. In lines 1-3, J1 proposes an identification with J4 in terms of feeling how the latter feels, and indeed, in his opening statement (excerpt 4), he clearly favored conviction. Next, in lines 3-7, J1 re-asserts the primacy of the legal criteria for guilt in relation to his decision. Then, J1 invokes his experience with his son (lines 7-10) and uses this experience to propose what "every kid" does as a result of watching television commercials (lines 10-15). Finally, this experience and proposal are cited as a reason for relating to the possibility that the defendant "bought a picture" (lines 15-18). This is what "could be" (line 20), and, according to J1's earlier talk (excerpt 8), raises a doubt as to whether Larry "knew" he possessed a firearm. Thus, J1's testifying suggests that a vote for acquittal can be consistent with the judge's instructions and a hardline orientation.

Juror 10's testifying turn of talk, following upon J1's, has a similar organization but a different rationale.

(13)

J10: Uh I found myself feeling real down last night. I was aware of the weight that's on each one of us as a juror, and I was aware of the facts y'know, evidence, facts in the case, and I thought hey, this guy's guilty. Is there some way out of him being adjudged guilty by us. Could I live with, my writing guilty, for this particular person. Boy I mashed around with that for awhile, and I said, if there's any justice really, it's in drawing attention to this man's personal situation and limitations. Getting rid of the firearm is okay too. But judging him not guilty, then I can

10. believe in jury. I mean, that's where I find myself.
11. J1: Ah but, let's say-- let's say we take a vote.
12. J8: ((to J4)) Do you feel better, worse, y'know I think we have to
13. really consider how he feels.
14. J1: I don't think he really feels good about the decision.
15. J8: No no no but he-- y'know he said he would vote guilty even
16. though he would feel bad and wouldn't y'know-- and I-- I don't
17. feel good about that.

In lines 1-2, J10 identifies with the other jurors, presumably including J4, because of the "weight" that is on each of them. She also reports her awareness of the facts, evidence, and guilt of the defendant (lines 2-4). Her person experience is of asking whether there was "some way out" of this judgment, wondering whether she could live with such a judgment (line 5), and mashing "around with that" (line 6). Finally, in a re-specification of a position that originated in embryonic form in the jurors' opening statements, she concludes (lines 6-9) that *justice* would draw attention to the defendant's situation and limitations. She thus re-introduces the kind of extra-legal factors that the hardliners considered irrelevant. More than this, J10 implies that justice would permit "judging him not guilty" (line 9), which would, in turn, permit her to "believe in jury" (lines 9-10). J10 thereby once more fits the giving advice to the role of the jury; it is something that they can do, given the circumstances of the case.

To depart briefly from our concern with the concept of justice, it is relevant to consider how this case was resolved. In the above excerpt, following J10's turn, J1 proposes that they vote again. However, juror 8 exhibits great concern for the "feelings" of J4. Indeed, after this, there are further efforts on the part of the jury to convince J4 of the legitimacy of his decision to vote. Ultimately, J4 admits to having a "very weak reasonable" doubt, and it has to do with the linkage between the defendant being a felon and the buying of the firearm:

(14)

1. J4: I think he knows that he was a felon, and I think he knew that he
2. bought the firearm. The possibility of the two together would be
3. the weakest point for me.
4. J2: Okay and I think-- I think that is everyone-- uh one of the basic
5. problems everyone's having.

We do not wish to explicate the "real" reason for J4's doubt here.[5] Rather, the efforts that the jurors exert to obtain some display of a "rational" rather than "coerced" vote from him illustrate Garfinkel's (1967:114) argument that deliberative *outcomes* precede the actual *decision* in the sense that having achieved a verdict, members of the jury work to assign that verdict its "legitimate history". The jurors in this case could have voted an acquittal much earlier than they actually do; that they do not largely reflects their efforts to achieve unanimity in process *after* having reached the potential for a unanimous vote. Note also a further feature of the above exchange; Garfinkel (1967) maintains that, based on the ways they determine "what actually happened", jurors can expect "social support" for the verdict they choose; such an expectation does not waver even when the grounds for a decision change. To the contrary, when, after "holding out" for the defendant's guilt for so long, juror 4 here exhibits the possibility of a "reasonable doubt", J2 proposes that his reasoning is shared by "everybody". He suggests, in other words, that J4 is now a part of the majority, not just because of his willingness to vote with the other members, but because he shares a reservation they all have. Finally, J4 does not, however, show the same concern for justice that some members of the jury do; his position remains closest to J1 in calling in to question whether all three criteria for the defendant's guilt have been met.

In summary, we can briefly give some flesh to what we have heuristically referred as the stages of the deliberative process and the role of justice in therm. First, posing a puzzle or dilemma involves searching for an account or reason to acquit the defendant in the face of legal guilt. According to one of the jurors' opening statements, this would mean invoking the role of the jury as having a conscience and not being a computer. Acquittal might mean correcting an "injustice". Second, maintaining the hardline initially refers to being legalistic and favoring conviction. The role of the jury is to decide the law in terms of evidence and testimony, not to be speculative about the defendant's intentions or understandings. Those matters are for the judge to decide upon. Third, the discovery of justice involves filling the place for making an exception or for finding a solution to the puzzle with the concept of justice. The facts of the case remain intact. Fourth, referencing the knowledge of the defendant means remaining legalistic but finding grounds within the legal criteria for acquittal. The facts of the case are re-cast. Fifth, convincing the last holdout does not mean obtaining agreement upon the grounds for acquittal; it means arriving at a unanimous verdict while retaining an orientation both to the law and to justice.

Conclusion

We have suggested that "justice" has been something of an archetype in social science, an inherited idea that investigators have found functional in assessing the merit of whole social systems, their specific arenas, such as criminal processing, and the relationships among people in small groups. Thus, social science is replete with the attempts to determine whether these systems, arenas, and relationships, are just or perceivably just social enterprises in terms of some model. Seldom are there inquiries into how members of society themselves might administer the concept when confronted not only with deciding the "facts" of "what happened" in some past event, but also with theorizing about why they occurred and, correspondingly, what the proper sequelae are (cf. Garfinkel, 1967:111). This tendency to view the actualities of concerted activity through a stipulated model might be the product of a society and its professions, in which the "abstractive habits" of literacy have essentially "remodeled" (Havelock, 1978:337; our emphasis) those actualities into forms that would suggest structure and organization are to be found elsewhere than in the concreteness of that activity itself. Thus, it is not only that, in measuring behavior according to their models, investigators presume the latter to be more organizationally real than the former; it is that they also examine outcomes as structured according to the variables of age, class, gender, or race, and other statuses, which are abstractly anchored in purported relationships in the larger society rather than in the mundaneity of the jury's own talk and activity.

In Pitkin's (1972:274) terms, justice has been something with which social scientists have "fiddled" in order to make it useful to their investigations. In approaching justice as a phenomenon of order, we wish to recover the concept at work in the activities of the jury's own members. This does not mean making the social scientist a hostage to ordinary people and what they might say about justice; the strategy, instead, is to analyze the produced regularities of conduct (cf. Pitkin, 1972:16-18). As Garfinkel and Wieder (1991) have suggested, every possible "topic" of order, such as justice, is capable of respecification as a phenomenon of order. From this standpoint, we can develop a sociology of justice that is formal. Our starting point is not with what is presumably relevant to people, and our concern is not with what do people think. Rather, we ask how people act in concert with one another, and how such venerable concepts as justice are embedded in this acting and thus in and as the orderliness that comprises everyday activities.

Justice *became* part of the talk and activity of jury members, emerging formally as what they would do as a contrastive performance to following the facts of the case, obeying a strict interpretation of the judge's instructions, and finding the defendant guilty. For these same jurors, injustice was what was done to the defendant under the circumstances in which he was arrested and tried, so that justice is also something the jury could do to counteract or offset this prior activity of the police and prosecutor. Doing justice, accordingly, is finding the defendant not guilty in spite of the strict interpretation of the facts and because of particular circumstances, which both provide a particular texture for the case-as-a-whole and are reciprocally textured by it. And finally, for these members, doing justice is how they find themselves as jurors. "Justice" is what jurors do. Formally, then, justice as a phenomenon of order that resides in and as actual activity can have both a relational component, when it exists in contradistinction to other modes of activity, and a functional component, when it is the manner in which a group, in performing justice, thereby defines itself.

Not all of the jurors, however, affiliated with the position that they were doing justice. There were two holdouts who, when they changed their vote from conviction to acquittal, nevertheless adhered to the "hardline". What they show is that the concern with doing justice is not all-pervasive. A more fundamental matter for jurors is the legal accountability for their decisions. For the two holdouts, the judge's instructions provided such accountability. For those who were dissatisfied with the outcome those instructions might otherwise dictate, doing justice provided them with a "place" simultaneously to admit the validity of these instructions and to transcend them, while preserving the observably arguable legal validity of what they decided. In all, then, jurors never lost sight of the legal framework and consistently worked to fulfill the image of the "good juror" that this framework provides (Garfinkel, 1967), which suggests that there was also a deep moral component to their deliberations. This finding brings into question the orthodox sociological view of jurors' expertise and ability to provide "legally valid" decisions (cf. Reskin and Visher, 1986), which suggests that jurors do not display much expertise in legal reasoning.[6] That view, along with charges of racial or gender-related bias, have cast a cloud over the jury system. Our research suggests that jurors display a profound appreciation for legal accountability even in the course of aiming to transcend it. Our point here is not to defend the jury, however, but to suggest that analyzing actual deliberations reveals an orderliness to the deliberation process that may be missed in other types of investigation.

Finally, we propose that a sociology of justice necessarily starts with what Garfinkel (1988) discusses as phenomena of order, for it is in the actualities of concerted activity, in the particularities of conduct, that a society exhibits how it is organized with respect to such a venerable concept. The sociological quest for justice, rather than being guided by abstract models and definitions, can involve further uncovering of the "grammar" of the concept. In Wittgensteinian (1958) terms, this means analyzing the patterns and regularities with regard to its usage--the practices of perception, talk, and action that are known in terms of their employment but which do not necessarily operate at the level of discursive awareness (cf. Pitkin, 1972:82-3). Our study has scratched the surface of such a grammar. In examining deliberative *discourse*, we study the *yield* from jurors' own perception and analysis of a trial and the events within it. Further phenomenal elucidation of "justice" would involve understanding its role in that more primary perception and analysis.

Notes

1. Of course, justice has been a topic of interest among philosophers for centuries, and there is an important set of contributions to this legacy. Most famous of these is the work of Rawls (1971, 1985). While Rawls' position is not universally accepted (see e.g. Nozick, 1974), it warrants brief discussion as both a paragon and a paradigm in the contemporary philosophy of justice. Rawls (1971:11) maintains that the nature of justice will vary from society to society based on what he calls the "original position" in which principles of justice are chosen to fit with a society's political and social constitution:

    > The guiding idea is that the principles of justice for the basic structure of society are the object of the original agreement. They are the principles that free and rational persons concerned to further their own interests would accept in an initial position of equality as defining the fundamental terms of their association.

    In specifying the kind of justice which should obtain in a democracy, Rawls (1985) has articulated the principle of "justice as fairness", which differs from a strictly analytic definition because of reference to a specific form of society. Thus, because of his concern with historical and social context, Rawls would seem to have a sociological element to his theory. However, in discussing what justice is or should be, Rawls' works are ultimately speculative and miss the phenomena with which we are concerned, and that is how justice, in the first place, inheres in the real performances of people engaged in actual courses of action in ordinary society.

2. We are referring to what appears to happen in our jury deliberation, but similar matters have been discussed in previous studies. As Kalven and Zeisel (1966:488-489) argue,

    with very few exceptions the first ballot decides the outcome of the verdict. And if this is true, then the real decision is often made before the deliberation begins ... The deliberation process might well be likened to what the developer does for an exposed film: it brings out the picture, but the outcome is pre-determined.

    Garfinkel (1967:114) suggests,

    In the material reported here, jurors did not actually have an understanding of the conditions that defined a correct decision until after the decision had been made. Only in retrospect did they decide what they did that made their decisions correct ones. When the outcome was in hand they went back to find the "why", the things that led up to the outcome, and then in order to give their decisions some order, which namely, is the "officialness" of the decision.

    Finally, Simon (1967), in her study of insanity trials, conducted pre- and post-deliberation interviews with jurors. She found that among jurors who, during deliberations, voted differently than their pre-deliberation positions, only 65% actually changed their minds in the course of discussions. Fully 35% did not change their position but apparently conformed publically (changed their vote) in a mechanical kind of way; i.e. they "went along" with the other jurors while privately disagreeing about the defendant's guilt or innocence.
3. It was not until Plato's dialogues in the *Republic* that Greek culture fully develops justice as a definition and as an abstract concept. There are precursors, such as Hesiod's identifying the "justice" and assembling examples of its occurrence in concrete situations (Havelock, 1978:230), where justice itself is an agent who does something or experiences something. But Hesiod never said what justice "is", apart from these particular instances of its agency, in the way that Plato eventually does.
4. Hertzberg's "Inside the Jury Room" was aired on *Frontline* on April 11, 1986.
5. Such explication could only be, at best, speculation. Juror 4 provides an *account* for his change of vote, and we consider such an account not as a cause for his action but as a constitutive feature of it.
6. For a more thorough discussion and critique of this view, particularly in regard to the "amateurism" of the jury, see Galanter (1990:201-2).

References

Cohen, R. (1982), 'Perceiving Justice', in R.Greenberg (ed.), *Equity and Justice in Social Behavior*, Academic Press, New York.

Furby, L. (1986), 'Psychology and Justice', in R.L.Cohen (ed.), *Views from the Social Sciences*, Plenum Press, New York.

Galanter, M. (1990), 'The Civil Jury as Regulator of the Litigation Process', *The University of Chicago Legal Forum 1990*, pp.201-271.

Garfinkel,H. (1967), *Studies in Ethnomethodology*, Prentice-Hall, Englewood Cliffs, N.J.

Garfinkel, H. (1988), 'Evidence for Locally Produced Naturally Accountable Phenomena of Order, Logic, Reason, Meaning, Method, etc., in and as of the Essential Quiddity of Immortal Ordinary Society (I of IV): An Announcement of Studies', *Sociological Theory*, vol. 6, pp.103-106.

Garfinkel, H. and Sacks, H. (1970), 'On Formal Structures of Practical Actions', in J. McKinney and E. Tiryakian (eds), *Theoretical Sociology*, Appleton Century Crofts, New York, pp. 338-366.

Garfinkel,H. and Wieder, D.L. (1991), 'Evidence for Locally Produced, Naturally Accountable Phenomena of Order*, Logic, Reason, Meaning, Method, etc., in and as of the Esssentially Unavoidable and Irremediable Haecceity of Immortal Ordinary Society IV: Two Incommensurable, Asymmetrically Alternate Technologies of Social Analysis', in G.Watson and R.Seiler (eds), *Text in Context: Contributions to Ethnomethodology*, Sage, Newbury Park, CA., pp.175-206.

Havelock, E.A. (1978), *The Greek Concept of Justice: From Its Shadow in Homer to Its Substance in Plato*, Harvard University Press, Cambridge.

Homans, G. (1961), *Social Behavior: Its Elementary Forms*, Harcourt, Brace and World, New York.

Kalven, Jr., H. and Zeisel,H. (1966), *The American Jury*, Little, Brown and Co., Boston.

Leventhal, G.(1980), 'What Should Be Done with Equity Theory?', in K. Gergen, M. Greenberg, and R..Willis (eds), *Social Exchange: Advances in Theory and Research*, Plenum, New York.

Manzo, J. (1988), 'Jury Deliberation as Members' Accomplishment: The Achievement of a Unanimous Decision', Unpublished M.S. Thesis, Department of Sociology, University of Wisconsin, Madison.

Manzo,J. (1991), 'Jurors' Narratives of Personal Experience as Interactional Phenomena in Deliberation Talk', Unpublished manuscript.

Maynard, D. (1984), *Inside Plea Bargaining: The Language of Negotiation*, Plenum Press, New York.

Maynard,D. (1986), 'Offering and Soliciting Collaboration in Multi-Party Disputes Among Children (and Other Humans)', *Human Studies*, vol. 9, pp.261-286.

Maynard,D. (1988), 'Language, Interaction, and Social Problems', *Social Problems*, vol.4, pp.311-344.

Newman, D. J. (1966), *Conviction: The Determination of Guilt or Innocence Without Trial*, Little, Brown and Co., Boston.

Nozick, R. (1974), *Anarchy, State and Utopia*, Basic Books, New York.

Pitkin, H. (1972), *Wittgenstein and Justice*, University of California Press, Berkeley.

Pomerantz, A. and Atkinson,J.M. (1984), 'Ethnomethodology, Conversation Analysis, and the Analysis of Courtroom Interaction', in D.J. Muller, D.E. Blackman, and A.J. Chapman (eds), *Psychology and Law*, Wiley, New York, pp.183-87.

Rawls, J. (1971), *A Theory of Justice*, Harvard University Press, Cambridge, MA.

Rawls, J. (1985), 'Justice as Fairness: Political not Metaphysical', *Philosophy and Public Affairs*, vol. 14, pp.223.

Reskin, B. and Visher, C. (1986), 'The Impacts of Evidence and Extralegal Factors in Jurors' Decisions', *Law and Society Review*, vol. 20, p.423.

Rosett, A. and Cressey, D.R. (1976), *Justice by Consent: Plea Bargaining in the American Courthouse*, J.B. Lippincott, Philadelphia.

Rytina, S. (1986), 'Sociology and Justice', in R.L.Cohen (ed.), *Justice: Views from the Social Sciences*, Plenum Press, New York, pp. 117-151.

Sacks, H. (1966), Unpublished Lectures, University of California, Irvine.

Sacks,H. (1984), 'Notes on Methodology', in J. M. Atkinson and J. Heritage, *Structures of Social Action: Studies in Conversation Analysis*, Cambridge University Press, Cambridge, pp. 21-27.

Schegloff, E. (1987), 'Analyzing Single Episodes of Interaction: An Exercise in Conversation Analysis', *Social Psychology Quarterly*, vol. 50, p.101.

Schutz, A. (1943), 'The Problem of Rationality in the Social World', *Economiça*, vol. 10, pp.130-49.

Simon, R. (1967), *The Jury and the Defense of Insanity*, Little, Brown and Co., Boston.

Thibaut, J. and Walker,L. (1975), *Procedural Justice: A Psychological Analysis*, L.Erlbaum, Hillsdale, N.J.

Von Neuman, J. and Morgenstern, O. (1947), *Theory of Games and Economic Behavior*, Princeton University Press, Princeton, N.J.

West, C. and Zimmerman,D. (1985), 'Gender, language, and discourse', in T. A. van Dijk (ed.), *Handbook of Discourse Analysis, Vol. 4: Discourse Analysis in Society*, Academic Press,London, pp. 103-124.

Wittgenstein, L. (1958), *Philosophical Investigations*, MacMillan, New York.

10 Remorse, Redress, and Reform: Blame-Taking in the Courtroom[1]

MARTHA KOMTER

Introduction

The criminal law process can be seen as a moral arena where the boundaries between good and bad are established and maintained. It has been proposed that the law and morality mutually influence each other in the sense that the elite that makes laws does not usually ignore the dominant moral culture, and that the criminal law process confirms and sometimes leads morality (cf. Garland, 1990, p. 53). Thus those who consider crime to be a result of 'moral decay' may argue that this can be remedied by intensifying the moral message conveyed by the criminal justice system. However, it has also been argued that the criminal law system itself cannot produce moral authority, it can only confirm the existing moral order. A strong moral order, therefore, only needs symbolic punishment to maintain itself, while a weak moral authority must take recourse to coercion (Garland, op. cit., p. 60; Hart, 1961, p. 197). This supports the idea that coercion and morality are intrinsically irreconcilable (Hart, 1963), and that there are limitations to the power of the criminal law system to manipulate morality. Obviously the criminal law system cannot force offenders to become better persons or to develop a moral consciousness.

In this chapter problems of morality and coercion will be investigated to the extent that they are acted out in the courtroom.[2] The material for this study consists of observations of 48 trials of violent crime in three district courts in the Netherlands, of which 31 have been audio-taped and transcribed.[3] An inspection of this material shows that judges elicit a number of expressions of moral confirmation from defendants. Three modes of expression that may illuminate the defendants' moral consciousness will be distinguished. First of all, verbal expressions of remorse, such as apologies, and expressions of regret and shame will be examined. Next the more tangible expressions of remorse, such as paying for the damages or other attempts at redress will be studied. Finally, the promises defendants make to mend their ways will be analyzed.

These three modalities of moral consciousness are investigated as they are produced and made recognizable within their sequential environments, and within the framework of the tasks and interests of the participants at the trials.

Verbal Expressions of Remorse

An essential general feature of remorse is that it originates from inner conviction and is therefore impervious to direct observation. Because the sincerity of verbal expressions of remorse cannot be checked they must be taken at face value. Defendants know that others may judge their statements about their inner feelings with suspicion. They have already discredited themselves by their acts in the past, moreover it is in their interest to make a good impression on the judges. Defendants are potentially unreliable sources of information, and they know that others may think so. What distinguishes apologies in the courtroom from those made in everyday life is that they are made to a third party, and not directly to the injured party. Moreover, there is usually a considerable time-lapse between the offence and the apology. And finally apologies in the courtroom are made in public and to the official authorities.

The Sequential Environment of Verbal Expressions of Remorse

The question to be answered here concerns a first sequential step: what do judges do to induce defendants to apologize? The most frequent occasion for the defendants' expressions of moral consciousness is in their 'last word'. This is a more or less solemn speech ritual, where the defendant has the right to express his views on anything that may pertain to his case. The judge invites the defendant to speak, and the choice of topic is completely open:

(1)
J: → You have the last word. So you can still say something.
...
D: Yes of course that's very difficult.
For something as serious as this you surely cannot (express) your apologies.
I do want to, but I don't think that it- no:

It seems so weak.
Uh if you do something like that to somebody,
and then go and offer your apologies,
it won't give satisfaction.
You'll never be satisfied with that.
I don't forgive myself that I've done this.
Perhaps I'll be able to live with it.
It remains difficult.
Also for me.
((quietly:)) That's all.
J: Right. Then I close the examinations, ...
(8, p. 35)[4]

This fragment illustrates that the defendant's last word is in a 'loose' sequential environment in the sense that the topic is free, and there is no topical follow-up by the judge. The fact that a number of defendants express remorse in their last word indicates the relevance of a moral orientation at this stage of events. These expressions of remorse appear to be generated by a recognition of the harm and self-blame.

An inspection of the material reveals that judges and defendants also exhibit a moralistic orientation after the discussions about the 'facts'. This is shown in direct or implicit utterances of moral disapproval by the judges. The following fragment is from a rape trial:

(2)
J: But you have-
→ I think that we can still conclude from all this,
→ that you've gone further than you should have.
D: Yes.
J: Right
→ as long as we agree on that
whether it has been a complete intercourse or not,
D: No
J: that doesn't matter
→ but this won't do.
D: → No, I agree with you on that.
J: Yes.
D: → For that I feel- I feel somehow sorry for that.
(24, p. 5)

It can be seen from this fragment that the judge does two things: in the first place he puts a lot of emphasis on the expression of his moral disapproval ('you've gone further than you should have'; 'this won't do'), and secondly he almost forces the defendant to agree with him ('we can still conclude from all this'; 'as long as we agree on that'). The defendant then agrees with the judge on the wrongness of his deeds, after which he expresses his regrets.

Let us now consider how judges respond to the defendants' expressions of regret. It has been proposed that apologies It should be noted that expressions of regret are not offered as a direct response to the moral disapproval of the judges, but as a follow-up to the defendants' self-blame. are expressed with the aim of seeking forgiveness (Tavuchis, 1991, p. 22). Although expressions of remorse are appreciated by judges and public prosecutors (Hoefnagels, 1987, p. 56) they are not officially honoured by our criminal law system.[5] A feature of expressions of remorse in the defendant's last word is that they are not responded to by the judge. Judges typically continue after the defendant's last word by closing the examinations and the trials. Because this is an institutionalized feature of the trials, the lack of response of the judges cannot be taken as 'withholding' an acceptance or rejection of the defendants' expressions of regret.

A different situation arises in those instances where the defendants' expressions of remorse occur in the course of their interrogation by the judge. Let us return to example (2), which continues as follows:

(3)
J: that doesn't matter but this won't do.
D: No, I agree with you on that.
J: Yes.
D: For that I feel- I feel somehow sorry for that.
J: Yes.
→ And then a girl who was 15 then right.
D: I didn't know that myself.
...
J: → but you did know that she wasn't an adult woman let's be sure about that. (24, p. 5)

The defendant's expression of regret is followed by the judge's mentioning an aggravating circumstance: the girl was only 15 when the defendant raped her. It seems as if the judge is 'rubbing it in': it is the heinousness of the crime that is the topic of discussion, not the better feelings of the defendant.

In the next fragment the defendant's expressions of regret meet the following response from the judge:

(4)
D: It is a big mistake what I've done.
For yes never before I've taken part in that.
So (please) I'm wholly sorry.
J: → And now you're in jail.
D: Yes.
J: → That is no use to anybody and especially not to your wife and child of course right.
(7, p. 9-10)

Here the judge confronts the defendant with the consequences of his actions, rather than with possible consequences of his remorse. Her response points at the inevitability of the punishment, and at the responsibility of the defendant, not only for his offence but also for the problems he has created for his wife and his new-born baby. Thus expressions of remorse in our courtrooms confirm the guilt of the defendant and anticipate punishment instead of forgiveness.

Remorse and Defences

It has been argued that to apologize is to declare that one has no excuse or defence (Tavuchis, 1991, p. 17). By apologizing people fully accept moral responsibility for their deeds. Thus a risk of contrition in these circumstances is that it may lead to conclusions about an acceptance of punishment (Erikson, 1966, p. 195). This might explain the reactions of the defendant in the following example:

(5)
J: I do want to try and find out what you really think of it.
You might feel dead ashamed for example.
Perhaps you do, but I don't <u>see</u> it.
D: → Well I don't feel dead ashamed for that man.
J: ((interrupts)) No?
D: → I hate that man's guts.
J: → And do you think then that you can cut up his tyres?
D: <u>Hnooo</u> not really.

J: Did you compensate for the damage?
D: Partly.
(31, p. 8)

We see here that the judge's attempts to mobilize expressions of moral consensus fail initially. The defendant's resistance to admitting being ashamed is followed by an account: he hates that man's guts. This might be taken as an anticipation to a possible justification for his acts: there will have been a reason for his hatred, and the destruction of the man's tyres may have been a reaction to a provocation. The judge however overrules the defensive implications of the defendant's response by asking for his views on the appropriateness of his actions. After the defendant has conceded that his actions were wrong, the judge asks for a more tangible expression of the defendant's moral consciousness: his efforts at redress. The half-hearted way in which the defendant admits to the wrongness of his actions reflects the essential irreconcilability of remorse and defences. Showing remorse implies one drops one's defences, and good defences by-pass moral considerations. Defendants who successfully claim self-defence or insanity are not asked whether they think their actions are all right.

It has been shown, however, that the kind of defences that are usually brought forward in the courtroom serve as mitigation rather than as exculpation (Komter, 1994). This would mean that moral and defensive considerations may operate at the same time. In the next example the defendant, standing trial for armed robbery, has brought forward a number of extenuating circumstances to mitigate his guilt:

(6)
J: And then I do know you say that also to the police and it is in the report that mr. Spark has written about you, that you needed money, that it all went wrong, you couldn't find a job, the baby came early,
→ but do you yourself think that this is all right what you've done?
D: What do you mean
J: → How do you think back on it. How do you look back on it.
D: Yes. It is a big mistake what I've done.
For yes never before I've taken part in that.
So (please) I'm wholly sorry.
(7, p. 9-10)

After the judge has recapitulated the mitigations that have been presented, she asks for a moral evaluation of the defendant's acts. She seems to imply that although the robbery may have been induced by the defendant's personal circumstances, this does not make his acts all right. The defendant confirms this and expresses his regrets. The example shows that the judge is not satisfied just to establish the extenuating circumstances that may mitigate the punishment. In her question the judge invokes a moral framework, stressing his moral guilt. Although the extenuating circumstances may be legally significant for establishing the amount of punishment, they lack moral substance. They may make the offence understandable, but they cannot make it right.

The importance of this distinction between legal and moral guilt is also demonstrated in the next example from the rape case commented on before:

(7)

J: But you have- I think that we can still conclude from all this, that you've gone further than you should have.
D: Yes.
J: Right as long as we agree on that
→ whether it has been a complete intercourse or not,
D: No
J: → that doesn't matter but this won't do.
D: No, I agree with you on that.
J: Yes.
D: For that I feel- I feel somehow sorry for that.
(24, p. 5)

The defendant's defence is that the intercourse was not completed because he did not reach an orgasm. The judge underlines the irrelevance of this defence for the moral issues at hand by emphasizing their agreement on his disapproval of the act. The fact is, that this defence does matter from a legal point of view. In Dutch legal practice the offence was classified an 'attempted rape' when a rapist has not reached an orgasm.[6] In the course of this trial the public prosecutor drops the charges of rape and announces that the defendant will only be prosecuted for attempted rape. This means a reduction of the punishment by one third. Thus, although the defence of attempted rape is legally relevant, the judge underlines the fact that morally this does not count. The defendant agrees with him and subsequently expresses his regrets.

The defence counsel in this trial attempts to solve the tension between the relevance of defences and the moral relevance of remorse as follows:

(8)

C: Jansen says that he is deeply sorry,

and that well that he has behaved uh in a pushy way.
(24, p. 13)

A great deal of remorse for a small offence is less risky than a little remorse for a serious crime. This example shows that the defence counsel attacks the problem from two sides: he magnifies the regrets, and diminishes the harm. The defendant's original expression of regret ('I feel somehow sorry for that') is reformulated as 'he is deeply sorry', and the rape for which the defendant stands trial is described as 'pushy' behaviour. The toning down of the seriousness of the offence by means of alternative descriptions is a widely used defence strategy (Drew, 1990; Komter, 1994). The combination of remorse and defence strategies or other mitigations can help to moderate the consequences of remorse, such as the presumed acceptance of punishment. However, it does not solve the inherent incompatibility between defensive strategies and expressions of remorse.

Remorse and Moral Character

When defendants accept the moral responsibility for their acts this also has consequences for an assessment of their moral character. The next fragment is from a case where the defendant stands trial for an attempt at strangling his girlfriend:

(9)
J: Do you wish to say something yourself mr. Rijksman? It is now almost the end of the trial, and you may bring something forward now to close off,
D: Uh I am terribly sorry sorry for for the events,
as I have largely understood them at the police station,
as uh has also been put forward here,
it has been very difficult for me in the past months to to that sen- to say something that makes sense about something which you a did not not uh intend to do at all,
uh uh as uh is charged,
and on the other hand that I yes love mrs. Frankendaal an awful lot.
And I myself I cannot believe it about myself that this has happened.
That's all.
(9, p. 21)

In this trial the defendant has stated that he does not remember much of the events, because he acted in a blind rage. His lack of memory implicitly supports his claim of temporary insanity. He describes his acts as if he was not there: he has learned about the course of events at the police station and in the courtroom, and he cannot believe he has acted in this way. He seems to split himself into two parts, one part that commits an offence and another part that does not believe he is capable of such acts (cf. Goffman, 1971, p. 113). In this way he can at the same time confirm the morals, and indicate that he is not a bad man. Yet his moral confirmation also reveals that he is aware of the fact that his acts are morally wrong. His remorse may be a protection of his moral character, but it also makes him personally responsible for his own discrediting (Emerson, 1969, p. 197). Thus remorse is at the same time inclusive and exclusive: the defendant shows his commitment to the moral community, but by his acts he has placed himself outside it (cf. Erikson, 1966, p. 195).

The Limitations of Verbal Expressions of Remorse

In our culture there is a very limited set of actions available for contrite offenders. Moreover, expressions of remorse will exhibit feelings of moral solidarity rather than attempts to compensate for the harm (Goffman, 1971, p. 117-8). That defendants are aware of the limitations of expressions of remorse is illustrated in the following example, commented on before:

(10)
J: You have the last word. So you can still say something.
...
D: Yes of course that's very difficult.
For something as serious as this you surely cannot (express) your apologies.
I do want to, but I don't think that it- no.
It seems so weak.
Uh if you do something like that to somebody,
and then go and offer your apologies,
it won't give satisfaction.
You'll never be satisfied with that.
I don't forgive myself that I've done this.
Perhaps I'll be able to live with it.
It remains difficult.
Also for me.
((quietly:)) That's all.
(8, p. 35)

This defendant has fiercely attacked a policewoman, who wanted to inspect his motorcycle, with his helmet. The victim is present at the trial as a witness, and she has given a dramatic account of her mental and physical suffering. She has also explained why she considers the letter of apology, written by the defendant before the trial, insincere. The defendant starts by recognizing the seriousness of the harm, mentioning the inadequacy of an apology to compensate for the harm, and expressing his desire to apologize. He then continues with a reflection on the victim's refusal to forgive by stating that he does not forgive himself. This then serves as a negative compensation for the harm, consisting in this instance of his own suffering from his feelings of guilt: it is difficult for him too. The defendant's problems in expressing his apologies depend directly on his acknowledgement of the seriousness of the offence, combined with the fact that an apology cannot undo the harm. At the same time an apology is meant to restore the moral balance, but apparently this works only if the victim is willing to forgive. This means that any expression of remorse in this situation is inadequate. All the offender has at his disposal is speech, in exchange for the conversion of righteous indignation and betrayal into forgiveness (cf. Tavuchis, 1991, p. 35).

It has been shown that verbal expressions of remorse occur in those stages of the trial where an orientation to moral issues is relevant, that is, in the defendant's last word, and after the discussions about the 'facts' of the offence. The defendant's last word is a 'loose' sequential environment in the sense that it is not generated by what immediately precedes it, and there is no topical follow-up. In those cases where verbal expressions of remorse are elicited by what immediately precedes them, we have seen that the judges' moral disapproval results in the defendant's acknowledgement of the harm, which is then followed by defences or expressions of regret, and sometimes in a combination of the two. Verbal expressions of remorse may be both detrimental and expeditious to the defendants' interests. Moral confirmation may protect the moral character of the defendant, but it highlights the wrongness of his deeds. It commits him to accept his fate and anticipates punishment rather than mercy. The defendant's dilemma is to express his moral solidarity while dissociating himself from subsequent conclusions about his guilt. The combination of expressions of remorse and defences indicates the strategic repertory available to escape this dilemma. However, this creates another dilemma because defences and expressions of remorse are essentially irreconcilable: defences by-pass morality, and remorse signifies that one has no defence. Thus the defendant is caught in a web of dilemmas that lead him to combine remorse with defences, which may detract from his credibility in both areas. In these circumstances verbal expressions of remorse are credible only if they are accompanied by more tangible manifestations of remorse, such as offers to make amends or concrete plans to turn over a new leaf.

Redress

In the Dutch criminal law system there are not many possibilities for victims of crime to get some form of compensation, although there are now initiatives to broaden the scope for victim compensation. In court there are three ways in which forms of redress are brought forward. First, efforts at reconciliation or compensation that have taken place before the trial are sometimes referred to: some defendants have written letters of apology to the victims or have offered to pay for the damages. Secondly, the victim can join in the criminal trial as injured party, and claim material or immaterial damages. And, finally, material damages can be imposed as a 'special condition' of a sentence. In this case someone who has served part of his sentence has the choice to pay the damages as part of his probation, or serve the rest of his sentence.

Conditions of Redress

By the time someone appears before the court, earlier moments for redress have passed. In the trial of the man who had tried to strangle his girlfriend (see example 9) the victim had come to regret her report to the police. She wanted to forgive him, to go in therapy together, and to continue the relationship. However, the public prosecutor in the trial declares that he does not only protect the interests of the victim, but also of society:

(11)
P: but they do overlook, that uh in cases like these, of course it matters not only what uh what the parties concerned have in mind, ... but that it is indeed to an uh large extent also a matter of how society assesses this kind of action. (9, p. 15)

The victim's report to the police makes her conflict a responsibility of the state (cf. Christie, 1977) which, from that moment on, controls the ways in which the conflict is settled:

(12)

P: Uhm Rijksman and Dorien uh if I understand correctly would like to start therapy together uh preferably tomorrow, ... and uh then try and end the situation as soon as possible so that they could start living together again.
And then uh then I as uh representative of the Public Prosecution office as far as I'm concerned I must put a stop to this.
For I think that uh what has happened here, is too serious, to uh say uh well that's done, uh let's go back to normal and resume life as soon as possible. It clearly uh concerns here an uh attempt to take someone else's life, there are all kinds of degrees in that, uh and this case is not uh a very harmless one.
(9, p. 16)

This examples illustrates that in this stage of the criminal process the seriousness of the offence renders impossible a reconciliation as sought by the defendant and the victim.

This does not mean, however, that victims have no say at all in the way the conflict may be redressed. Victims must be willing to accept initiatives to this effect by the defendant. From the negotiations about this in the courtroom it appears that certain conditions must be met for the success of the defendants' efforts at redress. What is important is that they convince victims of the sincerity of their intentions. In the next fragment a policewoman, who is the victim of a battery assault (see examples 1 and 10), presents her opinions of the letter of apology that the defendant has written her:

(13)

W: You know how it was, the l- the letter started with uh I I have now the time to write or something for I have my holidays now. And two days later it was my birthday.
((sobbing:)) And six weeks after the events he found the time to write. ...
And he writes such a letter, in my eyes a piece of rubbish. I even think he hasn't even written it himself. But that is my feeling.
And when I realize that I believe two and a half months ago, he himself had the nerve to come to the station where I work, to ask for his motorbike, and the only thing then he asks my colleague who had been there when we checked on uh the motorbikes, and the only thing he asks is why all those things are missing from his motorbike, and doesn't even take the trouble to perhaps ask how I am doing, then I think the letter is a piece of rubbish.
(8, p. 18)

This victim concludes a lack of sincerity from a number of circumstances: it has taken six weeks before the defendant wrote the letter;

the style of the letter is such that she suspects he has not written it himself; when he came to the police station to ask for his motorbike he failed to inquire after her health.

Her suspicion about the defendant's sincerity will undoubtedly have been roused by the assumption that he will want to make a good impression on the court. Moreover, the defence counsel always acts as mediator in such cases between the defendant and the victim, and it is not unthinkable that such a letter is written on the advice of the defence counsel. In this case however, the defence counsel rejects such a suggestion:

(14)

C: Mrs. van Rijn has also mentioned here that she thinks the letter is a piece of rubbish, uhm I want to remark in any case that uh I haven't uh organized that letter so to say, I- the only part I've played in it is that I've eventually given the letter to Mrs. van Rijn's counsel.
(8, p. 34)

Only when the letter has been written on the initiative of the defendant himself, can it convince as an sincere expression of a sense of guilt. If redress is to be a true expression of the defendant's moral consciousness, it has to be voluntary. Yet any attempt at reconciliation, however sincere, can lead to rejection. In the last resort the victim's willingness to forgive determines the success of an attempt at redress.

Proportionality of Redress

Redress must in some way be proportional to the harm done. It the harm is too serious, any effort at redress can fail, especially when it concerns psychological suffering. The defence counsel's recognition of this is illustrated by the following fragment:

(15)

C: → It has been very serious, what has happened,
I've talked to Hans about it uh time and again,
→ and told him time and again that can never be redressed,
→ and a part of it cannot be redressed whatever he'd do for those people, ...
He wanted to try and uh and make amends, and I understand ... that it is eventually difficult, to uh to restore to someone the peace of mind to go out of doors.
(30, p. 12)

This fragment illustrates the dilemma of the defence when the defendant wants to repair the damages. An acknowledgement of the seriousness of the harm lends respectibility to the defence; at the same time this puts a heavy burden on the victim's acceptance of the redress. An anticipation of the victim's implacability may then be a reason to refrain from attempts at redress:

(16)
P: What have you- have you thought about it what you've done to those people, and how you could make it up to them somehow.
D: Yes, I've surely uh thought about that.
Yes I c- uh I could could compensate for the damage or uh or write a letter, or send flowers
but uh I don't think that uh that-
→ they will throw them in the wastepaper basket uh right away I think.
(29, p. 9-10)

This defendant has grabbed handbags from old ladies, and he suspects that they will not appreciate his efforts to undo the harm. The public prosecutor does not agree:

(17)
P: Anyway I also think, that-
and Visser has had uh time to think about it for at least 90 days as I said just now,
that something should be done about the damages.
Uh he has even been too callous to write a letter I must honestly say that I hold him greatly to blame for that.
(29, p. 12)

This defendant has been remanded in custody for 90 days. The idea of the public prosecutor is that this is a time to think and to repent (see also section 4 on reform). The fact that this defendant has failed to try and redress the harm is taken by the public prosecutor as a sign of callousness. The defence counsel however proffers a different interpretation:

(18)
C: The Public Prosecutor has blamed my client, uh for not having written letters to the victims.
My client has certainly thought about that, ...
and he has given me the reason for that, which I think is an excellent reason,
those 80 year old ladies have he understands that now fully, they have been

> frightened to death,
> and is it then sensible, to confront people, who perhaps because of their age have not such a good memory any more, now again with the letter of the offender. And <u>that</u> is the reason, why he hasn't done it.
> (29, p. 15)

Thus the same behaviour can be interpreted as callousness but also as sensitivity of the defendant. A sincere sense of the seriousness of the harm inflicted can lead to a recognition of the futility or insufficiency of any effort at redress.

Redress and Punishment

The more serious the offence, the greater the effort that is required to make up for it. Besides, the reparation of the damage also depends on the means the defendants have at their disposal. Everyone can afford writing a letter, but that does not mean that a defendant should make it too easy for himself. A defence counsel explains how he has tried to put the defendant back on the right track:

(19)
C: He's had to write all five of them. Not write one letter and then copy it, it has been a sort of schoolmasterish assignment. You write it out 5 times. And he did not object to that at all.
And that then was an attempt on my part ... to enable someone, to make himself a start with the restoration of uh social order.
(30, p. 11-12)

This 'schoolmasterish assignment' reminds us of the kind of punishment unruly pupils get at school: the defendant has to 'write lines', to write the same letter to his five victims. The defendant's willingness to comply with this assignment is brought forward by the defence counsel as his contribution to the restoration of social order. The more effort the redress requires from the defendant, the greater its cogency as restoration of the moral balance. If the defendant suffers under the strain of undoing the harm, this can counterbalance the victim's suffering. In this respect redress can be seen as an anticipation of, or an alternative for his punishment.

Let us now compare this example with fragment (14), where the defence counsel emphasizes that the defendant has written the letter on his own initiative. We have proposed that redress as a sincere expression of moral consciousness depends on voluntariness. On the other hand redress has to be proportional to the harm done. In this case redress becomes convincing through the suffering of the defendant under the coercion of the criminal law system. This tension between voluntariness and coercion is most noticeable in those cases where damages are demanded by victims who have joined in the trial as injured party. In these cases the defendant is asked whether he is willing to pay an amount of money to the victim as compensation for the harm. In this way the defendant can show his good will, but at the same time he has no real opportunity to refuse, because the payment can be imposed in the verdict. Something similar occurs when damages are demanded as a special condition of the punishment. In this case a defendant who gets a (partially) suspended sentence will have to pay for the damages in his probation period:

(20)

J: Well yes that uh those damages that uh only starts to count when you're released again, then such an uh probation starts,
and then you'd <u>have</u> to go to work right away, so not like I don't feel like it then you'd have to go to work to compensate for the damages.
...
And if you would <u>not</u> do it, yes then you'd still have to be locked up for another period.
But you'd have that in your own hands then.
But that really only starts to <u>re</u>ally count, after you've been released again.

D: Yes.
(29, p. 15-16)

A period of probation is considered as an opportunity where the offender can demonstrate that he has renounced his criminal past. We see here that the defendant has a choice between a prison sentence and paying for the damages, but that choice is imposed by the verdict of the court. The obligation to earn money to be able to pay his debt works as an extra burden on his probation.

What is also noticeable in this trial is the fact that this defendant might have paid for the damages earlier, in exchange for a suspension of his custody:

(21)

C: I have also thought about damages, my client too, uhm I have that wrong-misjudged the case apparently when I proffered this to the examining judge and to the court in chambers as an argument to release my client, or to suspend him, **then he could keep his job and he could have paid for the**

damages.
(29, p. 15)

This defendant lost his job on account of his being taken in custody. The defence counsel's request to suspend the custody was rejected. Thus the defendant was first deprived of the opportunity to compensate for the damages more or less voluntarily, when he still had his job, while eventually he was forced to pay for the damages as special condition of his punishment.

All these examples show that several forms of redress are available to defendants to make up for the harm, but these have to fit in the framework of the criminal law system. Because the state, at the same time, mediates between defendant and victim, and decides on the fate of the defendant, tensions arise between coercion and voluntariness. As a result redress can at the same time be taken as an alternative for, and as form of, punishment. The retributive and reparative functions of the criminal law system overlap, while they are in principle irreconcilable (cf. Davis, 1992, p. 148).

Redress can be seen as a tangible manifestation of the moral consciousness of the defendant, and is therefore more amenable to inspection than verbal expressions of remorse. However, if redress is to be a true expression of the defendant's moral sense it must be made voluntarily, whereas this stage of the criminal law process is dominated by coercion. The defendant's compliance with redress that is forced on him can only be interpreted as obedience, and thereby he is deprived of the opportunity to demonstrate his moral consciousness.

Reform

Most defendants indicate to the court that they want to turn over a new leaf, and most judges stimulate this by asking them to elaborate on it. When defendants are asked to describe the nature of their plans for the future, they appear to harbour common aspirations:

(22)
J: What are the plans when you'll be released,
D: Well I hope to be released as soon as possible,
and to get my girlfriend back.
For uh <u>that</u> really worries me.
And uh yes then I'll have to get new housing again, and you name it.
J: Yes. But also other con- concrete plans?

D: Well yes in any case to stay away from the drugsscene right,
uh yes try to find a job or whatever.
J: yes,
D: For this is no fun either.
(14, p. 14-15)

Such elementary attributes of citizenship, like a steady relationship, a home, a job, or an education, are mentioned very often as the substance of a new life. These plans for the future need no further justification as they correspond with commonly held values in our society. Consequently the negotiations about the defendants' future concern the feasibility rather than the substance of their aspirations.

Future and Past

Plans for a better future often stand in direct relation to the background circumstances and motives presented to explain the offence (Komter, 1993). A connection is assumed between what has driven defendants to commit the offences, and how they can avoid this in the future. If the offence has been committed under the pressure of a drug addiction, the defendant says he wants to kick the habit; if the wrong friends have led the defendant astray he wants to break with them; if the offence is committed in a blind rage the defendant wants to go into therapy in order to control his temper in the future. A problem with this is that the more the defendant presents himself as a victim of circumstance, the harder it will be to avoid this in the future. The less responsibility the defendant assumes for his acts, the more difficult it is to explain that he will be able to take this responsibility for organizing his life in the future. A hopeless position in life may perhaps make the offence understandable, but it provides bleak prospects for the future. What the defendant gains in cogency at one level he loses at another.

On the other hand there may be circumstances conducive to reform without requiring much effort from the defendant. People sometimes point to the fact that the defendant is soon to become a father, that he has a good education, that his parents or friends support him in every way, or that he is becoming a little old to be addicted and that he will soon outgrow it. Just as it is assumed that circumstances may drive someone to commit an offence, they may apparently also protect him against criminal involvement. What is indispensible for this, however, is the will to start a new life, and the insight that it is necessary to change:

(23)

C: For the first time he has- in his career he has robbed a woman, and that is apparently necessary, to bring about the insight, and that insight is there, that he says I am going downhill. He says that to the examining judge. It is also the very first time president, that my client has confessed immediately, in an early stage, and not just now at the trial, but to the examining judge. That is in his case (extremely) unique.

...

It's important, that he has made that confession, it's important to him, that he co-operates with the examinations,

→ because it means, that he realizes himself, that it will have to change. (12, p. 12)

The defendant's insight into the hopelessness of his criminal career is an important condition for change. The defence counsel substantiates the authenticity of this insight by his statement that the defendant, who is an 'old acquaintance' of the court, has confessed for the first time and has cooperated with the investigations. This is to show that the defendant accepts the official morality and plans to behave accordingly in the future. Defendants often describe their confessions as 'starting with a clean slate'. This implies a moral turn from bad to good, and an acceptance of punishment. A defendant first has to put his past behind him before he can turn over a new leaf.

Reform and Punishment

It is noticeable that the effects of the criminal law process on the life of a defendant are usually not referred to in the courtroom. The judges' questions about the defendants' plans for their future resemble those in a 'career-planning' interview: how does the defendant imagine his future, what does he want to achieve, and what steps is he going to take towards it:

(24)

J: And after that ((=finish school)) you want to study biology right,

D: Yes,

J: Will you be moving into lodgings then, or don't you know yet.

D: I don't know yet.

J: What does that depend on then?

D: On what happens here.

J: On what happens here. Yes.

(8, p. 22)

(25)

J: Uh what are your plans with that study- well plans you have quit.
D: Yes your honour
J: ((interrupts)) (you've) quit definitively.
D: Uh that's right.
On account of what uh uh has happened I'm afraid that it will perhaps be definitive. But
J: On account of the grant or on account of the registration, or how is that.
D: Uh on account of all of that.
(9, p. 11)

These two examples indicate clearly that in this stage the defendants are not master of their fate. It is impossible for them to anticipate the punishment they will probably get, and its consequences for their future. The judges too approach the topic with some caution. In the first place they cannot anticipate the consequences of the punishment because they have not yet passed judgement, and secondly it is somewhat contradictory to stimulate the good intentions of the defendant, and then invalidate these by pointing at what is in store for them. In the two examples above this dilemma is shown by the defendants' vague references to the criminal process, and by the judges' apparent acceptation of this vagueness. Defendants seem to be aware that it is ill-advised to blame the criminal law system for their lack of perspective.[7]

Help and Punishment

It is well known that a criminal record is an obstacle to finding a job, and that prison is not very effective in discouraging drug use. The participants in the courtroom often refer to the possibility that defendants may not be able to reform when left to their own devices, especially when it concerns stopping their drug habit:

(26)

J: He has said that you uh are planning to quit.
D: That's right. Yes.
J: Yes Mr. Sahil we don't want to be unpleasant, but we hear so many people here say that right?
Almost everyone who sits here,
D: I've never said it.
J: You've never said it.
D: No.

J: And what are you going to do about it?
For simply <u>quitting</u>, hardly anyone succeeds in that.
D: No, that's true, but I want to work I want to
J: yes,
D: → I want uh to be admitted somewhere where I'll be he- helped.
(21, p. 4)

This judge expresses his doubts about the perseverance necessary to get clean of drugs, to which the defendant replies with the request to be admitted to a drugs rehabilitation center. However, his defence counsel has not managed to secure a place for him. The public prosecutor formulates the problems he is confronted with:

(27)
P: If you read that then it doesn't look <u>very</u> hopeful. There are <u>too</u> few opportunities for Moroccans who are addicted...
Where can he go, he cannot go to his parents, at least he doesn't want to, and then yes then I somehow get the impression that the best thing for Mr.. Sahil is to be locked up for the time being, until everything is completely arranged.
(21, p. 7)

This example illuminates the two aims of the criminal law system of treatment and punishment. Punishment should not only function as retribution for the harm, but also to rehabilitate the offender. Even when a defendant is motivated to cooperate with this, help is not always available. The only thing that remains is punishment. The probation service also has a double task: it has to assist defendants in finding their way back to law-abiding society, and it has to provide information to the court about the defendants' prospects. In the next example the judge reads from the report of the probation officer:

(28)
J: It's a rather short report, and uh ... Mr. uh Spies affirms my client has had a chance and he has not taken it.
...
My client is reasonable enough to realize that within the judicial framework he won't be offered any chances any more for the time being.
(12, p. 9)

This is a fragment of the trial of the defendant who had for the first time in his life robbed a woman, and then realized that he would have to change (see fragment 23). In spite of these good intentions the defendant has not made use of the program of the rehabilitation center because, according to him, he was badly treated there. By defining the situation in terms of 'chances' offered to the defendant, his own responsibility for his failure is stressed, and the adequacy of the help is not taken into account (cf. Emerson, 1969, p. 188).

Moral Improvement, Deterrence, and Retribution

A defendant is assumed to rehabilitate himself not only by way of help, but also through punishment. The idea is that prisoners have all the time for reflection and repentance. Example (17) has shown that a public prosecutor has this opinion, and in the next fragment the defendant expresses the same thought:

(29)

J: Thank you Mr. Zegers what do you want to say yourself.

D: Well. Yes. I've just told you that I've had uh for three months I've had the time to think, and uh yes I've come to the conclusion that I uh don't want to do this uh to others and to myself any more. And I hope that we'll then get another chance to start work, and to uh and my girlfriend to be able to lead a normal life. Thank you.

J: Fine.

(16, p. 27-28)

The idea that detention leads to repentance and moral improvement may perhaps seem outdated, yet the participants in the courtroom sometimes appear to endorse it. Besides it is assumed that the hardships of imprisonment will induce people to avoid it in the future. If the moral sense of convicts does not develop in prison, their future behaviour may be guided by their fear of punishment. If prison does not rehabilitate, it should at least deter:

(30)

P: What uh is the case actually, that is that uh little by little it does contain a lot of three twelves, uh violent theft, and uh that also apparently longer prison sentences that have been imposed, that they don't work.

(12, p. 11)

Punishment is supposed to work if a convict keeps clear of the law after his release. However there can be several reasons for this. Someone can start using smarter methods so that he will not get caught. He can abide by the law out of fear of punishment, or for moral considerations. If a suspect gets caught this may mean that he is either not smart enough, or not afraid enough, or not virtuous enough. This way of measuring the effectiveness of punishment does not take into account the underlying motives and circumstances, and does not discriminate between cunning, fear, and virtue.

Although example (23) shows that the defendant has by now come to the conclusion that his life will have to change, the public prosecutor only considers his criminal record. While the defence counsel suggests moral improvement, the public prosecutor concludes a failure of the deterrent effects of punishment. This then provides him with the argument to demand an extra long term in prison:

(31)

P: Considering all this Mister president, I demand a prison sentence for the duration of two years, with deduction.
Besides I very consciously do not ask to impose part of it as suspended sentence, ...
on account of the fact that Rutten is such an old acquaintance of the law, and has been sentenced so many times, that he should know by now what the effect of punishment ought to be, and I deem a surplus value uh of a suspended part, I deem that out of the question.
(12, p. 11)

The length of the sentence is justified here not by the seriousness of the offence, but by the defendant's recidivism. This reflects the ambiguity of a criminal law system where both retribution and moral improvement is sought. Punishment becomes retribution, not only for the harm that has been inflicted, but especially for the incorrigibility of the defendant. This demonstrates the helplessness of a criminal law system that at the same time provides the defendants with opportunities for a better future, and deprives them of it.

Conclusion

Three themes have been discussed here that may each reflect on the moral position of the defendant in the courtroom: remorse, redress, and reform. If remorse, redress and reform are to be genuine expressions of the defendants' moral consciousness, they have to be sincere, voluntary, and feasible. A sequential feature that differentiates these expressions of morality from those made in everyday contexts is the absence of forgiveness. Our criminal law system is concerned with justice rather than with mercy. Although the court appears to respect these manifestations of morality, the circumstances in which they must be expressed deeply influence their interpretation. Thus verbal expressions of remorse can be taken as mere strategy to mollify the judges; the defendants' willingness to compensate for the harm may be taken as mere obedience in view of the coercion of the court; and plans to turn over a new leaf may be invalidated by the prospect of punishment. In other words, expressions of moral consciousness may be overshadowed by their strategic consequences, by the coercion of the criminal law system, and by the threat of punishment.

This is consequential for the moral persuasiveness of the criminal law process. The defendants' moral confirmation underlines the ritual of 'justice' that is being enacted in the public arena of the courtroom. The fact is that submissive defendants are easier to convict than recalcitrant ones. The defendants' moral confirmation is of symbolic importance for the moral credibility of the criminal law process, because their recognition of the harm legitimates the activities of the court. Ritualized confirmation of the moral order reassures the public and the professionals, and reinforces existing relations of authority. It can be suggested that judges appreciate expressions of moral sense from the defendants because this may be taken as the first step towards rehabilitation, and might induce the court to be lenient in their sentence. Yet the defendants' efforts to restore the moral balance anticipate punitive rather than reconciliatory reactions. The trial may, therefore, lead to the alienation of defendants, instead of an improvement in their conduct.

Notes

1. This study was presented at the 13th World Congress of Sociology, Bielefeld, Germany (1994). A different version, focused on dilemmas, will appear in Komter (forthcoming).
2. I am indebted to Herman Franke, Ellie Lissenberg and Marca Schasfoort for their comments on earlier versions of this paper.
3. In the Netherlands we have a combination of an inquisitorial and an adversarial criminal justice system. The inquisitorial aspects are shown in the examinations of the defendant by the judge, and in the importance of the 'preliminary examinations'. Prior to the trial, defendants and witnesses have been heard by the police and by the examining judge, and their depositions have been recorded in the defendant's dossier. In court this dossier is an important source of

information for the judges, next to the statements of the defendants on the spot. Witnesses are only seldom summoned to appear in court. The most important phases of the trial are: the opening of the proceedings by the presiding judge, the public prosecutor's presentation of the indictment, the examination of the defendant by the judges, the public prosecutor's summing up and advice on punishment, the defence counsel's address, the defendant's last word, and the closing of the proceedings by the presiding judge. Defendants have the right to remain silent, and they swear on oath that they will speak the truth.

4. Transcription conventions:

J	judge
D	defendant
C	defence counsel
P	public prosecutor
underlined	stress
(parentheses)	unclear utterance
((double parentheses))	transcriber's note
((24, p. 5))	trial no. 24, p. 5 of transcription etc.
. full point	falling intonation
, comma	slightly rising intonation
?	rising intonation

The names have been changed for reasons of privacy.

5. In contrast to, for example, Japan. Braithwaite (1989, p. 165) describes the different consequences of remorse in Japan and the USA. Two Americans in Japan stand trial for rape. On the advice of their Japanese attorneys they had secured the reconciliation with the victim, who had written a letter to the court stating that she had been compensated and that she absolved the Americans completely. During the trial however they claimed their innocence. Because they showed no remorse they were sentenced to the maximum term of imprisonment. In contrast to this Braithwaite describes an incident of a Japanese woman arriving in the USA with a large amount of American currency which she had accurately declared on the entry form. This would not normally be prosecuted. Then she wrote a letter acknowledging her violation of the law, apologizing profusely and seeking forgiveness. This blatant confession of guilt obliged the Justice Department to prosecute her.
6. Since the revision of the law on rape in 1991, this distinction has lost its relevance. This trial took place before the law was changed.
7. There is one exception. A denying defendant says to the court that if he is sent to prison he will end up in the criminal circuit, for which the court will be responsible. The judge replies: 'if you are proven to be guilty, you are already in the criminal circuit. Then you yourself are to blame for that'. Two weeks later he is pronounced guilty.

References

Braithwaite, J. (1989), *Crime, shame and reintegration*, Cambridge University Press, Cambridge.

Christie, N. (1977), 'Conflicts as property', *The British Journal of Criminology*, vol.17, pp.1-15.

Davis, G. (1992), *Making amends. Mediation and reparation in criminal justice*, Routledge, London.

Drew, P. (1990), 'Strategies in the Contest between Lawyer and Witness in Cross-examination', in N. Levi and A.G. Walker (eds), *Language in the Judicial Process*, Plenum Press, New York, pp.39-64.

Emerson, R.M. (1969), *Judging Delinquents. Context and Process in Juvenile Court*, Aldine, Chicago.

Erikson, K.T. (1966), *Wayward Puritans: A study in the sociology of deviance*, John Wiley and Sons, New York.

Garland, D. (1990), *Punishment and Modern Society. A study in Social Theory*, Clarendon Press, Oxford.

Goffman, E. (1971), *Relations in Public. Microstudies of the Public Order*, Harper & Row, New York.

Hart, H.L.A. (1961), *The Concept of Law*, Clarendon Press, Oxford (Herdruk uit 1992).

Hart, H.L.A. (1963), *Law, Liberty and Morality*, Oxford University Press, Oxford.

Hoefnagels, G.P. (1987), *Rituelen ter terechtzitting (Rituals in Court)*, Kluwer, Deventer.

Komter, M.L. (1993), 'Onderhandelen in de rechtszaal over verklaringen voor geweldsmisdrijven' ('Negotiating in the courtroom about explanations for violent crime'), in C. Bouw and B. Kruithof (red.), *De kern van het verschil. Culturen en identiteiten*, Amsterdam University Press, Amsterdam, pp. 129-150.

Komter, M.L. (1994), 'Accusations and Defences in Courtroom Interaction', *Discourse and Society* 5/2, pp.165-187.

Komter, M.L. (forthcoming), *Dilemmas in the Courtroom: A Study of Trials of Violent Crime in the Netherlands*, Lawrence Erlbaum Associates, Hillsdale, New Jersey.

Tavuchis, N. (1991), *Mea Culpa: A Sociology of Apology and Reconciliation*, Stanford University Press, Stanford.

11 Practicing Law: A Study of Pedagogic Interchange in a Law School Classroom

STACY BURNS

"Isn't that the way we operationalize in lawyer lingo the point you've just made? We didn't go in 'I would...' We go in real time and say just what we said...You see the point I'm trying to get at? Start talking as a lawyer would talk on that occasion with that problem in front of him/her... Got it?"
(Law Professor to civil procedure students at the end of a pedagogic interchange.)

Introduction

Upon first glance into almost any American law school classroom, the observer is struck by the distinctive nature of the interactions which routinely occur there. It is quickly apparent that instruction in law school is characteristically different from teaching in other types of university classes where lecturing is the primary format (Stevens, 1971; Goffman, 1981). Central to the uniqueness of law school training are the locally organized pedagogic interchanges which make for the real time practice, development and material display of a distinctively legal competency and expertise.[1,2] What is being taught and learned in law school is not just the substantive legal curriculum, but more generally, a mode of professional conduct.

Some existing studies of socialization (Brim and Wheeler, 1966; Goffman, 1961; Lofland, 1966) or rites of passage and conversion (Turner, 1974, following van Gennep, 1960; Sargant, 1957) are potentially applicable to the law school training process.[3] Other research deals directly with legal educational practice and interprets it as instruction in the use of legal jargon and the acquisition of the "cant" (Philips, 1982) or as learning the lawyer's professional "role" and the proper "role distance" from its sometimes alienating aspects (Pepper, 1986 and Luban, 1988).[4,5]

Such social scientific, educational and jurisprudential literature broadly outlines, but is ultimately independent of the detailed orderliness of pedagogic interchanges and how they unfold in real time and in the first place in the law school classroom. What is reported by conventional studies leaves largely unaddressed many matters of central practical concern, relevance and consequentiality to law professors and their students. Traditional analytic approaches are unable to specify what connection, if any, there may be between the observable detail and contingent ordering of pedagogic tasks in the law classroom and the skills identifying of professionally competent legal practice.

Garfinkel (1989) refers to such a state of affairs as a "gap" in the research literature. As Heritage describes it, this gap "consists of all the missing descriptions of what occupational activities consist of and all the missing analyses of how the practitioners manage the tasks which, for them, are matters of serious and pressing significance..." (Heritage, 1984, at p. 299). Significant promise for closing the gap and locating this orderliness is demonstrated in the ground-breaking studies and findings of ethnomethodology and conversational analysis (Garfinkel, 1967; Garfinkel and Sacks, 1970; Sacks, Schegloff and Jefferson, 1974; Sacks, 1992 and Heritage and Drew, 1992).

An analysis of the phenomenon of law school training requires a close empirical investigation of what actually happens in the times and places where legal instruction occurs. This study examines the recurrent methods by which law class participants organize and concertedly accomplish their practical pedagogic and legal tasks, *in situ* and in observable detail. Through pedagogic exchanges with the law professor, students recurrently attempt to publicly display the technical legal "practice" just then called for in addressing the specific legal problem in front of them. This study details some of the technical ways class members are taught improvisationally and in material detail how to engage in competent legal discourse and argumentation.

The analysis centers on the "professionally led" nature of pedagogic exchanges between the law professor and his students, although the student's spontaneous participation in the interchange also significantly influences the developing direction of the pedagogic exchange.[6] Indeed, key to the pedagogy in many law school classes are the technical practices by which the professor uses the student's emergently detailed responses as the material resources with which to engage the student in the performance of a variety of practical legal tasks, such as making legal objections, offers of proof, requests to amend the pleadings, motions for judgment on the pleadings, etc.[7,8]

The law professor commonly requires students in pedagogic interchange to make use of newly found legal knowledge in asserting competent courses of legal argumentation, often with the student knowing little about what technical legal discourse is. The professor rarely tells his students "in so many words" just what to say in the unfolding pedagogic interchange to resolve a given legal problem and it is left up the student to provide the words of a competent lawyer then confronting that task (see Garfinkel and Sacks, 1970, at p. 351 and Macbeth, 1991, at p. 292 and Macbeth, 1994). Hence, in such exchanges, students are asked to demonstrate the very legal competency that is ongoingly being taught to them.

The law professor regularly puts students to the task of asserting cogent and properly articulated legal arguments and positions and demonstrating the use of legal terms, rules, concepts, principles, etc. Yet, under the professor's rigorous scrutiny, the law students quickly learn that their exposition and invocation of legal concepts, terminology, rules or principles alone does not in fact establish the legal competency of their practice or the cogency of their asserted position. Like the new army recruit at an inspection, it may seem to the student that no preparation is ever sufficient and no response is ever good enough (see Sargant, 1969).

However, unlike a practicing lawyer in adversarial interchange with an opponent, the law professor's pedagogic task is *not* to win the argument and completely annihilate the students. Although the professor obviously understands the legal subject matter and the techniques of legal practice to a skill level far beyond that of the novice student and could easily prevail in any adversarial interchange, such a stance would not best serve the aims of the pedagogic exchange. Indeed, the law professor's pedagogic endeavor is to teach students the skills of legal reasoning and exposition without being overly intimidating. At the same time the law pedagogue instructs the students in adversarial techniques, s/he also tries to engage them in legal discussions and encourage them to think for themselves.

But the fact remains that the context of many work day tasks of lawyers can be characterized as generally adversarial, if not downright hostile. Accordingly, the law school pedagogy constrains students to use certain non-optional techniques of legal practice which can only be mastered through their real time engagement in adversarial interchange.

The public nature of the pedagogic interchange is also an important and consequential feature of law teaching.[9,10] It is not uncommon for law graduates to recount their experience in law school in terms of being placed on the "hot seat" in front of their peers in class and being compelled to partake in a series of interchanges or "grillings" with the professor which are often humiliating, perplexing and technically exacting. In large part, the law professor's expertise consists of the ability to reveal in front of the whole class just what is irrelevant, faulted and deficient in the student's response. The professor makes evident in real time and in detail the untenability of the students' asserted propositions, the inapplicability of their arguments, the incompleteness of their rule citations, their vulnerability to unanticipated counter-positions, etc. Thus, class members are taught moment-by-moment how to advance particular partisan aims by asserting and sustaining cogent legal argumentation and exposition in the face of a variety of adversarial obstacles ongoingly interjected by the professor.

The fact that the pedagogic practice of legal argumentation is done publicly makes observable to the entire class the particular legal task being posed for the selected student and exhibits the adequacy of the student's attempt to address that task. Thus, through these public pedagogic interchanges, the class witnesses and is made accountable for learning the objects constitutive of civil procedural law and the skills of competent legal practice. During the pedagogic exchanges, the non-participating law students, who are subject to the ever-present possibility of being called upon next by the professor, closely monitor the unfolding interchange and stay persistently "on their toes".

Setting and Methodology

The law classroom was selected as a perspicuous setting in which to examine how, over the course of three years of law school training, students learn increasingly to think, act and be in the world as a lawyer. The examination of the law school classroom as a research site was tied to my member's knowledge of what went on there.[11]

The law school class seemed especially intriguing for gaining access to the embodied development and exercise of the professional legal craft in real time and in material detail. Specifically, I knew that there I would find and observe novice law students repeatedly stumbling while attempting to learn and demonstrate the skills of legal practice. Law school "practice" provided fertile material grounds for specifying both the methodic competencies common to professional legal training and some of the orderly skills constitutive of competent legal practice.

The data relied upon in this project consists of video and audiotape recordings of class sessions in a first semester civil procedure course, along with my own observations of the unfolding classroom events. Through videotape recordings, I obtained detailed, real time records of the pedagogic interchanges which preserved for analysis the moment-by-moment embodied day's work of classroom participants in addressing their practical tasks.

The episode presented in this paper is just one extract from a rich array of potentially analyzable events. It was specifically selected for presentation because it provoked understanding of the professional practices and pedagogy of legal exposition and argumentation.

Data Analysis: "In Court" Episode

The interactive structure of the "in court" episode exhibits as well as formulates a recurrent feature of pedagogic interchange in the law school classroom.[12] Neither law school training nor professional legal practice ever happen hypothetically, in general, in the abstract or in principle. Rather, professional training and work are unavoidably practice centered and addressed to the particular pending problem of practical concern and consequentiality for the participants within an actual case and specific course of professional interchange.

In this episode, the professor requires the student as counsel "in court" to participate with him in a technical course of legal exposition. The pedagogic interchange involves a consideration of "loss of use" damages which was the subject of a published decision reprinted in the course casebook and assigned as reading for this day's class session. In particular, the interchange addresses the fact that loss of use damages were not specifically sought as a remedy by the plaintiffs in their pleadings.[13] Thus, the "legal practice" involved in this exchange engages the student in articulating in real time and in legally competent material detail a request by plaintiff's counsel (the student) for permission from the court (the professor) to amend her pleadings to seek recovery for this additional item of damages. Our focused attention begins at line 14.

"In Court" Data[14]

P=Professor
S=Student [Subsequent participating students are designated by S2, S3, etc.]

P: ... And one might say look, to the defendant, if you are saying that the issue wasn't preser:ved, you have some kind of obligation to help close the door. To say that the only issue is the market value of the plane at the time, and you weren't very specific about that--but, the way this language in the pretrial order is it says--and the uh the losses resulting to the plaintiff therefrom--well, what does that mean. Okay, there's that possibility. Second, this appellate court may not li:ke doorclosers. (.2)
And therefore, it it requires unequivocal ah um failure by the plaintiff to tender the issue.

(4.8)

((P calls on student with raised hand))

S: Um I was going to say that Rule Fifteen B of the Federal Rules of Civil Procedure allows for amendments in the form of the evidence ((?)) n' that n' so that IF the defendant had objected to the question on the grounds that it did not comply with the procedure, it says that the um objecting party ((if it)) ((quoting)) "fails to satisfy the (court) that the admission of such evidence would prejudice him in maintaining his action or defense upon the merits". So therefore a=

P: =Yeah but read the whole sentence.

S: Okay huh ((laughter)) It says ((quoting)) "If the evidence is objected to at trial on the ground that it is not within the issues made by the pleadings, the court may allow the pleadings to be amended and shall do so freely when the presentation of the merits of the action will be subserved thereby and the objecting party fails to satisfy the court that the admission of such evidence would prejudice him in maintaining his action or defense upon the merits".

(1.0)

P: Alright. If you wish to avail yourself of the benefit of that rule (.6) in Reynolds against the Bank (1.0) and the situation is (.2) that the objectuve--you, you're representing the plaintiff--you've asked the question, the objection is made (1.0) uhh: your line of uh uh argument I suppose is that the issue was fairly tendered by the pre-trial statement (1.2) Granted Your Honor that the pre-trial statement is not elaborate in its detail (.8) °you wouldn't say you wouldn't say (.2) granted Your Honor we didn't put it in the pre-trial statement-you'd say° ((slight laughter)) granted Your Honor the pre-trial statement is not elaborate in its detail (.6) nevertheless the very generality of the language of the pre-trial statement encompasses whatever the damages might be (.5) particularly in the absence of any suggestion by the defendant (.3) that that the issues ought to be particularized.

(1.0) ((Professor crinkles face and leans over to impersonate elderly JUDGE))

P: We:ll (1.0) I still believe in pleading though.

(3.0) ((Laughter from class, including S))

P: Ya don't Ya don't plead, in this court ya don't prove!

(4.5) ((More laughter))

((Professor resumes normal conduct))

P: Now: what do you say? ((gestures toward S))

S: Okay, basically the purpose of the rule (.3) which (.5)
[
P: ((JUDGE)) Now
LAdy, I want an Ah-gument from you.

(1.0)

P: ((Normal)) I want you to pretend now that you're in that Court (.2) and Judge J. has just ruled (.5)

P: ((JUDGE)) We::ll, without the pleadings you can't ((prove)) it.

((laughter))

(6.8)

S: Well=

P: ((Normal)) =What do you say now?

(.6)

S: Ba:sically, I would offer=

P: ((Normal)) =Yer not-I don-I want you to Shift into (.6) ((I
want you to)) we're in that Court-I don't want you telling me
what you Would do, I want you to Act the behavior of counsel-
What (.3) Words come out.

(3.0)

S: The Proof of the damages sustained by the plaintiff (.3) in
terms of Loss of use, loss of ((business)) profits (.2) um (.3)
although not alleged specifically in the pleadings (.2) would be
(.2) relevant in this ca:se (.2) because (.2) they (2.0) ((the
contention here)) would not be that (.2) the defendant was caught
unawares (.2) of the possibility (.2) tha t
[
P: ((JUDGE)) What are you TAlking
about!

((laughter (3.0)))

P: ((JUDGE)) You SAYing that the pl-it's Already an Issue?

(2.5)

P: ((JUDGE)) I ruled against you on that. (.6) I'll rule against you
aGAin (.3) so you'll know.

((laughter (12.0). S shakes head at 2 and 12 seconds))

P: ((Normal)) What'll you do no:w?

S2: It Is in the pleadings (.2) ((Isn 't))
[
P: ((JUDGE)) I just ruled it Isn't.

((laughter (1.8)))

P: ((JUDGE)) When I say it isn't, it isn't.

S2: If (.4) I as counsel can (.3) put (the complaint) in front-under
your nose and it SHOWS it is obvious=

P: ((JUDGE))=it's UNder my nose.

(1.0)

S2: According to ((laughter)) ((inaudible)) of the opening brief
they say the subject of appeal involves paragraph six of the first
count and paragraph three of the sec on
[
P: ((JUDGE)) I can Read it. (.8) All it
talks about is damage ((as a result of the loss of the plane)) (.4) I
don't think that sufficiently tenders the difference between (.2)
loss of use (.2) 'n that new fangled rule you're pushing for (.2) 'n
market value which is the good o::ld rule.

((laughter (8.0)))

S3: For the record Your Honor I'd just like to state my objection
to your ruling (.2) I'm not going to argue it further but I'd like t a
[
P: ((JUDGE)) You
can take it on apPEA:l
((laughter (6.0)))

P: ((JUDGE)) Well I guess I'll have to let you do that.

(3.0)

P: Is that all we have?

(.8)

S4: Offer proof.

(2.0)

P: ((JUDGE)) ((You want-maybe)) ask the question again ((?))
(.2) Sonny?

(1.4)

S4: ((inaudible))
[
P: ((JUDGE)) I'll susTAin it again.

S4: ((I'll just)) offer proof of uh=

P: ((JUDGE)) =You want to make an offer of proof?

S4: ((uh)) Yes. (.2) Yes Your Honor.

P: ((JUDGE)) That's better.

((laughter (3.0)))

P: Is that All we're gonna Hear?

(2.5)

S5: Your Honor on the basis of the rule just cited I request
permission to amend the pleadings.

(.3)

P: ((JUDGE)) OOO::HH! (2.5) Would you care-would you uh
exPOund on that Counsel?

(1.0)

S5: I forget the (.2) number of the rule
[
((laughter (5.5)))

P: You're only ma--able to make lim:ited (.2) use of this new found knowledge.

((laughter (4.5)))

P: ((Normal)) You would say I think (.2) that (.2) the rule as I
understand it (.2) fifteen B permits the pleadings to be aMEnded
(.4) when doing so would not (.3) result in-when doing so would
Further the cause of substantial justice (.2) and when the
opposing party cannot show (.2) that (.3) uh: (.2) that party
would be prejudiced as a result of the amendment. (.3) Is that
what your argument is? (.3) And therefore with respect Your
Honor I ask that the (.2) that the comPLaint and the
pretrial order (.2) be amended (.2) to state that the plaintiff
wishes-that the plaintiff's losses inCLuded lo:ss of use of the
airplane in question.

(2.2)

P: How's that? (2.0) Isn't that the (.2) the way we operationali::ze
in Lawyer Lingo in Court (1.0) the point you've just made (1.0)
'n we didn' go in I Would (.8) We go in (.2) Real Time and say
(.2) just what we said. (1.0) You see the point I'm trying to get
(.2) at which is (.2) to start talking (.2) as a lawyer would talk on
that occasion with that problem (.) in front of him-her. (.2)
Hmm? (.4) Got it?

(9.0)

P: Enough?

Analysis

The "in court" interchange begins when a student raises her hand and proposes that the plaintiffs in the case in question could have made use of Rule 15(b) of the Federal Rules of Civil Procedure to request the court's permission to amend their pleadings and seek recovery for loss of use damages. The student's question occurs right after a brief statement by the professor about whether the plaintiffs might be precluded at trial from asking for the additional item of ("loss of use") damages because they failed to clearly specify in their original pleadings that they intended to seek such damages.[15]

The student begins to state her proposal at lines 16-23 as follows, "Um...Rule Fifteen B of the Federal Rules of Civil Procedure allows for amendments in the form of the evidence...so that IF the defendant had objected [to the introduction of loss of use evidence, Rule 15(b)]... says that the um objecting party if it (quoting) 'fails to satisfy the (court) that the admission of such evidence would prejudice him in maintaining his action or defense upon the merits.' So therefore a".

At this point in the student's comment, the professor interrupts her, "Yeah but read the whole sentence" (line 25). The student is immediately alerted to at least two things: First, the professor is familiar with the rule and his interruption indicates that she has failed to properly cite the rule. Secondly, the professor suggests that the omitted portion of the rule is relevant and necessary to her proposal to invoke the rule in requesting an amendment of the pleadings in the case.

The student laughs, perhaps acknowledging her abbreviated reading of the rule with, "Okay huh" (line 27). She then reads the whole sentence as suggested by the professor and then stops (lines 27-34). At this juncture, the inquiry for the student (and the other class members) focuses on the relevance of the previously omitted portion of the rule which the professor has identified as necessary so that the student's suggested amendment procedure may meaningfully and consequentially proceed.

With the further recitation of the rule now "on the record", the professor begins to transform the student's suggestion (that plaintiff's counsel could have advanced her partisan aims by using Rule 15(b)) into an actual instance of "in court" invocation of the rule. The legal problem posed by the professor is that the present pleadings are insufficient and in need of amendment in order to set forth a valid claim for recovery of lost use damages. The professor creates this real time legal task for the student by witnessably adopting a new persona as the cantankerous elderly "judge", who responds on the video record by crinkling his face and leaning over (lines 54-55), to suggest that the matter has not been sufficiently pleaded, "Well I still believe in pleading though" (line 57). This attempted embodiment of the "judge" evokes laughter from the class, including from the participating student (line 59). The professor continues as "judge" at line 61, "Ya don't plead, in this court ya don't prove!" More laughter from the class follows (line 63). For competent counsel, the statement by a judge that, "Ya don't plead, in this court ya don't prove!" may be heard as an indication that the judge believes that the loss of use issue has *not* been properly pleaded in the pretrial documents, nothwithstanding "counsel's" assertion to the contrary.

From the persona of the "judge", the professor shifts his voicing back to sotto voce to ask the student, "Now what do you say?" (line 67). The professor-guide thus indicates that, without more, the "judge" is inclined to disallow the plaintiffs the opportunity to prove that they suffered any loss of use damages. The student responds, "Okay, basically the purpose of the rule which" (line 69). The professor quickly overlaps her, again visibly adopting the persona of the "judge" and with a facial expression of scowl and hearably annoyed states, "Now lady, I want an argument from you" (lines 71-72). The professor "judge" perjoratively addresses the student as "Lady", perhaps to suggest that her attempt was not that of competent counsel. Pedagogically, the professor also shows that the student's prior attempt to explain "the purpose of the rule" was not the legal argument that was called for.

Following a 1.0 second gap which is not taken up by the student (line 74), the professor switches to normal voice as professor-guide to direct the student to what she is next competently expected to do. He states at lines 76-77, "I want you to pretend now that you're in that Court and Judge J. has just ruled". He then witnessably changes his voicing and facial expression to locally invoke and make evident the persona of judge with, "Well, without the pleadings you can't prove it" (lines 79-80). The class laughs at the judge impersonation by the professor (line 82), who changes to sotto voce and says, "What do you say now?" (line 88). The student states at line 92, "Basically, I would offer-". Again, with gesticular emphasis, this incipient effort is cut off by the professor, visibly waiving off the student's in-course response immediately after it is recognizable as other than the words of competent counsel: ".I want you to Shift...we're in that Court-I don't want you telling me what you *would* do, I want you to *act* the behavior of counsel-What... Words come out" (lines 94-97).

The student, with hearable hesitancy, ventures an articulation of "counsel" at lines 101-106 with, "The proof of the damages sustained by the plaintiff in terms of Loss of use, that is loss of business profits um although not alleged specifically in the pleadings would be relevant in this case because they the contention here would not be that the defendant was caught unawares of the possibility that". The professor "judge" curtly interrupts the student in a way which indicates that her argument misses the mark with, "What are you *talking* about!..." (lines 108-109). The class apparently finds this amusing and again laughs (line 111). The "judge's" interruption serves to reprimand "counsel". However, it leaves pedagogically unspecified exactly what was faulted about the student's immediately preceding effort.

The professor next gives a clue as to how the student's attempt was deficient when demonstrably as "judge" he counters with, "You saying that...it's already an issue?" (line 113). No response is forthcoming from the student and after a 2.5 second gap (line 115), the professor, still witnessably as the "judge", continues, "I ruled against you on that...I'll rule against you again...so you'll know" (lines 117-118). The class laughs prolongedly for twelve seconds (line 120). This comment plays on the local fact that previously in the interchange the "judge" had already ruled that the present pleadings do not tender the issue of loss of use.

The video shows the student witnessably shaking her head in displayed befuddlement about how to proceed at about two seconds and again at twelve seconds into the class' concerted laughter (line 120). She says no more and appears to have relinquished her attempted articulation as competent counsel. The professor then opens up the forum at line 122 by observably shifting his gaze from the student to address the entire class, asking, "What'll you do now?".

Brief interchanges ensue between the professor and three more students in pursuit of what competent plaintiff's counsel should do at this point in the proceedings to be permitted to introduce evidence of lost use damages (lines 124-191).[16] Interestingly, they all miss the pedagogic point, although each seems to be attempting to exhibit the conduct of "counsel". Just like the first student, the second student (S2) tries to insist that the pleadings were already sufficient to tender the issue of loss of use, which the "judge" again rules against. The third student (S3) wants to make an objection, which the judge permits him to do, but that does not solve the problem. The fourth student (S4) wants to make an offer of proof, but that also fails to resolve the pending task.

At last, at lines 195-196, a fifth student "co-counsel" proffers, "Your Honor on the basis of the rule just cited I request permission to amend the pleadings". The professor, observably as "judge", makes it crystal clear that co-counsel number five has finally hit upon the "words of counsel" which solve the legal task he had pedagogically posed. The "judge" becomes observably very attentive, exclaiming in a loud voice at lines 200-201, "OH!...Would you uh expound on that Counsel?" The respectful form by which he addresses this student as "Counsel" and requests him to "expound" upon his argument notably contrasts with the "judge's" prior pejorative forms of addressing other students as "Lady" (line 72) and "Sonny" (line 172).

Following a 1.0 second gap (line 203), "counsel" number five reveals the limits of his efficacious legal practice and his true "student" status by conceding, "I forget the ...number of the rule" (line 205). The class laughs (line 207) and the professor underscores the humor of the student's drift back into ineptness, noting, "You're only...able to make limited...use of this new found knowledge" (lines 209-210). More class laughter occurs (line 212).

With the pedagogic point of the preceding interchanges in hand, the professor begins to sum up by stating what a competent lawyer in the case would have to say to invoke the rule allowing amendment of pleadings (at lines 214-219) with, "You would say I think...that...the rule as I understand it...permits the pleadings to be amended...when doing so would further the cause of substantial justice... and when the opposing party cannot show...that ...that party would be prejudiced as a result of the amendment".

The professor then visibly returns his gaze to the first student (S1) with whom the pedagogic interchange initially began and asks her, "Is that what your argument is?" (lines 219-220). He then completes the words of competent counsel, "And therefore with respect Your Honor I ask...that the complaint and the pretrial order be amended to state...that the plaintiff's losses include loss of use of the airplane in question" (lines 220-224).

The end of the episode is marked by the professor demonstrating the point of the interchange, namely that counsel must be able to exhibit and advance in real time and in material detail their partisan aims when faced with the particular legal problem then confronting them. He instructs the students to notice the crucial difference between asserting a hypothetical or in principled argument about what the student "would do" if she were counsel and the student's professionally competent exposition in real time of the actual "words of counsel".

With the motion by plaintiff's counsel to amend the pleadings to seek lost use damages placed competently "on the record", the professor concludes the pedagogic point at lines 228-234 stating, "How's that....Isn't that...the way we operationalize in lawyer lingo in court...the point you've just made...We didn' go in 'I Would...' We go in real time and say just what we said... You see the point I'm trying to get at which is to start talking as a lawyer would talk on that occasion with that problem in front of him-her....Got it?". (Sometimes, the insightful pedagogue makes the sociologist's job easy!)

The pedagogic point having been made and summed up and after a long 9.0 second gap with no uptake by the class (line 236), the professor closes this exchange by querying, "Enough?" (line 238).

Implications and Conclusions

This study has been an attempt to specify some of the distinctly legal features of pedagogic interchange in the law school classroom. In the episode, the professor pedagogically crafted a legal task which required the student(s) to articulate in the "words of counsel" a competent request to amend the pleadings. While this is a specifically delineated legal task with a particular substantive civil procedural content, what is taught and learned through such pedagogic exchanges in law school are, more generally, the practical skills of legal reasoning, argumentation and exposition.

In this initial inquiry, only a single pedagogic interchange was presented and we have only scratched the surface of a rich and largely unexplored analytic territory. The professionally led, collaboratively organized and locally detailed interactive work of pedagogic interchange in the law class makes available to students the relevant legal concepts, terms, rules, principles, etc., which comprise civil procedural law. But not only that. Through pedagogic dialogue with the professor, the students learn in real time and in material detail techniques which are necessary for dealing with a given day's specific legal problems and emergent practical tasks.[17]

In the end, the import and consequentiality of such analyses of pedagogic and practical interaction in legal settings do not depend upon their tie to more large-scale and received topics of interest in the social science literature, such as the performance of ideology or power in the classroom. The practical tasks and problems of practicing lawyers are not on that order of abstraction. Rather, their professional workways are unavoidably addressed to particular pending problems and matters of practical relevance, concern and consequentiality for attorney and clients within a specific case, course of professional interchange and place in the proceedings. In the end, if a student learns to be a competent lawyer, this is in the first place done and demonstrated as a locally detailed and emergent practical achievement.

Acknowledgements

I would like to acknowledge several persons in the settings where I have been privileged to work and conduct research. At the UCLA Sociology Department, I thank Harold Garfinkel who first prompted me to attend law school. Many of the ideas in this paper developed from the keen insights of his ethnomethodological investigations and lectures on Instructions and Instructed Action and from collaborative discussions with Professor Garfinkel. I am grateful to Robert Emerson whose deep familiarity with the situated practices and hurdles of ethnography offers me thorough guidance as a fieldworker. This analysis is also indebted to the seminal research and findings of Harvey Sacks, Emanuel Schegloff, John Heritage, Paul Drew and others in the analysis of natural conversation. John Heritage's characteristic generosity, intellectual interest and encouragement enhanced my understanding of numerous issues.

Most especially, I gratefully acknowledge the continuing support and kind care of Geoffrey Hazard of Yale Law School who generously opened up his classroom to me, gave of his time and otherwise inconvenienced himself to advance this research. Professor Hazard's craftsmanship led me further and further into the phenomenon of legal pedagogy and his critical reflections about pedagogic practice stimulated significant adjustments in my thinking.

I also wish to thank my friends Richard Boldt, Doug Macbeth and Mark Peyrot whose support, guidance and exceptional scholarship have eased immeasurably my transition to law school and back to sociology. I have tried to acknowledge specific debts to Doug Macbeth's exemplary educational studies in the notes, but they fail to make apparent how important his unselfish colleagueship has been to me over the years. Finally, a special debt is owed to my husband John Horwitz for his loving encouragement in the face of all my challenges.

Notes

1. A concern with the practices distinctive to the pedagogy of law and the intelligibility of law's objects implicates a sociological topic no less central and enduring than the Durkheimian interest in the objectivity and reproduction of social structure or what Garfinkel, 1989, calls the "immortal ordinary society" (also see Garfinkel, 1988 at p. 103). See A. Rawls, forthcoming.
2. The task of this paper is to restore the tie between social facts and the real time, materially detailed orderliness of interchange in the law school classroom.
3. For example, Goffman, 1961, sets forth a "total institutional" model of re-socialization. He specifies certain features of total institutional life and issues of identity management there which are arguably applicable to law school training, including the "basic split" between "inmates" and staff, stripping and mortification practices and the use of secondary adjustments by "inmates".
4. The concept of role distance originates with Goffman, 1961, at pp. 85-152.
5. It is notable that the educational program of the legal realists emanates from a critique of the disengaged nature of legal formalism and Langdellian legal education, although the critique is not grounded in the study of interaction. The realists urged the restoration of an apprentice-like "clinical lawyer school" to expose students to the "law in operation" in "courtrooms and law offices" (Frank, 1933A at p. 911 and Frank, 1933B and 1935. See also Stevens, 1971 and

Llewellyn, 1930.). Yet the realist program presumes a distinction between classroom pedagogy and real-worldly professional activity which treats classroom teaching and learning as inadequate to "equip students for real work in the world" (Macbeth, 1996 at p. 271). Thus, even the realists fail to specify just what are the core practices and problems distinctive to teaching and learning law or how law students and professors address their practical daily tasks. Similarly, in the recent educational research literature, there is a growing collection of "situated studies" which assert that "classrooms produce 'thin' versions of the affairs they teach" (Id., at p. 273). For a trenchant review and critical examination of this literature, see Macbeth, 1996.

6. The professionally led character of pedagogic exchange in the law class was suggested to me by Harold Garfinkel.
7. The usage of "etc." is borrowed from Garfinkel's discussions of the "et cetera" problem (see e.g. Garfinkel, 1967).
8. Of course, some law professors primarily lecture, answer questions and do not call on students to participate in compulsory pedagogic interchange.
9. Macbeth's (1991) review of the conversational analytic research in the classroom points out that several studies identify a "two party" speech exchange system of teacher vis-a-vis students in class. Characteristically, teachers address the entire class and, for the most part, these utterances are made publicly available to all class members. Each individual student is treated by the instructor to be generally available for address and there is an asymmetry in the teacher's right to allocate next turns (notwithstanding the various systematic ways for selecting which student will speak next, such as by raising of the hands). The teacher also has the prerogative to shape turn development and content. Moreover, the teacher also usually determines the length of the turn and their right to a continuing turn at talk is not impaired by 'lapses' within it.
10. On the public nature of classroom interaction, see Macbeth, 1991 and 1994. Also see discussion in Garfinkel and Burns, 1978, of a "locally historicized reference" which in retrospect becomes part of the local history of events shared by class members over a series of course meetings and which may subsequently be embodiedly re-invoked and oriented to be class participants as a matter known in common. The fixed seating arrangements characteristic of law school classes facilitates use of a given student's seating location as a locally historicized reference for the pedagogic point which was covered with them.
11. I began this focused investigation when I was a third year law student in the Fall of 1981. I was granted open access to attend and make observations in a first semester civil procedure course taught at one of the nation's top law schools by the law professor, a renowned jurisprudential scholar and expert in legal ethics and civil procedural law. I was an observer in this law class, but not a bona fide member of the class enrolled for a grade.

12. On the use of formulations, see Garfinkel and Sacks, 1970 at p. 353. See also J. Heritage and D.R. Watson, 1980. As described by Peyrot, 1982, p. 266, "[t]he work of all formulations is to claim the existence of a structure which has been implicit to that point and invoke that structure as a principle for organizing activity...".
13. The case from which this pedagogic interchange begins is the California Supreme Court case of *Reynolds v. Bank of America National Trust & Savings Ass'n.* (1959) 53 C2d 49, 345 P2d 926. *Reynolds* stands for the proposition that a plaintiff may recover damages for loss of use of a vehicle based on the reasonable value of the use of the property and that such damages are recoverable only for the time period necessary to repair or replace the damaged property. However, in the classroom "practice", the facts of the case are extended to raise other issues of legal pleading and practice which were not present in the original case, including a request by plaintiff's student-counsel at trial to amend the pleadings. The student's proposal is technically incorrect in that it suggests the use of a federal civil procedural rule (Federal Rule of Civil Procedure 15(b)) which is not applicable to the California state court proceedings in *Reynolds*. The "pleadings" are the formal allegations by the parties of their respective claims and defenses. In both federal and California state court, the pleadings may be amended to conform to proof at trial. In federal court, unlike in state court, a pretrial conference may be ordered by the trial judge (F.R.C.P. 16) and is mandatory in some federal districts under their local court rules. At the end of a pretrial conference, a pretrial order is entered and this document supercedes the pleadings to control the issues at trial (F.R.C.P. 16). Under Federal Rule of Civil Procedure 15(b) cited by the student and utilized in the "in court" practice scenerio, if evidence is objected to on the grounds that it is not encompassed by the issues framed in the pleadings, the proponent of the evidence may seek leave to amend the pleadings. Specifically, the text of F.R.C.P. 15(b) provides that "the court may allow the pleadings to be amended (during trial) and shall do so freely when the presentation of the merits of the action shall be subserved thereby and the objecting party fails to satisfy the court that the admission of such evidence would prejudice him in maintaining his action or defense upon the merits".
14. The transcript should be considered a "simplified" transcript in that certain fine grained conversational features not addressed in the analysis presented have been omitted. The notations in the transcript use the conventions developed by Gail Jefferson (in Atkinson and Heritage, 1984 at pp. ix-xvi). The principal symbols are as follows:

( )	Numbers in parentheses indicate the occurrence and duration of pauses in tenths of a second
[	Marks the point at which overlapping talk begins
]	Marks the point at which overlapping talk ends

=	Notes the end of one utterance and the start of the next with no gap or overlap
-	Indicates the point at which a word is cut off
(( ))	Double parentheses indicate the transcriber's descriptions
doing	Underlining indicates emphasis by means of pitch
OOOHH	Capital letters are used to indicate that an utterance or part of an utterance is produced with louder amplitude than the surrounding talk
° °	Dialogue between these symbols is quieter than surrounding talk.
ca:se	Colons indicate a stretch of the immediately prior sound
. , ?	punctuations note falling, continuing and rising intonation, respectively

15. See Footnote 13, *supra.*
16. Consideration of much analytically rich material has been omitted from this presentation of this episode (e.g. lines 120-189).
17. Future research is needed to focus on the case-specific legal content and task-oriented nature of lawyer's work in the various settings within which actual legal practice occurs, for example, the methods by which diverse forms of partisan examination of witnesses at trial are accomplished, including the routine practices used on cross-examination to impeach an adverse witness (see Burns, 1996).

References

Atkinson, J. M. and Drew,P. (1979), *Order in Court: The Organisation of Verbal Interaction in Judicial Settings*, MacMillan, London.

Atkinson, J. M. and Heritage,J. (eds) (1984), *Structures of Social Action: Studies in Conversational Analysis*, Cambridge University Press, Cambridge.

Atkinson, P. and Delamont, S. (1977), 'Mock-Ups and Cock-Ups: The Stage-Management of Guided Discovery Instruction', in P. Woods and M. Hammersley (eds), *School Experience: Explorations in the Sociology of Education*, St Martin's Press, New York, pp. 87-108.

Becker, H. (1972), 'School is a Lousy Place to Learn Anything', *American Behavioral Scientist*, vol.16, pp. 85-105.

Berger, P. (1963), *Invitation to Sociology*, Doubleday and Company, New York.

Boldt, R. and Feldman,M. (1992), 'The Faces of Law in Theory and Practice: Doctrine, Rhetoric and Social Context', *Hastings Law Review*, vol.43, p. 1111.

Brim, O. and Wheeler,S. (1966), *Socialization After Childhood: Two Essays*, John Wiley and Sons, New York.

Burns, S. (1996), 'Lawyers' Work in the Menendez Brothers' Murder Trial', *Issues in Applied Linguistics*, vol. 7, pp. 19-32.

California Evidence Code, section 210.

Chapple, E. (1980), 'The Unbounded Reaches of Anthropology as a Research Science and Some Working Hypotheses', *American Anthropologist*, vol. 82, pp. 741-758.

Dillon, J.T. (1980), 'Curiosity as Non Sequitur of Socratic Questioning', *Journal of Educational Thought*, vol. 14, pp. 17-22.

Emerson, R. (1983), *Contemporary Field Research*, Waveland Press, Prospect Heights, Ill.

Emerson, R. and Messinger,S. (1977), 'The Micro-Politics of Trouble', *Social Problems*, vol. 25, pp. 121-135.

Federal Rules of Civil Procedure 15 and 16.

Frank, J. (1933A), 'Why Not A Clinical Lawyer School?', *University of Pennsylvania Law Review*, vol. 81, pp. 907-923.

Frank, J. (1933B), 'What Constitutes a Good Legal Education?', *ABA Journal*, December, 1933, pp. 1-15.

Frank, J. (1935), *Law and the Modern Mind*, Tudor, New York.

Garfinkel, H. (1988), 'Evidence for Locally Produced, Naturally Accountable Phenomena of Order, Etc.: An Announcement of Studies', *Sociological Theory*, vol. 6, pp. 103-109.

Garfinkel, H. (1989), Unpublished Lectures, Department of Sociology, University of California, Los Angeles.

Garfinkel, H. and Burns,S. (1978), 'Lecturing's Work of Teaching Introductory Sociology', Department of Sociology, U.C.L.A., presented at the Sociolinguistics Program, Ninth World Congress of Sociology, Uppsala, Sweden.

Garfinkel, H. and Sacks,H. (1970), 'On Formal Structures of Practical Actions', in J.C. McKinney and E.A. Tiryakian (eds), *Theoretical Sociology*, Appleton Century Crofts, New York, pp. 338-366.

Goffman, E. (1961), *Asylums*, Doubleday and Company, Inc., New York.

Goffman, E. (1981), *Forms of Talk*, Blackwell, Oxford.

Heinz, J.P. and Lauman,E.O. (1978), 'The Legal Profession: Client Interests, Professional Roles and Social Hierarchies', *Michigan Law Review*, vol. 76, p. 1111.

Heritage, J. (1984), *Garfinkel and Ethnomethodology*, Polity Press, Cambridge.

Heritage, J. (1985), 'Analyzing News Interviews: Aspects of the Production of Talk for an "Overhearing" Audience', in T. van Dijk (ed.), *Handbook of Discourse Analysis, vol. III, Discourse and Dialogue*, Academic Press, London, pp. 95-119.

Heritage, J. and Drew,P. (eds) (1992), *Talk at Work*, Cambridge University Press, Cambridge.

Heritage, J. and Watson,D.R. (1980), 'Aspects of the Properties of Formulations in Natural Conversation: Some Instances Analyzed', *Semiotica*, vol.30, pp. 245-262.

Kennedy, D. (1968), 'How the Law School Fails: A Polemic', Unpublished Paper presented at Symposium on Legal Education, Yale Law School.

Kennedy, D. (1982), 'Legal Education as Training for Hierarchy', in D. Kairys (ed.), *The Politics of Law*, Pantheon, New York, p.40.

Lave, J. (1988), *Cognition in Practice*, Cambridge University Press, Cambridge.
Lave, J. and Wenger,E. (1991), *Situated Learning: Legitimate Peripheral Participation*, Cambridge University Press, Cambridge.
Llewellyn, K. (1930), *The Bramble Bush*, Oceana Publishers, Inc., New York.
Lofland, J. (1966), *Doomsday Cult*, Prentice-Hall, Englewood Cliffs, New Jersey.
Luban, D. (1988), *Lawyers and Justice*, University of Michigan Press, Ann Arbor, Michigan.
Macbeth, D. (1991), 'Teacher Authority as Practical Action', *Linguistics and Education*, vol.3, pp. 281-313.
Macbeth, D. (1994), 'Classroom Encounters with the Unspeakable: "Do You See, Danelle?"', *Discourse Processes*, vol. 17, pp. 311-335.
Macbeth, D. (1996), 'The Discovery of Situated Worlds: Analytic Commitments or Moral Orders?', *Human Studies*, vol. 19, pp. 267-287.
Mehan, H. (1979), *Learning Lessons*, Harvard University Press, Cambridge, MA.
Moerman, M. (1988), *Talking Culture*, University of Pennsylvania Press, Philadelphia.
Moore, W. (1963), 'The Temporal Structure of Organizations', in E. A. Tiryakian (ed.), *Sociological Theory, Values and Socio-Cultural Change*, The Free Press, New York.
Moore, W. (1969), in D.Goslin (ed.), *Handbook of Socialization Theory*, Rand McNally Publishers, Chicago.
O'Barr, W. (1982), *Linguistic Evidence: Language, Power and Strategy in the Courtroom*, Academic Press, New York.
Osborn, J.J. (1971), *The Paper Chase*, Houghton Mifflin: Boston.
Pepper, S. (1986), 'The Lawyer's Amoral Ethical Role: A Defense, A Problem and Some Possibilities', *American Bar Foundation Research Journal*, p. 613.
Peyrot, M. (1982), 'Understanding Ethnomethodology: A Remedy for Some Common Misconceptions', *Human Studies*, vol. 5, pp. 261-83.
Peyrot, M. (1995), 'Therapeutic Preliminaries: Conversational Context and Process in Psychotherapy', *Qualitative Sociology*, vol. 18, pp. 311-328.
Philips, S. U. (1982), 'The Language Socialization of Lawyers: Acquiring the "Cant"', in G.Spindler (ed.), *Doing the Ethnography of Schooling*, Waveland Press, Prospect Heights, Ill., pp. 176-209.
Rawls, A. (forthcoming), 'Durkheim's Epistemology: The Neglected Argument', *Sociological Theory*.
Sacks, H. (1984), 'Notes on Methodology', in J.M. Atkinson and J. Heritage (eds), *Structures of Social Action: Studies in Conversational Analysis*, Cambridge University Press, Cambridge, pp. 21-27.
Sacks, H. (1992) (1964-1972), *Lectures on Conversation*, 2 vols, Gail Jefferson (ed.), Blackwell, Oxford.
Sacks, H., Schegloff,E. and Jefferson,G. (1974), 'A Simplest Systematics for the Organization of Turn Taking in Conversation', *Language*, vol. 50, pp. 696-735.

Sacks, H., Schegloff,E. and Jefferson,G. (1977), 'The Preference for Self-Correction in the Organization of Repair in Conversation', *Language*, vol. 53, pp. 361-382.

Sargant, W. (1957), *Battle for the Mind*, Doubleday and Company, Inc., New York.

Schegloff, E. (1988-9), 'From Interview to Confrontation: Observations on the Bush-Rather Encounter', *Research on Language and Social Interaction*, vol. 22, pp.215-240.

Sinclair, J. and Coulthard,M. (1975), *Towards An Analysis of Discourse*, Oxford University Press, Oxford.

Stevens, R. (1971), 'Two Cheers for 1870', in B. Bailyn and D. Fleming (eds), *Law in American History*, Cambridge University Press, Cambridge, pp. 404-548.

Turner, R. (1962), 'Role Taking: Process Versus Conformity', in A. Rose (ed.), *Human Behavior and Social Processes*, Routledge and Kegan Paul, London, pp. 20-41.

Turner, V. (1974), *Dramas, Fields and Metaphors*, Cornell University Press, Ithaca.

Turow, S. (1977), *One L*, Penguin Books, New York.

Index

For Product Safety Concerns and Information please contact our EU representative GPSR@taylorandfrancis.com
Taylor & Francis Verlag GmbH, Kaufingerstraße 24, 80331 München, Germany

www.ingramcontent.com/pod-product-compliance
Ingram Content Group UK Ltd.
Pitfield, Milton Keynes, MK11 3LW, UK
UKHW022003180926
475701UK00003B/170
* 9 7 8 1 1 3 8 2 5 0 1 6 1 *